The Dynamics of Corporate Co-evolution

ORGANISATION AND STRATEGY: CASE STUDIES IN THEIR CONTEXT

Series Editors: John Child, *University of Birmingham, UK* and Suzana B. Rodrigues, *Erasmus University, the Netherlands*

We are actively commissioning new books for this important new series. It will showcase high-quality research on strategy and organisation in order to inform theory and policy. Books in the series will highlight the value of the best case study research, offering a holistic approach, sensitive to theory, context and history.

Titles in this series include:

The Dynamics of Corporate Co-evolution

A Case Study of Port Development in China

John Child

Emeritus Professor of Commerce, University of Birmingham and Professor of Management, University of Plymouth, UK

Kenneth K.T. Tse

Senior Research Fellow, University of Birmingham, UK and Adjunct Professor, the Chinese University of Hong Kong

Suzana B. Rodrigues

Professor of International Business and Organization, Erasmus University, the Netherlands

ORGANISATION AND STRATEGY: CASE STUDIES IN THEIR CONTEXT

Edward Elgar

Cheltenham, UK • Northampton, MA, USA

Published by
Edward Elgar Publishing Limited
The Lypiatts
15 Lansdown Road
Cheltenham
Glos GL50 2JA
UK

Edward Elgar Publishing, Inc.
William Pratt House
9 Dewey Court
Northampton
Massachusetts 01060
USA

A catalogue record for this book
is available from the British Library

Library of Congress Control Number: 2012948842

This book is available electronically in the ElgarOnline.com Business Subject Collection, E-ISBN 978 1 84980 744 9

ISBN 978 1 84980 743 2 (cased)

Typeset by Columns Design XML Ltd, Reading
Printed and bound by MPG Books Group, UK

FURTHER ACCLAIM FOR THIS BOOK

'There are two reasons for recommending this highly readable book. It offers a careful explanation of how interaction between investors, operating firms, local politicians and central administrators shapes the corporate governance of new Chinese multinationals and their contracts in a highly regulated infrastructure industry such as ports. Based on the outcome of the empirical study of China's largest container terminal, the book further convincingly argues how the interaction between firms and local politicians or central administrators specifies the missing link in Co-Evolution Theory, namely the mechanism by which firms can convert their demand for a better fitting business environment into corresponding institutional policies. In short the book offers both additional insights into the new business system in China (and suggestions for foreign firms on how to better cope with such a system), and the process by which good theory gets refined.'

– Professor Barbara Krug, Professor of Economics of Governance, Rotterdam
School of Management, Erasmus University, the Netherlands

'The dramatic progress of many societies in recent decades has rested – often without full acknowledgement – on the hybridizing of different business systems, and on the flowing together of the resulting blended organizations with their political, social and cultural surroundings. This is nowhere better illustrated than in China's Pearl River Delta where the long heritage of Hong Kong as a western trading outpost meets the longer heritage of China as a state-dominated society. In this book the co-evolution of the world's largest matrix of transport hubs is analysed in fine detail by another hybrid: that of world class exponents of both organization theory and the practical managing of complexity.'

– Professor Gordon Redding, Adjunct Professor of Asian Business and Comparative
Management, Formerly Director of the Euro-Asia Research Centre
INSEAD; Secretary-General, HEAD Foundation

'The Dynamics of Corporate Co-evolution provides an excellent exploration of co-evolution from the perspective of power relations within a hierarchical system. It is relevant not only to firms working within a political environment, but also useful for people working in think tanks and policy analysis. Its treatment of relationship management has universal implications.'

– Professor Huijiong Wang, Former Vice President, Academic Committee,
Development Research Center, The State Council, PRC

v

Contents

Figures

Tables

Acknowledgements

This book is the product of the collaboration between three authors, each of whom has some special thanks to give. The two academics, John Child and Suzana Rodrigues, owe a considerable debt to Kenneth Tse for the way in which he opened the doors of Yantian International Container Terminals, the focus of this book, to numerous research investigations. These included the projects conducted by 21 Master's students at the University of Birmingham for whom their stay at YICT was a learning experience of immense value. Without wishing to indulge in mutual self-praise, the long-term collaboration between academia and industry that has given rise to this book has proven to be of substantial benefit to both parties, but unfortunately happens far too rarely. The partnership both nurtured academic learning about management and supported YICT as a learning organization.

Kenneth's PhD research has made a significant input into this book. He would like to acknowledge how his academic colleagues – first as doctoral supervisors and now co-authors – insisted on 'evidence based' accounts and justified conclusions. Dr Leanne Chung helped the process of triangulation which confirmed the validity of Kenneth's interpretations of events, given his unusual dual role as both researcher of, and key actor in, the story. Ken Everett played the role of devil's advocate, questioning Kenneth at various points as he progressed with his thesis. Professor C.K. Mak read the entire thesis and has become a keen supporter of the co-evolutionary perspective embodied in this book. Kenneth's colleagues at YICT made the successful development of the port possible, which this book charts. To all of them, Kenneth owes a sincere debt of thanks.

All three of us wish to thank the managers and staff at YICT, those in Shenzhen's Yantian Port Group, and in various Chinese government agencies, who gave their valuable time to be interviewed and cited, as well as to share their views informally. There are far too many to mention by name here, but without them the YICT story would not have taken place, nor would it have been recorded here.

Suzana would also like to give particular thanks to the Dinalog Project Ultimate, the Erasmus SmartPort Community and Europe Container Terminal at Rotterdam for the opportunity to learn more about ports as organizations and how they operate. Participation in the Dinalog Project Ultimate not only provided valuable understanding for her contributions to this book, but also the financial support to conduct research in the port sector.

Above all, we owe a debt to our spouses. Karen Tse has always been there to support Kenneth during his long journey in pursuit of his doctorate and preparing materials for this book, with an encouraging word and smile. Anielo Rodrigues has never ceased to support Suzana in her duties far from home in Birmingham and then Rotterdam, which enabled her to contribute to the production of this book. Elizabeth Child likewise has tolerated the rivalry of the computer for John's attention as words turned into chapters. Without the encouragement and tolerance of our spouses, this book would not have been written and we dedicate it to them.

John Child
Kenneth Tse
Suzana Rodrigues

PART I

Introduction, perspective and method

1. Introduction

This book has two principal objectives. One is to report a remarkable corporate success – the rapid development of China's largest and most advanced container terminal from its foundation in 1993.[1] The other objective is to increase our understanding of corporate co-evolution – how firms and their environments evolve together over time – by closely examining the development of the company running this terminal within its changing environment. This includes ways in which the company was able to influence the evolution of that environment.

The book has contributions for both academics and practitioners. For academics, it offers new theoretical and empirical insights on the processes lying at the heart of co-evolution. Theoretically, it adopts and takes forward a political perspective that focuses on the role of power and influence, a perspective that has largely been absent from previous work on co-evolution.[2] Detailed examination of the company's history will illustrate the relevance of this perspective and offer some detail about the actors, the issues and the sources of power that came into play in its dealings with the environment. For practitioners, we identify ways in which the company was able to chart its own evolution through successfully managing key external relationships. In reporting a major turnaround from a vicious to a virtuous cycle of port development, we describe how a coherent strategy can emerge from positive engagement with the environment. We distil implications for corporate practice into seven approaches that can be taken to generate change that has positive consequences not only for a company but also for its environment. These are presented in the final chapter.

The terminal is located at Yantian in the Shenzhen Special Economic Zone [SEZ] just three kilometres across the Mainland Chinese border from Hong Kong. The company that owns and runs it is Yantian International Container Terminals [YICT]. This is a joint venture, which was established in 1993 between Hutchison Port Holdings [HPH] based in Hong Kong as the majority owner and the Yantian Port Group owned by the Shenzhen government as the principal minority shareholder.[3] Its story is a fascinating one of how a company achieved its strategic objectives within China's complex environment, and actually went on to set new standards of practice within its sector both in China and internationally. It enlightens our understanding of the strategic possibilities that companies can create even within highly challenging and controlled environments.

Although the booming economy of southern China provided a propitious environment for the new port, YICT experienced a difficult first few years. It had a major problem persuading shipping companies to switch their business to its new facilities from the well-established and efficient berths of nearby Hong Kong despite offering competitive rates. The shippers' fear was that Yantian, being located in Mainland China, would suffer from all the restrictions of Chinese bureaucracy to the detriment of being able to offer them a reliable and efficient service. So through the years 1993 to 1997, the young joint venture was investing heavily in its new facilities while at the same time losing money fast. The agreement under which the YICT was established specified a number of reforms in the procedures of government agencies located in the port that could directly affect its operations, such as the Customs Administration. In practice, it took several years of careful and persistent relationship management at different levels in the Chinese system, as well as investment in advanced equipment for the agencies to use, before these reforms started to be put into practice. By 1996, the Chinese central authorities formally endorsed the principles of port reform and they officially recognized Yantian as the 'pilot site' for national reforms in port administration. From that point on, the company was able to institute a series of initiatives that gave it a leading place first within China's port industry and then worldwide. Yantian won a series of Chinese industry awards and in 2005 it was chosen by the Global Institute of Logistics to be the 'Global Terminal of the Year'. While YICT had to continue with innovations in order to maintain this leading position, against growing competition from other local ports, it also had to contend with another issue which was actually stimulated by its success. This was the desire of its Mainland partner to secure a larger stake in what had become a highly profitable business.

THE CO-EVOLUTIONARY PERSPECTIVE

Good theory and research can inform practice. In order to do full justice to our subject, we shall adopt and add to what has come to be called a 'co-evolutionary perspective'. This perspective, which is described in Chapter 2, draws attention to ways in which firms and environments evolve together and how, through their relationships, each can impact on the other. The practical significance of this is that, while firms have to adapt to changes in their environments, they may also be able to influence external organizations so as to create better conditions for meeting their strategic objectives. This is not achieved easily and requires a strategy for building and using channels through which corporate leadership can relate with key people outside of the firm. This 'relational framework' offers opportunities to influence the perceptions and thinking of these external people (Meyer and Scott, 1983).

The environment of a firm consists of institutional and non-institutional segments (Lewin et al., 1999). The latter primarily comprises other firms – as customers, suppliers and competitors. The institutional environment comprises government agencies and public institutions, such as the legal system. This segment is becoming increasingly important to business because of the growing economic significance of emerging markets, which have a tradition of heavy regulation and in view of the more interventionist policies of governments in most countries following the global financial crisis of 2008.[4]

We need to have a better understanding of how firms can be proactive toward their environments with the intention of both securing some strategic leeway for themselves while at the same time recognizing that their legitimacy depends on their responding responsibly to social and political concerns. There has been a longstanding debate around the question of how much strategic leeway firms can realistically hope to secure. On one side are those who adopt a Darwinian perspective, which maintains that ultimately firms and other organizations have to adapt to externally-imposed pressures if they are to survive. This is the theory that only the fittest survive through a process of 'natural selection' by the environment. The only role it accords to corporate strategy is the reactive role of monitoring external changes and ensuring that the firm adjusts to them. The influence of the environment is therefore seen to be ultimately decisive. On the other side are those who stress that firms actually have a considerable degree of choice as to the strategies they adopt because their dependence on the environment is only conditional. For example, if they deem it to be necessary, they may be able to move from one environment (industry or country) to another. They are not necessarily dependent on one set of external conditions. While this option is not available to a physically fixed unit like a port, it may also be possible to exercise some influence over environmental conditions through other means such as market leadership, innovation and effective lobbying. The extent of this influence may be a function of the power firms can wield through their size or their ability to act collectively, as well as their negotiating skills. Only a close empirical examination of the respective initiatives and pressures arising from both firms and relevant external bodies can shed light on this issue and highlight the practical ways in which both parties are able to exercise influence effectively. The co-evolutionary perspective has a special attraction and relevance precisely because it encourages this particular empirical focus.

WIDER RELEVANCE OF THE STUDY

The institutional environment has been of key importance for YICT. This is because it is a major infrastructural facility of strategic importance to the Chinese authorities and, in addition, it is located in a country where government is closely involved with business and intervenes actively in it (Redding and Witt, 2007). At first glance, these two characteristics might seem to make it a rather non-typical case, with only limited general relevance. Certainly, infrastructural companies have not been studied as much as other categories by management researchers. But this does not mean they should be considered as out of the mainstream. Actually, infrastructural industries such as transportation, energy, power and water are both large and of central importance to economies, so they can hardly be dismissed as 'of less consequence'. Ports play a vital role in economic development, and ideally should enable the increasing volume of exports and imports associated with a growing economy to be handled without delay or undue cost. In reality, the combination of historical and bureaucratic impediments can create a serious barrier to the effective performance of this function, as is the case today in a major emerging economy such as Brazil. Despite being a greenfield facility, YICT also had to overcome some of these problems.

In all countries, ports tend to be highly regulated. However, in some countries such as China their regulation is more subject to political forces than in others. While the general level of political intervention in business by government and institutions is particularly high in China, government and its bureaucracies also impose significant constraints on business activities in other emerging economies. The World Bank's 10 indicators of 'doing business' in 183 countries point clearly to the added difficulties of conducting business in most emerging economies due to bureaucratic requirements and restrictions, with the situation often exacerbated by political instability (World Bank, 2012). Active government involvement can create considerable uncertainty for firms regarding the strategies they should pursue, especially when political considerations predominate. The other side of the coin, however, is that this involvement also provides channels to government ministries and agencies through which firms themselves have the potential to exercise influence. Using such channels, proactive companies possessing valued specialized competencies have an opportunity to inform the evolution of government policies and practices (Child and Tsai, 2005).

So although YICT does have some special features, there are many other situations to which the insights it furnishes into co-evolutionary processes are likely to apply. YICT's senior management engaged proactively with Chinese government ministries and their local agencies whose support was essential for the company to achieve its objectives and to secure the port's profitable growth. Lessons of wider significance can be drawn from the company's success in doing this.

Companies like YICT, operating within the heavily institutionalized context of a major emerging economy, have received less attention in studies of how firms evolve than companies in western contexts that do not generally impose the same level of constraint. With the exception of anti-competition and consumer protection legislation, political and regulatory forces may well touch many companies relatively lightly in developed western countries. As a result, studies of corporate evolution have tended to focus on the growth strategies companies have taken in their marketplaces rather than on how they relate with governments and institutions. Burgelman's investigation of how strategy and environment co-evolved in the case of Intel is one such example (Burgelman, 2002a; 2002b). Such investigations naturally tend to adopt an economic perspective rather than a political orientation that is attuned to dealings with governments. There are some studies that have examined the political processes through which companies have evolved over time within heavily institutional environments (for example, Rodrigues and Child, 2008; Dieleman and Sachs, 2008), but they are exceptional.

THE SPECIAL CONTRIBUTION OF THIS BOOK

It is a major undertaking to explore how a company has evolved over time in keeping with changes in its environment. It requires the collection of information that satisfies a number of criteria. It should, first, relate to a historical time-period that is sufficiently extensive to enable changes and trends to emerge clearly. Second, the information secured must also be comprehensive enough to permit the various strands in the development of both the firm and its context to be understood in order to provide a balanced and holistic picture. Third, as we note shortly, shedding light on how a firm and its environment evolve in relation to each other requires that insights be obtained into the interactive processes involved.

The opportunity to secure this quality of information and insight occurs only rarely in business and organizational research. Indeed, one can virtually count on the fingers of one hand the number of studies that have come close to meeting even the first two criteria: Jacques (1951), Chandler (1962), Pettigrew (1985), Johnson (1987), Burgelman (2002a), Rodrigues and Child (2008), and not many more. There are, of course, many business histories and biographies of entrepreneurs. Valuable though these are, they tend to concentrate on their story rather than analyzing it in ways that contribute to theory-based generalizations and practical implications of wider relevance.

The concept of co-evolution suggests that firms have the capacity to *interact* with their environments, rather than being obliged simply to *react* to external events and trends. It draws attention to the dynamic interaction of forces in an organization's environment with the capacity of its leadership to respond to these forces, and indeed intentionally to shape aspects of the environment. A co-evolutionary perspective therefore has the potential to inform research on organizations that spans levels of analysis and involves adaptation over time (Lewin and Volberda, 1999). It offers a lens through which the development of organizations and their populations can be better understood. There is, however, still uncertainty among scholars as to what 'co-evolution' means (Murmann, 2010). Does it simply mean that the organizations and environments develop along parallel paths, or does it mean something more, namely that there is interdependence in their development which arises because environments 'influence' organizations and vice versa? In this book we adopt the latter interpretation in which co-evolution refers to interdependence in the respective development of organizations and their environments.

If both organizations and environments are influencing each other's development, the key question then becomes 'how does this take place?' The way in which this interdependence plays out necessarily lies at the heart of any theorizing on the subject (Volberda and Lewin, 2003), yet our understanding of it remains underdeveloped. A number of studies have traced events in detail to provide evidence of whether changes in the environment were followed by apparently related changes in organizations, and vice versa (for example, Jones, 2001; Flier et al., 2003). However, there is still the question of how co-evolution is driven forward.

For example, in discussing the co-evolution of multinational enterprises [MNEs] and institutions, Cantwell et al. (2010: 572) refer to both MNE experimentation and institutional entrepreneurship as potential drivers, but they do not go further into the processes by which co-evolution might come about. While they identify MNEs as 'change agents' in co-evolution, they pass over the issue of how MNEs can mobilize and apply sufficient influence to have an external impact. There is a longstanding debate concerning the influence of the firm vis-à-vis that of the environment on co-evolution (White et al., 1997; Volberda and Lewin, 2003). However, only recently have co-evolutionary studies come to refer to the political processes that may be involved (for example, Rodrigues and Child, 2008; Dieleman and Sachs, 2008; Dieleman and Boddewyn, 2012). We still lack a systematic analysis of how the power and influence held by organizations and relevant external parties might impact on their respective evolution. A major aim of this book is therefore to advance the understanding of how co-evolution takes place by examining the ways in which key actors both in a focal firm and its environment were able to influence aspects of each other's evolution. This will help us move towards a more adequate theoretical perspective on the subject.

At a more applied level, this book also adds to our understanding of how a company can successfully achieve sustained strategic development over a long period of time. It contributes guidelines on this issue, which are of interest to executives as well as to specialists in port operations. The book provides a detailed account of how a strategy for a new large container terminal emerged through a process of learning about the unfamiliar market and other conditions that it faced. The ways in which the company developed its external relations, especially with government, in order to implement its strategy are of wide relevance. Insights are also provided into how YICT's management came to develop a clear intentionality, which accelerated the company's growth and took it to a position of being a global benchmark for its industry.

It is generally very difficult to obtain valid information into the processes through which a company's strategy emerges and how strategic opportunities are conditioned by interactions with other organizations in its environment. It can be even more difficult to secure valid insights into the intentions of external actors, especially when they are government personnel who are subject to political restrictions. So research on the subject is often handicapped by the very real problem of gaining access to the appropriate informants. Concerning as it does strategic issues and sensitive negotiations, the information required is normally confidential and carefully guarded from the prying eyes of investigators. This is not an easy obstacle to overcome and it is undoubtedly a major reason why so few studies are available of this central issue. Gaining adequate insights into what goes on may depend largely on serendipitous good fortune, such as finding participants in the process who are interested in collaborating with scholars. This book would not have been possible without such collaboration between two scholars and the former chief executive of YICT, Kenneth Tse. Our collaboration has provided a unique opportunity to examine the process of the company's evolution comprehensively, in detail and over its total lifespan. It is another factor lending special interest to this study of YICT, to complement the remarkable achievements of the company itself.

PLAN OF THE BOOK

This book is divided into three parts. The task of Part I is to introduce the book, its perspective and its methodology. The purpose of Part II is to present the story of how YICT evolved and the context within which this happened. Part III draws various strands of the story together and builds on them in order to offer new theoretical insights as well as practical lessons for managers.

This initial chapter is introductory, indicating what the book is about, what it claims to do, and what it will cover. Chapter 2 provides a more detailed account of the co-evolutionary perspective we adopt. Knowledge of the perspective and its rationale will assist an appreciation of how it is applied to the case study later on in the book and the analytical value it provides. The chapter traces the development of evolutionary and co-evolutionary thinking and its application to firms and other organizations. It compares co-evolution with other perspectives, such as environmental determinism, institutional theory, resource dependence, path dependency and strategic choice. It argues the case for bringing a political dimension into co-evolution, which is one of the distinctive contributions of this book.

Chapter 3 focuses on relevant methodological issues. It considers the strengths and limitations of case studies such as the one that this book is based on. It reviews the additional contributions one should expect from longitudinal case studies, such as an insight into processes, into cause and effect, and into complex systems of relationships. The chapter also describes the specific methods used to construct the YICT case study.

The opening chapter in Part II, Chapter 4, puts YICT and the Yantian port 'on the map' and describes the changing context in which it evolved. The general 'macro' context was that of China's Reform and Development Program, launched at the end of 1978, which accelerated rapidly from 1992 just before YICT was founded. This context was one of high growth, expanding international trade, and a political agenda to introduce institutional reforms. This agenda, however, did not necessarily carry forward easily into implementation. The chapter also describes YICT's 'meso' context – the Shenzhen SEZ and the port industry in Hong Kong and Mainland China. In these ways Chapter 4 provides an understanding of YICT's competitive and institutional environments.

Chapters 5, 6 and 7 focus on the 'intentionality' of YICT's management in the process of the company's co-evolution with its environments. Chapter 5 analyses the stages through which YICT evolved during the first 15 years of its operation, giving particular attention to the ways in which its management developed a strategy vis-à-vis its environment. This emergent strategy resulted from a process of learning about how to adapt to the serious difficulties that the company faced during its early years. The chapter also charts the growth of the port and changes to its joint venture ownership. The latter were the subject of difficult and protracted negotiations.

Chapter 6 examines four areas of innovative management practice that YICT introduced in order to provide an internal capability to realize its strategic intent. These concern development of a service mentality supported by productivity improvements, a strategic orientation toward port construction and development, innovations in port marketing, and establishing a favourable ecological system. The advanced practices introduced by the company's management also played a significant role in adding substance and lending credibility to the firm's proposals for reform in the Chinese port industry and in its external relations.

How the company developed its external relational framework is the subject of Chapter 7. This chapter concentrates on three areas – relations with the Chinese joint venture partner, relations with Chinese government ministries over the port's expansion and relations with government regulatory authorities operating in the port. While the need for companies to manage their external relations in China is often mentioned, the rationale and skills required for it to be effective are less well understood. Chapter 7 contributes valuable insights into this process.

The purpose of Part III is to analyze the main themes from the Yantian story and then to apply them to advance our understanding of the practice and theory of co-evolution. Chapter 8 identifies two forms of co-evolution. The first consists of actions taken by the company or external parties that are primarily adaptive. The second consists of actions that influenced the way in which complementary domains evolved. These include managerial actions that influenced the way in which the environment evolved over time and external actions or event that influenced the way the firm evolved. The chapter illustrates both forms of co-evolution through an examination of the interactions of YICT and HPH with the Chinese government and its agencies.

Chapter 9 then develops a systematic analysis of the political dynamics of co-evolution, illustrating these primarily by reference to interactions between the company and government agencies on the issue of port practices. This issue was of vital importance both to the firm because it directly impacted on the port's productivity and the level of service it could offer, and to government authorities because it concerned their ability to regulate the country's frontier. The chapter demonstrates the relevance of applying a political perspective. It develops a theoretical analysis of power and associated processes of influence in corporate co-evolution. This recognizes that while the power bases available to firms and external organizations provide a potential for exercising influence, translating that influence into actual evolutionary change requires specific initiatives.

The closing chapter, Chapter 10, applies insights drawn from the YICT case to formulate guidelines for managers operating in complex environments such as those of China and some other major emerging countries. These guidelines are drawn from what YICT achieved and how this was accomplished. YICT's experience suggests seven key approaches which, together with the gains they produce, can generate a positive cycle of co-evolution over time.

NOTES

1. A terminal is a single operating unit in one port location. It is the maritime equivalent of a manufacturing plant. Ports like Rotterdam and Shanghai comprise several terminals. The port at Yantian in Shenzhen China, featured in this book, has one terminal which has grown through several phases of new investment, so we shall use both 'port' and 'terminal' synonymously.
2. We define 'power' as the potential to ensure the compliance of others, and 'influence' as the exercise of power over others.
3. We shall refer to the joint venture company as YICT and to the terminal itself as Yantian. There were also some other smaller equity-holders, notably the international shipping company Maersk with 10 percent. The Chinese partner was initially called the Dong Peng Industry Company Limited, which later in January 1995 changed its name to the Yantian Port Group.
4. Each year the World Bank compiles a ranking of countries according to the ease of 'doing business' in them in the light of government regulations and practices. The generally lower ranking of emerging economies reflects a high level of government intervention in, and restriction of, business activities. See http://publications.world bank.org.

REFERENCES

Burgelman, R.A. (2002a), *Strategy Is Destiny: How Strategy-Making Shapes a Company's Future*, New York: Free Press.

Burgelman, R.A. (2002b), 'Strategy as vector and the inertia of coevolutionary lock-in', *Administrative Science Quarterly*, **47**, 325–57.

Cantwell, J., J.H. Dunning and S.M. Lundan (2010), 'An evolutionary approach to understanding international business activity: the co-evolution of MNEs and the institutional environment', *Journal of International Business Studies*, **41**, 567–86.

Chandler (Jr), A.D. (1962), *Strategy and Structure*, Cambridge, MA: MIT Press.

Child, J. and T. Tsai (2005), 'The dynamic between firms' environmental strategies and institutional constraints in emerging economies: evidence from China and Taiwan', *Journal of Management Studies*, **42**, 95–125.

Dieleman, M. and J. Boddewyn (2012), 'Using organization structure to buffer political ties in emerging markets: a case study', *Organization Studies*, **33**, 71–95.

Dieleman, M. and W.M. Sachs (2008) 'Coevolution of institutions and corporations in emerging economies: how the Salim Group morphed into an institution of Suharto's crony regime', *Journal of Management Studies*, **45**, 1274–1300.

Flier, B., F.A.J. Van Den Bosch and H.W. Volberda (2003), 'Co-evolution in strategic renewal behaviour of British, Dutch and French financial incumbents', *Journal of Management Studies*, **40**, 2163–87.

Jacques, E. (1951), *The Changing Culture of a Factory*, London: Routledge.

Johnson, G. (1987), *Strategic Change and the Management Process*, Oxford: Blackwell.

Jones, C. (2001), 'Co-evolution of entrepreneurial careers, institutional rules and competitive dynamics in American film, 1985–1920', *Organization Studies*, **22**, 911–44.

Lewin, A.Y., C.P. Long and T.N. Carroll (1999), 'The coevolution of new organizational forms', *Organization Science*, **10**, 535–50.

Lewin, A.Y. and H.W. Volberda (1999), 'Prolegomena on coevolution: a framework for research on strategy and new organizational forms', *Organization Science*, **10**, 519–34.

Meyer, J.W. and W.R. Scott (1983), *Organizational Environments: Ritual and Rationality*, Beverly Hills, CA: Sage.

Murmann, J.P. (2010), 'Reflections on co-evolutionary research in organization science', Presentation to the Organization Science Winter Conference, Steamboat Springs, CO, February.

Pettigrew, A.M. (1985), *The Awakening Giant: Continuity and Change in Imperial Chemical Industries*, Oxford: Blackwell.

Redding, G. and M.A. Witt (2007), *The Future of Chinese Capitalism*, Oxford: Oxford University Press.

Rodrigues, S.B. and J. Child (2008), *Corporate Co-evolution: A Political Perspective*, Chichester: Wiley.

Volberda, H.W. and A.Y. Lewin (2003), 'Co-evolutionary dynamics within and between firms: from evolution to co-evolution', *Journal of Management Studies*, **40**, 2111–36.

White, M.C., D.B. Marin, D.V. Brazeal and W.H. Friedman (1997), 'The evolution of organizations: suggestions from complexity theory about the interplay between natural selection and adaptation', *Human Relations*, **50** (11), 1383–1401.

World Bank (2012), *Doing Business 2012: Making a Difference for Entrepreneurs*, accessed at http://www.doingbusiness.org/reports/doing-business/doing-business-2012.

2. The co-evolutionary perspective[1]

Evolutionary thinking on how different species, including human beings, have developed over time from their originally primitive forms has a 200 year history. It actually predates Charles Darwin's landmark *On the Origin of Species*, which was first published in 1859. The interdependence of species with their environments has been central to this area of inquiry. Most discussions of evolution have centred on the Darwinian theory of natural selection. This holds that there are variations within a species at any one time, but only those members with features best suited to their environment are 'selected' to survive. This 'survival of the fittest' ensures that the best adapted genes are retained and then inherited by the next generation. In this way, species evolve so as to fit their environments. Hence as environments evolve, so inevitably will the species living in, and depending on, them. According to this theory, there is co-evolution but it is driven entirely by the environment.

More recently, evolutionary theory has come to be applied to the social sciences at the 'macro' level of whole economies and societies, the 'meso' level of industries, sectors and regions, and at the 'micro' level of organizations. Veblen (1919) was among the first economists to favour an evolutionary perspective, which implied that economies should be regarded as open evolving systems rather than systems tending toward equilibrium as classical economic theory assumed. Schumpeter (1934) is celebrated as a leading evolutionary thinker in economics, but interestingly his theory of economic evolution under capitalism was one in which development was initiated by firms rather than proceeding through natural selection. It emphasized innovation by individual entrepreneurs as the driving force of change. Although evolutionary thinking has now acquired a strong voice within economics (for example, Nelson and Winter, 1982; Hodgson, 1993), there continues to be a lack of agreement on what is specific about its application to the discipline (Witt, 2008). We shall note later in this chapter how evolutionary and co-evolutionary thinking is today also being informed by other theoretical perspectives drawn from sociology, business strategy, and political science.

There are several reasons why we should be concerned with how firms evolve. The most fundamental is that since they create value for society, it is clearly of interest to understand how firms are able to survive and develop over time. Evolutionary theory also reminds us that firms, like biological species, operate within environments. Their decision-makers have to be extremely mindful of those environments. In a world characterized by continual change, a firm may well fail to survive if it does not adapt to new conditions. To a significant extent, then, firms have to evolve in ways that respond to the evolution of their environments. This, however, applies more to some than to others. There are firms that appear to have the power to dominate their environments, sometimes to an extent that becomes a cause for public alarm. For instance, the ways in which some large companies have misled their customers and investors, and induced politicians to act against the public interest, has fuelled concern over the ethics and accountability of business. By contrast, many smaller companies complain that they are completely at the mercy of external forces.

Firms and their environments therefore evolve together but it seems that how far one drives the other depends greatly on their relative power (Child and Rodrigues, 2011). That is why in this book we espouse a political view of co-evolution. The influence firms and external parties can exercise on each other is an important policy issue. If a firm is subject to too much external constraint or pressure, its leaders may have little room to apply creative strategies that both sustain its evolution and make a real contribution to society. Equally, if a firm is subject to weak external control, it may evolve through irresponsible policies that have a negative impact on its environment.

Before we go further in exploring the co-evolutionary perspective applied to firms, it will be helpful to take a quick look at the historical discourse on evolution that took place within biology. A short historical overview will identify certain fundamental issues that remain very much alive in present-day debate.

DISCOURSE ON EVOLUTION AND ITS CONTEMPORARY RELEVANCE

Evolution refers to the development of a form – an organism or other unit – from a simpler to a more complex or advanced state (*Shorter Oxford English Dictionary*, 2003: vol. 1, 876). The term assumes that the pre-existing form from which evolution proceeds contains the rudiments of the parts of the evolved form. This is consistent with the inheritance of biological genes. As mentioned, discourse on how evolution takes place has centred on Darwin's theory of natural selection. The key question is whether this theory provides an adequate explanation for how a species evolves over time. An alternative view recognizes the possibility that some species, or some members of a species, can adapt to their environments through a process of learning. The debate between selection and adaptation is of direct relevance, by analogy, to an understanding of how firms interact with their environments and the consequences of that interaction for their evolution.

Darwinism applied to firms starts from the premise that they belong to a species – a definable population such as an industry or sector. The criteria for defining a population of firms refer to competitive, regulatory and/or other significant conditions that all member organizations experience in common. Darwinism assumes that firms evolve towards a form that becomes typical of their population as a whole. The process involved is one of natural selection comprising the core Darwinian principles of variation, selection, retention and inheritance. At any point of time, there will be variation in the characteristics of firms constituting a particular population and sharing a common environment. This variation is maintained primarily through the entry of newcomer firms into the population. Within the range of this variation, some firms in the population will possess features better suited to their environment than others. They will eventually be selected to survive, while the others will fail. This means that the fittest firms – those best suited to the environment – will be retained. The more appropriate characteristics which they possess will be then inherited via the passing on of their 'genes', the organizational equivalents of which are their 'routines' in the form of their norms, practices and rules. In this way, the strategic and organizational characteristics of firms are seen to be determined by the environment, which selects those that survive and those that become extinct. If and when the environment changes, the characteristics that firms require for survival will change accordingly. A fundamental assumption of Darwinism is that the individual members of a species have an inherent inertia which prevents them from transforming themselves so as to adapt to the environment. Applying the same logic to firms similarly assumes that they suffer from structural inertia which prevents those less suited to their environment from making adaptations necessary to their survival (for example, Hannan and Freeman, 1977).

The main challenge within biological evolutionary thinking to this environmentally deterministic view came from Lamarckism. The essential thesis that Lamarck (1809) advanced, half a century before the first publication of Darwin's *On the Origin of Species*, is that an organism can pass on to its offspring characteristics which it acquires during its lifetime. This means that the organism can (1) *adapt* to its environment during its lifetime, and (2) pass on that adaptation to its offspring. Lamarck saw adaptation occurring through two processes. One was the way that more frequent use strengthens and develops the features of an organism that are best suited to its environment. The other is the process of inheritance, which was seen to occur through those adapted features being preserved by reproduction. Lamarck also argued that these two processes caused organisms to evolve from simple to complex forms. Although Darwin did not entirely dismiss the idea that organisms could adapt to their environments and that these adaptations could be inherited, Lamarckian thinking became overshadowed by the thesis that evolution is based essentially on natural selection (Gould, 2002). It nevertheless retains its supporters among biologists (Jablonka and Lamb, 2005).

Baldwin (1896) advanced 'a new factor' in evolution which did not rely on Lamarck's inheritance of acquired characteristics, but which at the same time also qualified Darwinism. This was 'organic selection'. The Baldwin factor recognized that organisms could adapt to their environments through applying their *intelligence*. Their adaptation could then be disseminated through at least part of a population through 'conscious imitation', 'maternal instruction' and similar processes. Successful adaptation of this kind helps to account for evolution within the wider regime of natural selection, but it does not rely on the principle of genetic inheritance. Although he did not use the term, Baldwin was actually identifying the role of learning in evolution, for he defined organic selection as 'the organism's behaviour in acquiring new modes or modifications of adaptive function' (1896: 444). Adaptive learning and the dissemination of its outcomes, through informal exchange (socialization) or its formalization into explicit guidelines and rules (externalization), are today recognized as playing a vital role in the ability of firms to adapt to their environments.[2]

The legacy of early evolutionary thinking is evident in the longstanding debate as to whether the forms that firms take are the outcome of environmental selection or of adaptation resulting from strategic choices made by their decision-makers. An increasing number of scholars see merit in drawing upon both selection and adaptation traditions. For example, while Hodgson and Knudsen (2006) argue that there is no plausible alternative to core Darwinian principles for explaining how populations of firms evolve, they admit that a neo-Lamarckian emphasis on human intentionality and the possibility of passing on acquired characteristics can complement Darwinism. The two perspectives are complementary insofar as they focus on different levels of analysis and, hence, emphasize different sets of factors as drivers of the evolutionary process. Neo-Darwinists tend to focus on *whole populations* of organ-izations. They emphasize the economic and institutional features operat-ing in a particular environment that create pressures towards conformity among constituent organizations. These pressures are regarded as un-avoidable and non-negotiable, and hence decisive. Neo-Lamarckians focus on the capabilities of *individual organizations*, or more precisely their decision-makers, to adapt in creative and therefore potentially divergent ways to their environments including migrating from one environment to another. They also acknowledge the potential for decision-makers to pass on such adaptations over time through embed-ding them in organizational routines such as behavioural norms and formal rules. Even organizations with a risk of sclerosis due to their age and size are not necessarily incapable of changing strategic direction, though for them the process may be traumatic and involve the replace-ment of their leadership and substantial restructuring.

Others have argued that it would be advantageous to bridge the dualism within organizational analysis between environmental determin-ism and strategic adaptation. For example, White et al. (1997: 1385) proposed that complexity theory may offer a fruitful context 'in which to view the interplay between self-organization (conscious adaptation) and natural selection'. Child (1997) advanced an evolutionary framework that focused on the dynamics of social interactions both between actors within organizations, and between them and external parties. He argued that 'Within this evolutionary framework, strategic choice only makes sense with reference to both pro-action and re-action ... the mutuality of action and constraint ... It therefore regards the polarization of determin-ism and voluntarism in organizational analysis as misleading' (Child, 1997: 72).

Although they may remain controversial within the biological sciences, the Baldwin and Lamarckian perspectives are each of considerable relevance for understanding the evolution of firms. They encourage a realization that firms, through a process of learning that both informs and results from decisions made by their key actors, can adapt to their environments and to changes in them. This implies that the firms which survive in evolving environments are not just those which happen to be best suited to the new external conditions from the outset, but will also include some which have learned how to adapt to the new circumstances and even take action to change those circumstances. This means that firms have the potential to co-evolve with their environments in a proactive manner. The very notion of organizational strategy is premised on this point.

When drawn together, the strands of debate within both biology and the social sciences suggest that the evolution of firms can take place via three processes. Each is informed by a different perspective in the literature. The first process is evolution through Darwinian selection. This maintains that firms suited to their environment are the ones that survive and prosper. It assumes that many firms suffer from internal inertia due to embedded routines and structures. This inertia is seen to handicap them in adapting to environmental change. The population of firms is therefore maintained by a combination of existing ones which 'fit' the environment and new entrants who also have suitable characteristics. The assumption of isomorphism between firms and their environment generates more interest in how whole populations of firms evolve rather than individual cases. It is assumed that outliers are unlikely to survive and they are therefore not considered to be of much consequence.

The second process is consistent with the 'Baldwin effect' in recognizing the possibilities for firms to adapt to their environments through learning and the sedimentation of that learning into repositories of organizational knowledge. McKinley (2011) argues that the emergence of unfamiliar characteristics in an organization's environment encourages its managers to engage in a fresh interpretation of the new environmental state leading to its 'objectification' as a coherent entity that can guide their actions. This is consistent with the notion of organizational strategy as a process that depends on learning about and assessing the organization's environment – both present and future. Based on that knowledge, a strategy will ideally reflect the needs of the organization to adapt to that environment in terms of: (1) the organization's capabilities (strengths and weaknesses); and (2) the opportunities and threats presented by the environment.[3]

The third perspective goes beyond mere adaptation to the environment. While acknowledging the need for firms to adapt in order to safeguard their long-term survival, this perspective brings in another process, whereby firms not only adapt to the evolution of their environments but also shape that evolution. This is the most developed and complex form of co-evolution, in which the evolution of firms and the evolution of their environments are interdependent through a process of mutual influence. The relative power of firms vis-à-vis external bodies is a key factor in this process, because it is only likely to take place if firms have the power to influence their environments and also know how to use this power (Child and Rodrigues, 2011). Some powerful firms may be able to shape certain features of a given environment to suit their interests and preferred pattern of evolution. This process involves mobilizing the potential of a firm's power through interaction between its leaders and their external counterparts. Such interaction can include informal exchanges of views and information, lobbying and negotiation. There may be opportunities for corporate leaders to alter external circumstances, such as proposed legislation, through negotiation and persuasion. This perspective also recognizes the reciprocal possibility, namely that external bodies such as government agencies and competitors may themselves have the power to shape, even terminate, a firm's evolution. For example, a governmental or other institutional agency could impose regulations that either permit or close off certain evolutionary paths, while a competitor might have the resources to acquire the firm.

Although the three possibilities just outlined reflect the level of influence that a firm can muster vis-à-vis the players in its environment, taken together they also depict a progression whereby a firm has the potential to learn how to become increasingly proactive over time. This progression is represented in Figure 2.1. The first stage is one in which a firm is not adapting to changes in its environment or has not yet learned how to do so. If the firm fails to progress beyond this stage, its relationship with the environment is not likely to last very long. In which case, unless the firm is specially privileged or subsidized in some way, it will not survive. The next stage is more complex in that the firm is now active in securing information about the environment, and engaging with external people and organizations, for the purpose of learning how to adapt better to conditions in that environment. The third stage is more complex still and it may take a firm some time to reach it. Here the firm is doing more than just learning about and evaluating the implications of its environment. It is proactively mobilizing support for its intended strategy, building relationships with key external actors and organizations, consciously articulating the case for its objectives, and building a favourable corporate image. The firm is now trying to shape its environment in order to exercise strategic choice (Child, 1972; 1997). In these circumstances, the environment and the firm are likely to co-evolve to an appreciable extent based on their intensive mutual interaction. This interaction may be cooperative or coercive in nature and can rest upon one or several different forms of power possessed by the interacting parties.

There is another process through which a firm can accommodate environmental conditions in a way that preserves its strategic choice. It entails the selection by firms, or strictly speaking their decision-makers, of the environments in which to operate. This contrasts with the selection of organizations by environments emphasized in the first perspective. If a given environment exhibits characteristics to which it is not possible or is too costly to adapt, the question arises as to whether corporate decision-makers can select a more attractive environment in which to operate. Can

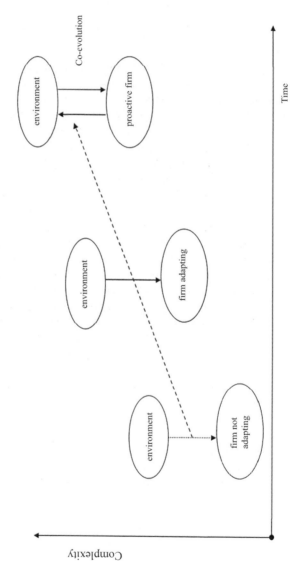

Figure 2.1   The progression toward co-evolution in the relationship between a firm and its environment

they successfully migrate from an unfavourable environment to a more favourable one? They may, for example, consider a more attractive environment to be a country or market in which competitive pressures or political risks are not as extreme as elsewhere. Many firms have in recent years moved some activities 'offshore' to a more favourable environment. Firms may be in a position to choose new environments through new market entry or investment, or to move their capital away from an environment that has become hostile or unrewarding. This process of environmental re-selection is not without cost and may only be achievable in the longer term, but it introduces the possibility that firms may, in this way, be able to reduce external constraints on how they wish to evolve. Environmental re-selection is likely to require considerable negotiation with stakeholders and regulators, which again brings political consider-ations into the picture.

The latter two processes involve pro-action on the part of firms as a factor that impacts on how they evolve. Both envisage that corporate decision-makers can aim to achieve their goals through seeking accom-modations with external parties *within* given environments and through selection *between* environments. These behaviours, in conjunction with external changes and initiatives, are central to the dynamics of co-evolution between firms and their environments.

Both natural selection by the environment and organizational pro-action are expected to give rise to an increasing similarity over time between the characteristics of firms operating in a similar context. Natural selection does this through promoting an organizational profile that best suits the environment. Co-evolution in which corporate initiative is an active force may also make for greater similarity between the firms in a given sector through the effects of leading firms acting as exemplars to other firms, and through the potential they may enjoy of being able to shape some environmental conditions through the influence they have with external organizations. Other firms then have to adapt to these conditions. While anti-trust and similar laws render it hazardous to manipulate the competitive environment through inter-firm collaboration, this constraint does not necessarily apply to a firm's cooperation with government and other agencies in the institutional environment.

CO-EVOLUTION AS A UNIFYING PERSPECTIVE

The concept of co-evolution applied to firms has come to be known as 'corporate co-evolution' (Rodrigues and Child, 2008). It draws on two key insights from evolutionary thinking in biology and economics. The first is a recognition that firms and their environments are inter-dependent – they interact in ways that lead to them developing together over time. The second insight is the realization that, while firms certainly cannot ignore environmental conditions, they are not simply passive in the face of such conditions, waiting to be selected for either survival or extinction. Corporate co-evolution draws attention to the dynamic interaction of forces in a firm's environment with the capacity of its leadership to adapt to these forces, and even in some instances to shape the environment. A co-evolutionary perspective therefore has the potential to inform research on firms that both spans macro and micro levels of analysis and examines adaptation over time (Lewin and Volberda, 1999).

This potential contribution of the co-evolutionary perspective is particularly attractive because it offers a more comprehensive theoretical approach to firms and their environments than any available alternative. In their path-breaking statements on the co-evolutionary perspective, Lewin and Volberda (1999) and Lewin et al. (1999) define its scope to embrace most of the theories that have hitherto contributed partial insights into corporate evolution. These theories contrast with each other in a number of respects:

1.   The level at which they see the main driving force for economic behaviour. Some theories see attributes of the environment as the main determinant of firm behaviour and performance, while others regard the attributes of firms themselves as the most significant determinants. Environmental factors may include the competitive structure and attractiveness of an industry, and the regime of institutional regulation. For example, neo-liberal thinkers argue that less external regulation tends to foster greater dynamism among firms. Attributes of firms themselves may include their corporate governance, their idiosyncratic resources, and their dynamic and entrepreneurial capabilities including the ability to learn and adapt. The co-evolutionary perspective takes both levels into account, as well as the interaction between them.

2.   Related to the question of levels is the contrast among different theories in the degree of freedom they acknowledge corporate decision-makers have to shape events, including environmental conditions. Some theories regard the survival of firms as depending primarily on the extent to which they are able or willing to adopt industry or other externally specified norms. Other theories allow scope for executives to negotiate or influence such norms, including the extent to which they should apply to a given firm, through

social interaction or networking with influential external actors. The co-evolutionary perspective allows for all these possibilities.

3. Existing theories also contrast in the role they ascribe to material forces as opposed to ideational forces as drivers of corporate evolution (Child, 2000). Material forces act on firm evolution primarily through the resources of finance, technology and human competence that firms require for their development. Such resources may be secured from markets based on the ability to pay or to promise future returns, or from public sources such as subsidies or economic rent obtained through governmental protection. An economy achieving rapid growth, such as China during the evolution of YICT, provides a favourable opportunity for a firm to evolve through accumulating material resources. Ideational forces at the macro level are most evident in the form of prevailing ideologies to which firms may feel obliged to conform. At the micro (firm) level, they manifest as entrepreneurial visions and corporate cultures. The YICT story will demonstrate how the material and ideational resources deployed by both the firm and external agencies played an important role in their co-evolution.

4. A fourth contrast is between perspectives that focus on initial conditions for corporate evolution, such as the ownership of a firm or the sector in which it is located, as opposed to focusing on the dynamic properties that affect the course of evolution itself, such as the ability of a firm's leaders to learn and to manage change successfully. Doz (1996) was one of the first analysts to make this distinction. Initial conditions shape the ideational and material foundations of a company, notably its vision and resources respectively. These provide it with the potential to chart a course within its environment through establishing an image and a position in the market. Although subsequent learning and change may be substantial, it has been argued that an organization's initial profile has a residual impact on its form and character through subsequent stages in its development (Stinchcombe, 1965). A similar distinction between initial conditions and ensuing dynamics can inform our understanding of the influence that firms and external organizations respectively have over their co-evolution. Here the initial conditions concern the sources of power available to the corporate and external actors who are involved, while subsequently it becomes a question of how those actors can employ that power to advance their preferred evolutionary paths.

These distinguishing characteristics point to the different, and potentially complementary, contributions that different theoretical perspectives can offer to a study of corporate evolution. Each of them offers valuable insights. The challenge is how to combine these insights in a way that is sufficiently comprehensive and integrated. It is the co-evolutionary perspective's promise to do this that is so attractive.

With this in mind, we now review major contributing perspectives before proceeding to the more over-arching and integrative framework offered by the co-evolutionary approach. Each of these perspectives draws attention to potential drivers for corporate change and evolution. We first consider two approaches that focus on the firm's environment and tend to ascribe a determining role to it. These are the natural selection and institutional theory perspectives. We then turn to approaches which draw attention to the opportunity that the managers of firms may have for taking initiatives within their environments in order to exercise strategic choice.

POTENTIAL DRIVERS FOR CORPORATE EVOLUTION

Natural Selection

Drawing from Darwinism, the natural selection perspective regards the environment in which a firm is located as the main determinant of its performance and hence its capacity to evolve. While firms may have the possibility of moving from one economic environment to another, this is regarded as a costly, difficult to achieve and long-term move. Essentially, firms are seen to be situated in a given environment. This environment determines the action possibilities available to firms that are compatible with their survival. Ports such as Yantian are an almost totally fixed investment, so for their owning companies moving environments would mean taking the drastic steps of closing down or selling a port and establishing or purchasing a new one. When investing in a new port, as Hutchison-Whampoa and the Shenzhen government did in forming YICT, firms have to consider environmental conditions very carefully, particularly the future economic prospects of its hinterland and how favourable the political and regulatory regime is toward realizing those prospects.

Within the natural selection perspective, industrial organization theory (IO) and population ecology (PE) have been two of the most thoroughly researched approaches (Scherer, 1980; Hannan and Freeman, 1989). According to the structure-conduct-performance paradigm in IO (Bain, 1956), industry conditions, namely market concentration, entry barriers and product differentiation, determine market power and hence both the policy options open to firms and their potential performance. PE also assigns primacy to the environment, asserting that resource scarcity and competition select the firms that survive ('retention'), leaving little scope for managerial action to affect outcomes.

Natural selection is seen to reduce the variety of corporate strategies and forms that can survive within a given environment. Both IO and PE approaches assign causal primacy to the environment, so that corporate evolution is seen to be primarily a product of environmental evolution rather than the consequence of strategic autonomy on the part of firms themselves. This perspective gives little attention or credence to the possibility that firms can survive by adapting to their environments rather than being subject to a predestined fate. It certainly does not admit to the possibility that some firms may be sufficiently powerful or skilled to influence that environment and the way it evolves.

Porter (1990) built on the IO approach to extend the range of environmental influences bearing on a firm by adding the quality of resource provision, the presence of supporting industries and the institutional context. The last of these is particularly important in emerging and transition economies (Peng, 2000). It is also of greater significance to firms that are in public ownership and/or subject to direct regulation as are those providing major infrastructure facilities such as ports.

The Institutional Perspective

The institutional perspective is concerned with the ways in which institutions confer legitimacy on, or withhold it from, firms or other organizations and their actions. Institutions are defined here as collective and regulatory complexes consisting of political and social agencies. Institutions potentially dominate firms through their laws, rules and norms that constitute both 'formal rules' and 'informal constraints' (Henrique and Sadorsky, 1996; Lu and Lake, 1997; North, 1990; Powell and DiMaggio, 1991). Scott (1995) argues that there are three fundamental 'pillars' through which this process takes place. The regulative pillar entails formal systems of laws, rules and enforcement mechanisms sanctioned by the state. The second normative pillar exerts pressures for conformity by defining the legitimate means through which socially valued ends can be pursued. Codes of professional conduct and public statements of socially acceptable behaviour fall into this category. The cognitive pillar refers to embedded beliefs and values that are imposed upon, or internalized by, actors in society.

Governmental and social institutions impose regulatory constraints upon, and offer normative guidelines for, the policies of firms and hence the practices they can realistically follow. Institutions can also affect the ability of different groups in society to mobilize opposition to corporate policies, through the laws and regulations that are enacted governing the rights to organize such opposition. If, for example, employees are protected from intimidation when they join a labour union, and if such unions are given the right to organize industrial action, this introduces an additional potential constraint upon corporate actions. Institutions can therefore impose limits on the policy choices available to firms (North, 1990). The institutional perspective perceives that isomorphism – the willingness of firms to conform in their policies and practices with laws, courts, regulatory structures, educational systems, awards and certification and accreditation bodies – enhances their chances of success and survival (Powell and DiMaggio, 1991). While this view is broadly consistent with the natural selection theory of evolution, it does allow for the possibility that firms can learn to adapt to externally imposed requirements.

The institutional perspective is particularly concerned with the ways in which institutions confer legitimacy on organizations and their actions, or withhold it from them (Scott, 1995). Institutions are likely to have particular relevance for the corporate policies and forms adopted by companies managing infrastructure facilities of national strategic import- ance such as ports. Such companies are subject to a high degree of regulation, and the social approval they enjoy depends on how well they meet expectations concerning their contribution to the wider economy and society. This means that their policies and plans require the approval of social and governmental institutions (Powell and DiMaggio, 1991). Because ports require public investment in complementary infrastructure such as transport links, this dependency creates a further means through which institutions can impact on the companies running them (Parsons, 1956; Pfeffer and Salancik, 1978). Institutions can therefore in various ways impose limits on the choices available to corporate leaders (North, 1990).

An element in the successful evolution of any organization is that it learns to develop a configuration of policies and practices, and in doing so establishes a public image that is compatible with external require- ments (Moingeon and Soenen, 2002). Firms that are embedded in an institutional context have to accommodate political regimes (Clegg and Dunkerley, 1980; Granovetter, 1992; Simons and Paul, 1997). This has consequences for the degree of autonomy they enjoy in the definition of their own policies and practices. Private organizations have more autonomy in defining their combination of mission and distinctive competence. They have more choice between alternatives, and greater freedom to pursue different strategies for securing appropriate resources from the marketplace and satisfying stakeholders. Neo-classical economists have for this reason argued that governmental institutions generate organizational traits that lead to inefficiencies (Friedman, 1962). This argument implies that state ownership or heavy governmental regulation is a handicap for a firm and something to be avoided. It does, however, overlook the potential benefits of harmonious cooperation between business and government which the history of YICT will clearly demonstrate.

Institutions are also socializing agents that transmit values and ideas to firms (Hall and Soskice, 2001). Governmental or non-governmental agencies (such as NGOs and labour unions) can filter political pressures by reconfiguring them in terms of ideology, vision or models of organizing. In so doing, institutions do not necessarily operate at arm's length from firms, even from those that are not publicly owned. They can influence firms through specific social arrangements that comprise a 'relational framework' (Scott and Meyer, 1983), such as joint business-governmental committees or study groups, which permit networks or coalitions to form. Such networks are institutionally sanctioned arrangements that connect actors through participation in a common discourse. They cross system levels by involving people who occupy strategic decision-making roles within both institutional agencies and firms (Castilla et al., 2000). Relational frameworks are highly relevant to the process of accommodation between institutional priorities and firms' preferred strategies. They provide channels through which institutional bodies can express approval or otherwise of particular corporate policies and practices. At the same time, they can also provide a conduit for corporate executives to express their point of view, and through which leading firms may have an opportunity to shape institutional regulations by offering relevant and scarce technical expertise. It will become apparent that relational frameworks played a central role in the co-evolution of YICT, especially those it developed with the government regulatory agencies that directly affected its port operations.

Many writers within both the PE and institutional perspectives emphasize the ways in which institutions impose conformity on their norms and rules in a constraining and coercive manner (DiMaggio and Powell, 1991). However, the *interaction* between institutions and leading firms may also encourage normative and mimetic isomorphism on a more cooperative basis. This is evident in the case of corporate policies towards the natural environment. The trend of green strategic change, which usually commences in a particular industrial sector such as chemicals and spreads first among competitors, is a form of normative conformity and mimicry. However, this conformity among firms does not simply arise from external institutional pressures. For example, in the chemicals sector, although it initially resisted the Montreal ozone protocol, DuPont became a leader, recognized by governments and environmental professionals, in greening as well as in industrial and occupational safety. The company has been in a position to establish industrial standards for others to follow, including its competitors. In extreme cases, securing the legitimacy to remain in business may largely depend upon a firm's ability to conform to the superior environmental standards implemented by such leading edge companies (Nehrt, 1998). In emerging economies, governments are known to have utilized the environmental protection codes of large, reputable corporations – such as Dow Chemical, DuPont and ICI – as examples upon which to base their regulations (Child and Tsai, 2005). This encourages mimicry and normative conformity within the sector. YICT's role as a leader and propagator of advanced practices within China's port sector followed a similar pattern.

Resource Dependence

The institutional perspective, and the so-called 'new' institutionalism in particular (Powell and DiMaggio, 1991), argues for a deeper understanding of the interaction between institutions and organizations. However, it often conveys a sense of corporate passivity that can be quite misleading. Oliver (1991) therefore argued for a combination of the resource dependence and institutional perspectives. She built on this combination to identify five 'strategic responses' to institutional pressures, ranging from the passive to the proactive. This is a significant departure from new institutional theory's failure to recognize proactive firm behaviour, and from its emphasis on conformity, isomorphism, and adherence to norms and values as a condition of firms' survival. The main focus of the resource dependence perspective is a political one, namely the power that the availability of key financial, technical and other resources gives either to the people who provide these resources to firms or to the firms which themselves possess such resources (Pfeffer and Salancik, 1978).

The institutional perspective assumes that, in seeking social legitimacy, a firm will abide by external regulations, whether they are formal such as enacted laws, or informal as in the case of pressures from NGOs' environmental protection demands. The resource dependence perspective, however, points out that firms may be able to mobilize resources of finance, technology and expertise either to establish a degree of independence from institutional demands or to negotiate accommodations to them that are acceptable to the firms. In emerging economies, leading firms will often be in a position to offer government inducements, such as support for educational and other social programmes, as a *quid pro quo* for negotiating some flexibility in the extent and manner to which regulations are applied to them. The advanced expertise they possess can also, through relational frameworks, be applied to the framing of government policies and regulations within which they have to work. Even if institutional constraints are applied strictly, Porter and Linde (1995) note that companies may be able to take adaptive action by being more innovative in all aspects of their operations, including the pursuit of greater resource productivity, in order to reduce the burden of compliance.

Despite acknowledgment by resource dependence theorists that firms may mobilize resources to counteract institutional constraints, they join institutional theorists in tending to assume an asymmetry of power in favour of environmental bodies and against organizations. It is true that 'old' institutional theory did take into account political initiatives by organizational leaders, such as the successful lobbying and co-optation strategies of the Tennessee Valley Authority (Selznick, 1949). Pfeffer and Salancik (1978) also recognized that there may be some scope for organizational managers to exercise a degree of strategic choice in negotiation with external resource providers, a possibility to which Pfeffer gave rather more attention in subsequent works (Pfeffer, 1992). Nevertheless, the discussion of options for organizational leaders to take the initiative in their dealings with environmental bodies is generally underdeveloped within both institutional and resource dependence perspectives. A political perspective, which by definition is concerned with the mobilization and exercise of power, has the potential to make up for this shortfall by drawing attention to ways in which firms may proactively use resources in their dealings with institutional bodies.

Bargaining Power and Strategic Choice

Within the broad ambit of a political perspective, two specific theoretical focuses – 'bargaining power' and 'strategic choice' – explicitly draw attention to the need to take into account proactive as well as reactive strategic options. The 'bargaining power' perspective was advanced as a modification to resource dependence theory. It suggests that the bargaining powers and negotiating skills of a firm's management may mediate the control implications of resource dependence (Blodgett, 1991). Bargaining power can also be used as a strategic response to institutional pressure. A company may be able to negotiate a more favourable accommodation with institutional regulations through exploiting legal loopholes, or it may be able to negotiate favourable terms with regulators by offering other valued social benefits such as the creation of local employment (Leonard, 1988). Alternatively, it may negotiate on the basis of offering to contribute assets at its command, such as technical expertise or investment or socially-valued improvements, in return for securing favourable treatment in support of its own development concerning matters such as business licences, investment incentives, or infrastructure provision. Hence, the bargaining power perspective warns against an assumption that the impact of resource dependence is entirely deterministic.

The concept of 'bargaining power' takes into account both baseline sources of power and the dynamics of how a party may mobilize these so as to exercise influence over other parties. Thus a firm may be able to increase its bargaining power within the co-evolutionary process by establishing coalitions with other parties, co-opting other interests, and enhancing its legitimacy. The concept has been applied to the relations between firms and other parties, usually governments (Eden et al., 2005; Moon and Lado, 2000). Knowledge-based resources may offer particular leverage for enhancing a firm's bargaining power vis-à-vis governments (Lohrke et al., 2007). Students of marketing have drawn similar distinctions between a firm's structurally-based market power and its enhancement through persuasion and other non-coercive initiatives that may be adopted when relating with customers through marketing channels (Gaski, 1984; Weitz and Jap, 1995). While earlier studies focused on the material and symbolic sources of power (for example, Hickson et al., 1971), more recent scholarship has drawn attention to the capacity of firms to create relationships that help them to build upon such sources in order to achieve their business goals (for example, Frynas et al., 2006). The implication is that a firm may be able to increase its bargaining power within the co-evolutionary process through the initiatives it takes within its relational framework with external parties.

The strategic choice perspective reverses the assumption of environmental determinism by focusing on the role played by managers in shaping conditions and processes both outside and within the firm (Child, 1972; 1997). It draws upon the social action approach within sociology (Weber, 1964; Silverman, 1978) and strategic management theory (Miles and Snow, 1978) to advance the view that managerial intentions and actions can impact upon how an organization evolves and even upon its environment. On the one hand, the strategic choice approach accepts that environments have properties that cannot simply be enacted or negotiated away by corporate leaders. It therefore attaches considerable importance to the question of whether such leaders are able to select an attractive environment in which to operate. In recognizing this as a distinct possibility, the strategic choice perspective contrasts sharply with the IO approach. A firm's executives may, for example, consider an attractive environment to be one in which social or political pressures are not as extreme as elsewhere. They may be in a position to threaten to move their capital away from an institutionally hostile environment, which could cause embarrassment for a country seeking to attract foreign investment.

On the other hand, strategic choice analysis also recognizes that it may be possible at least to moderate some external conditions through personal interaction between key corporate personnel and their external counterparts. Such interaction can include informal exchanges of views and information, lobbying and negotiation. There may even be opportunities for executives to go further and actually amend external conditions through negotiation and persuasion. This is consistent with the bargaining power perspective. In other words, the strategic choice view sees key corporate actors as seeking to realize their goals both through selection *between* environments, and by seeking accommodations with external parties *within* given environments.

Strategy analysts recognize that managers have a potentially wide range of actions available to them (Grant, 2009). Cooperation with other organizations, including institutional agencies, is one of the strategic options available to firms. The possibility of cooperation with external agencies is given relatively little attention in the institutional and resource dependence perspectives. Both imply that the leaders of organizations come under pressure to comply with external demands, and hence that the relationship may be one of antagonism and even resentment rather than one of positive cooperation. Game theory (Axelrod, 1984) reminds us that two parties in a continuing relationship will usually in the long term secure their objectives better through cooperation than by attempting to maximize short-term gains at the expense of the other party. Thus the aspirations of governmental policy may be more effectively met through cooperation between regulatory agencies and companies, especially when the latter are, as a result, willing to contribute from their expertise and resources to the attainment of public goals. At the same time the companies are then better able to realize their business objectives in the absence of distracting legal processes or threatening political pressures.

The theoretical perspectives just reviewed focus on the respective roles of: (1) constraints on firms arising from the industrial and institutional contexts; and (2) the managerial actions and initiatives taken by the leaders of firms. Whereas attention to external constraints lends itself to an assumption of environmental determinism, attention to managerial action lends itself to the recognition of strategic choice achieved through the negotiation and selection of preferred policies. A number of scholars, however, have argued that both sets of factors are likely to be operative, and therefore that the relationship and interaction between the two have to be taken into account.

Initial Conditions and Adaptive Learning

The contrast between external determinants and adaptive behaviour also informs the distinction between the initial basis on which firms are established and their ability to adapt subsequently through a process of learning. Firms are created with a set of initial conditions. Initial conditions can be both ideational, such as the founding mission given to a firm; and material, such as the capital and competencies with which a firm is endowed. The industry in which a firm is first established creates a set of initial conditions. IO theorists tend to give primacy to initial conditions by assuming that it is not easy for firms to escape the industries in which they are founded. Thus a firm's initial conditions may be expected to have a significant residual effect on its subsequent evolution. They create a 'heritage' in terms of corporate identity and culture, and a 'legacy' in terms of inherited structures, practices, and endowments. A firm's initial conditions, along with its capacity to perform as expected, affect its subsequent evolution. As Stinchcombe (1965) illustrated in his seminal essay, organizations can bear the marks of their initial founding conditions for a very long time over the years of their subsequent development.

This suggests a number of possibilities. One is that the identity and public image attaching to a firm at its foundation, or formed in its early stages of development, will continue to be meaningful both for its members and for its other stakeholders even if conditions subsequently change. Another possibility is that the subsequent success of a firm, including its ability to adapt through learning, will depend importantly on the quality of resources provided, and on the appropriateness of the structure laid down for it, at its foundation. Thus initial conditions are likely to exert an influence on a company's subsequent evolution, including its ability to incorporate and adjust to learning, even though later decisions and events will also play a part. Doz (1996) concluded from a close study of three international strategic alliances that a combination of initial conditions and subsequent learning produced an evolutionary process leading to success or failure of cooperation.

Initial conditions may predispose to the retention of founding ideas and material provisions. By contrast, subsequent learning provides an impetus toward changing these. The conjunction of initial conditions and subsequent learning implies that corporate evolution will be characterized by both continuity and change. Several previous studies have pointed to the existence of this apparent paradox (for example, Pettigrew, 1985; Child and Smith, 1987). They indicate that in a study of corporate evolution it is necessary to be alert to instances of where continuity coexists with change (dis-continuity), and how this co-incidence is accommodated. One may postulate that a balance needs to be struck between each aspect if corporate evolution is to be maintained over time. If there is too much discontinuity, a firm may lose its distinctive competencies and the accumulated knowledge that is held by people declared redundant or encapsulated in discarded routines. If there is too much continuity, a firm may fail to adapt to a changing environment.

AN OVER-ARCHING PERSPECTIVE: CO-EVOLUTION

The theoretical perspectives considered so far in this chapter offer a set of distinctive contributions. They distinguish between levels of analysis – economy and society (macro), industry, sector or region (meso) and firm (micro) – although organizations can extend across these levels such as levels of government bridging macro and meso levels, and firms with ties to a parent company prominent in the global industry. Some perspectives emphasize the determination of firm behaviour and change by higher-level variables, while others emphasize the ability of managers to negotiate external conditions. Some, like institutional theorists, draw attention to the relevance of the ideas incorporated in norms, while others, like economists, focus their analyses on material factors. Some adopt a relatively static view, emphasizing the power of initial conditions like industry membership, while others adopt a more evolutionary view, stressing the role both of changing circumstances and the ability of organizations to benefit from learning.

Therefore, despite their undoubted value, each perspective on its own contributes only a partial insight. There is a need to bring them together within an over-arching approach that more adequately addresses the dynamics of corporate evolution over time. This is the aim and claim of the so-called 'co-evolutionary' perspective developed in recent years.

Here we introduce this perspective. However, we will return to it in Chapters 8 and 9 where it will be developed further by adding a political dimension.

The co-evolutionary perspective regards environments and organizations as evolving interactively over time (Murmann, 2010). It 'considers organizations, their populations, and their environments as the interdependent outcome of managerial actions, institutional influences, and extra-institutional changes (technological, sociopolitical, and other environmental phenomena)' (Lewin et al., 1999: 535). It posits a framework of analysis, focusing on firms, in which there are on-going recursive processes linking the evolution of institutional and extra-institutional environments with that of the firms themselves. These processes are mediated by managerial action, strategic intent, adaptation and performance achievement in each firm, as well as by the competitive dynamics established by the behaviour of all firms in a sector. It is important to note that while the focus on strategic evolution adopted by writers such as Burgelman (2002) and Johnson (1987) is essential to the co-evolutionary perspective, the scope of co-evolutionary inquiry is a broader one. Studies of strategic change do, of course, take the environment into account, but they tend to confine themselves to its economic and other material features. They have not generally considered the significance of institutional and political factors, including those that can be conveyed in influential ideas concerning the legitimacy of corporate management and its practices. In addition, their heavy focus on the firm tends to divert attention from external actors and how corporate leaders interact with them.

A co-evolutionary perspective has the potential to inform any research on organizations that spans levels of analysis, especially 'firm' and 'environment', and that involves development over time (Lewin and Volberda, 1999). By drawing attention to the continuing interdependence between the context and the organization, the co-evolutionary perspective offers a framework in which the development of firms and their populations can be better understood. It endeavours to take into account both the factors driving such development and the interactive processes that are involved. The co-evolutionary perspective also has the significant advantage of drawing attention to the dynamic confluence and interaction over time of forces stemming from an organization's environment and the capacity of its management, for its part, to respond to these forces and indeed in some measure to shape that environment.

Earlier in this chapter we noted the continuing debate between those who see organizations evolving primarily through a process of adapting to their environments and others who see firms or other organizations as having some potential to influence their environments, depending on their negotiating skills and the power they possess. This divergence of view gives rise to two kinds of interpretation that can be attached to the concept of co-evolution. The first interpretation is that co-evolution signifies the development of an organization alongside that of its environment largely through a process of the former adapting to the latter. This may be called 'asymmetrical co-evolution', in that the environment is its primary driver due to the ultimate sanction that actors and forces in the environment are seen to have over the survival of organizations. The second interpretation regards co-evolution as a process in which both the organization and constituents of its environment are able to actively influence the evolution of the other. This may be called 'symmetrical co-evolution' in that it is driven both by developments in the environment and by the actions of an organization's leaders. Power and influence is more evenly distributed between the two sets of actors.

While the co-evolutionary perspective has only been developed in a comprehensive form since the mid-1990s, it was foreshadowed in the insights of several scholars who were concerned with the dynamics of organizations' relations with their environments. Selznick's (1949) study of how the Tennessee Valley Authority sought to overcome opposition to its plans under the 'New Deal' was a pioneering analysis of how an organization contributed to the evolution of a community into which it was inserted. Another example is the model of context, structure and process that Pettigrew (1985) developed to interpret his detailed longitudinal study of ICI. Pettigrew was one of the first scholars to argue for longitudinal studies of organizational change within their environments that could advance theorizing on the interactions between context, structure and process. The strategic choice analysis offered by Child (1972) also presaged the co-evolutionary perspective in focusing on the potentially mutual impact that an organization's leading group and parties in the environment could have upon each other. In a later elaboration, Child (1997) distinguished two levels of dynamic interaction in the development of organizations and their environments, through the processes of what he termed inner and outer structuration.

More recent work has brought together a number of theoretical strands informing co-evolution. Particularly important contributions are to be found in the pages of three journal special issues (*Organization Science* (Lewin et al., 1999), *Organization Studies* (Lewin and Koza, 2001), *Journal of Management Studies* (Lewin, 2003)). Nevertheless, Rodrigues and Child (2008) in their book *Corporate Co-evolution* pointed out that two aspects of co-evolution remained under-researched. One concerned the processes whereby co-evolution actually takes place. Their study of the Brazilian telecommunications company Telemig during its 27-year lifespan explores these processes and in particular identifies and conceptualizes their political dimensions. The second under-researched aspect of co-evolution is how it proceeds within highly politicized and institutionalized environments that at first sight do not seem to allow much scope for corporate initiative. Only limited attention has been given so far to the evolution of firms that are subject to a high level of institutional control, through public ownership or regulation.

The present book addresses these under-researched issues. In so doing, it develops the work of Rodrigues and Child (2008) in several ways. Principally, it expands and explores, in more detail, the political perspective on how firms co-evolve with their governmental and institutional environments. YICT is a joint venture between a major multinational corporation, the Shenzhen local government and private minority shareholders. This means that, compared to Telemig which was wholly state-owned for most of its life, YICT has had greater formal autonomy from the state. At the same time it operates within an environment in which government regulation and influence is very strong. YICT has enjoyed a greater strategic flexibility when dealing with that environment because its formal link to (local) government is based on a joint venture contract, which specifically recognized its managerial autonomy. A study of YICT can therefore throw further light on the politics of co-evolutionary development, in the relations both between private and government joint venture partners and between the company and its wider environment. These relations have been hitherto difficult to penetrate.

A POLITICAL VIEW

The theory-building aim of this book is to develop a political perspective on corporate co-evolution. It focuses on the co-evolution of the firm and its political environment within a highly 'institutionalized' business system (Oliver, 1992). This contrasts with the traditional theory of the firm which assumes an economic entity and market competition free of political influences. A political perspective draws attention to the intentionality and power resources of relevant actors, and suggests that co-evolution is the outcome of relational processes between them. It recognizes the role of strategic choice on the part of individual firms and external organizations rather than seeing evolution as the product of transcendent deterministic forces operating on whole populations of organizations, as has been assumed by Darwinist evolutionary thinking (Hodgson, 1993; Aldrich and Ruef, 2006).

Child (1972) pointed out that the actions taken on behalf of an organization are likely to result from a decision process that is shaped significantly by internal politics (see also Child et al., 2010). This view received strong empirical support from Pettigrew's (1973) study *The Politics of Organizational Decision Making*. It was also reinforced by Johnson's (1987) detailed study of strategic change in the clothing retailer Foster Brothers. Johnson was concerned with understanding how managers' interpretations informed their actions (or inaction) as their competitive environment changed dramatically for the worse. Foster Brothers experienced greatly strengthening competitive pressures in the 1980s and it provides an example of externally-driven corporate evolution. Johnson's study provides insights into how corporate management attempted to achieve adaptive strategic change. It identifies political processes within the company, such as lobbying for change and mobilizing support, as conditions for strategic change to be formulated and implemented. Johnson's study is of a company that lacked the power to exert significant influence over its environment and where 'the business environment influenced and constrained strategy' (Johnson, 1987: 201). While a firm is always likely to face a degree of environmental constraint, the present study of YICT will reveal that the balance between environmental constraint and strategic choice can vary, and that this reflects the influence the leaders of a firm can create and exert within their environment. This balance could be said to lie at the heart of the co-evolutionary process.

In general, most attention has been accorded to how external actors, such as institutions, impose constraints on firms' choices and strategies through compliance mechanisms and regulations (Peng et al., 2006; Kostova and Roth, 2002). However, firms are also able to influence institutions or governments. Some firms are able to do this through building up political capital (Frynas et al., 2006), while others may induce significant changes in levels of competition by collectively mobilizing economic and institutional agents around a cause or business model (Rodrigues and Child, 2008). In emerging economies, firms can protect themselves against the risk of external political dependence through various buffering mechanisms (Dieleman and Boddewyn, 2012). Understanding these processes requires an analysis which goes beyond mere competitive advantage, and which considers how firms are able to deploy material and symbolic resources, and mobilize allies, to influence the evolution of their environments in pursuit of their goals.

Dieleman and Sach's (2008) study of how the Salim Group in Indonesia evolved in a close relationship with a 'crony regime' also augments the political view in important ways. It is one of the first studies into how individual companies can co-evolve with institutions and it makes several contributions to our understanding. One is that it shows how, under some circumstances at least, firms can shape institutions to their advantage through aligning their interests with those of governments and politicians. A second contribution is to identify the ways in which firms can develop their influence with external institutions. These include formulating a clear corporate vision that is sympathetically received by external actors, developing firm-specific competencies that those actors value, and establishing close relationships with them based on reciprocity. The study reported in this book will confirm the validity and value of these insights. It will also expand upon an important observation concerning the role of corporate power, that Dieleman and Sachs (2008: 1296) make in their conclusion:

> We find that classical institutional theory tracing corporate strategy to contextual factors provides a good explanatory framework when a firm is relatively small and insignificant. When a firm is more powerful, one must also look at managerial intentionality and at reciprocal influences between a firm and the institutions in which it is embedded.

Our study of YICT's evolution over a period of 16 years from inception to maturity addresses the two under-researched areas identified earlier – how corporate co-evolution takes place and how it can proceed within highly politicized and institutionalized environments. It examines the sequence of related events that brought about the co-evolution of the firm and significant players in its environment. It will become clear that the co-evolution cannot be understood without reference to a political perspective; it took place because of political actions both on the part of the Chinese government, in the name of its economic reform and modernization policy, and on the part of the company, in the name of its vision to become a 'world-class port'. An application of concepts and insights from political science – power, influence, ideology, mobilization, and legitimacy – will be key to this understanding. Bringing a political approach into co-evolutionary thinking means appreciating that corporate co-evolution does not come about automatically, like ripe apples falling from trees. Rather, it is driven by initiatives consciously taken by the firm and relevant external actors who are the central interacting parties to it. Each participant in the process has its own interests and way of articulating these ideologically. The main message of this book for both academic and practitioner readers is that power and politics matter in the processes whereby firms and environments evolve together.

NOTES

1. This chapter draws upon Rodrigues and Child (2008) and Child (2012).
2. Socialization and externalization, as two processes of converting knowledge into organizational property, were identified by Nonaka and Takeuchi (1995).
3. This is the classical SWOT (strengths, weaknesses, opportunities, threats) framework in business strategy analysis.

REFERENCES

Aldrich, H.E. and M. Ruef (2006), *Organizations Evolving* (2nd edition), Thousand Oaks, CA: Sage.

Axelrod, R. (1984), *The Evolution of Co-operation*, New York: Basic Books.

Bain, J.S. (1956), *Barriers to New Competition*, Cambridge, MA: Harvard University Press.

Baldwin, J.M. (1896), 'A new factor in evolution', *The American Naturalist*, **30** (June), 441–51.

Blodgett, L.L. (1991), 'Partner contributions as predictors of equity share in international joint ventures', *Journal of International Business Studies*, **22**, 63–78.

Burgelman, R.A. (2002), *Strategy Is Destiny: How Strategy-Making Shapes a Company's Future*, New York: Free Press.

Castilla, E., H. Hwang, E. Granovetter and M. Granovetter (2000), 'Social networks in Silicon Valley', in W. Miller, H. Rowen, C. Lee and M. Hancock (eds), *How Silicon Valley Works*, Stanford, CA: Stanford University Press.

Child, J. (1972), 'Organizational structure, environment and performance: the role of strategic choice', *Sociology*, **6**, 1–22.

Child, J. (1997), 'Strategic choice in the analysis of action, structure, organizations and environment: retrospect and prospect', *Organization Studies*, **18**, 43–76.

Child, J. (2000), 'Theorizing about organization cross-nationally', *Advances in International Comparative Management*, **13**, 27–76.

Child, J. (2012), 'Introduction', in J. Child (ed.), *The Evolution of Organizations*, Cheltenham, UK and Northampton, MA: Edward Elgar.

Child, J., S. Elbanna and S.B. Rodrigues (2010), 'The political aspects of strategic decision making', in P.C. Nutt and D.C. Wilson (eds), *Handbook of Decision Making*, Chichester: Wiley, pp. 105–37.

Child, J. and S.B. Rodrigues (2011), 'How organizations engage with external complexity: a political action perspective', *Organization Studies*, **32**, 803–24.

Child, J. and C. Smith (1987), 'The context and process of organizational transformation: Cadbury Limited in its sector', *Journal of Management Studies*, **24**, 565–93.

Child, J. and T. Tsai (2005), 'The dynamic between firms' environmental strategies and institutional constraints in emerging economies: evidence from China and Taiwan', *Journal of Management Studies*, **42**, 95–125.

Clegg, S.R. and D. Dunkerley (1980), *Organization Class and Control*, London: Routledge & Kegan Paul.

Darwin, C. (1859), *On the Origin of Species*, London: John Murray.

Dieleman, M. and J. Boddewyn (2012), 'Using organization structure to buffer political ties in emerging markets: a case study', *Organization Studies*, **33**, 71–95.

Dieleman, M. and W.M. Sachs (2008), 'Coevolution of institutions and corporations in emerging economies: how the Salim Group morphed into an institution of Suharto's crony regime', *Journal of Management Studies*, **45**, 1274–1300.

DiMaggio, P.J. and W.W. Powell (1991), 'The iron cage revisited: institutional isomorphism and collective rationality', in W.W. Powell and P.J. DiMaggio (eds), *The New Institutionalism in Organizational Analysis*, Chicago: University of Chicago Press, pp. 63–82.

Doz, Y.L. (1996), 'The evolution of cooperation in strategic alliances: initial conditions or learning processes?', *Strategic Management Journal*, **17**, 55–83.

Eden, L., S. Lenway and D. Schuler (2005), 'From the obsolescing bargain to the political bargaining model', in R. Grosse (ed.), *International Business–Government Relations in the 21st Century,* Cambridge: Cambridge University Press: 251–272.

Friedman, M. (1962), *Capitalism and Freedom*, Chicago: University of Chicago Press.

Frynas, J.G., K. Mellahi and G.A. Pigman (2006), 'First mover advantages in international business and firm-specific political resources', *Strategic Management Journal*, **27**, 321–45.

Gaski, J.F. (1984), 'The theory of power and conflict in channels of distribution', *The Journal of Marketing*, **48**, 9–29.

Gould, S.J. (2002), *The Structure of Evolutionary Theory*, Harvard: Belknap Harvard.

Granovetter, M. (1992), 'Economic action and social structure', in M. Granovetter and R. Swedberg (eds), *The Sociology of Economic Life*, Boulder, CO: Westview Press, pp. 53–84.

Grant, R.M. (2009), *Contemporary Strategy Analysis* (7th edition), Chichester: Wiley.

Hall, P.A. and D. Soskice (eds) (2001), *Varieties of Capitalism: The Institutional Foundations of Comparative Advantage*, Oxford: Oxford University Press.

Hannan, M.T. and J.H. Freeman (1977), 'The population ecology of organizations', *American Journal of Sociology*, **82**, 929–64.

Hannan, M.T. and J.H. Freeman (1989), *Organizational Ecology*, Cambridge, MA: Harvard University Press.

Henrique, I. and P. Sadorsky (1996), 'The determinants of an environmentally responsive firm: an empirical approach', *Journal of Environmental Economics and Management*, **30**, 381–95.

Hickson, D.J., C.R. Hinings, C.A. Lee, R.E. Schneck and J.M. Pennings (1971), 'A strategic contingencies' theory of intraorganizational power', *Administrative Science Quarterly*, **16**, 216–29.

Hodgson, G.M. (1993), *Economics and Evolution, Bringing Life Back into Economics*, Cambridge, UK: Polity Press.

Hodgson, G.M. and T. Knudsen (2006), 'Why we need a generalized Darwinism, and why generalized Darwinism is not enough', *Journal of Economic Behavior and Organization*, **61**, 1–19.

Jablonka, E. and M.J. Lamb (2005), *Evolution in Four Dimensions: Genetic, Epigenetic, Behavioral, and Symbolic Variations in the History of Life*, Cambridge, MA: MIT Press.

Johnson, G. (1987), *Strategic Change and the Management Process*, Oxford: Blackwell.

Kostova, T. and Roth, K. (2002), 'Adoption of an organizational practice by subsidiaries of multinational corporations: institutional and relational effects', *Academy of Management Journal*, **45**, 215–33.

Lamarck, J.-B. (1809), *Philosophie Zoologique*, Paris: Dentu.

Leonard, H.J. (1988), *Pollution and the Struggle for World Product*, Cambridge: Cambridge University Press.

Lewin, A.Y., M.P. Koza (2001), 'Multi-level analysis and co-evolution', Special Issue, *Organization Studies*, **22** (6).

Lewin, A.Y., C.P. Long and T.N. Carroll (1999), 'The coevolution of new organizational forms', *Organization Science*, **10** (5), 535–50.

Lewin, A.Y. and H. Volberda (1999), 'Prolegomena on coevolution: a framework for research on strategy and new organizational forms', *Organization Science*, **10**, 519–34.

Lewin, A.Y. and H.W. Volberda (2003), 'Beyond adaptation vs selection research: organizing self-renewal in co-evolving environments', special research symposium, *Journal of Management Studies*, **40** (8), 2109–10.

Lohrke, F.T., G.W. Simpson and D.M. Hunt (2007), 'Extending the bargaining power model: eighteenth century lessons from Panton, Leslie and Company in managing political risk', *Journal of Management History*, **13**, 153–71.

Lu, Y. and D. Lake (1997), 'Managing international joint ventures: an institutional approach', in P.W. Beamish and J.P. Killing (eds), *Corporate Strategies: European Perspectives*, San Francisco: The New Lexington Press, pp. 74–99.

McKinley, W. (2011), 'Organizational contexts for environmental construction and objectification activity', *Journal of Management Studies*, **48**, 804–28.

Miles, R.E. and C.C. Snow (1978), *Organizational Strategy, Structure and Process*, New York: McGraw-Hill.

Moingeon, B. and G. Soenen (eds) (2002), *Corporate and Organizational Identities*, London: Routledge.

Moon, C.W. and A.A. Lado (2000), 'MNC-host government bargaining power relationship: a critique and extension within the resource-based view', *Journal of Management*, **26**, 85–117.

Murmann, J.P. (2010), 'Reflections on co-evolutionary research in organizational science', *Organization Science Winter Conference*, Steamboat Springs, CO, 4 February.

Nehrt, C. (1998), 'Maintainability of first mover advantages when environmental regulations differ between countries', *Academy of Management Review*, **23** (1), 77–97.

Nelson, R.R. and S.G. Winter (1982), *An Evolutionary Theory of Economic Change*, Cambridge, MA: Harvard University Press.

Nonaka, I. and H. Takeuchi (1995), *The Knowledge-Creating Company*, New York: Oxford University Press.

North, D.C. (1990), *Institutions, Institutional Change and Economic Performance*, Cambridge: Cambridge University Press.

Oliver, C. (1991), 'Strategic responses to institutional processes', *Academy of Management Review*, **1**, 145–79.

Oliver, C. (1992), 'The antecedents of deinstitutionalization', *Organization Studies*, **13**, 563–88.

Parsons, T. (1956), 'Suggestions for a sociological approach to the theory of organizations – I', *Administrative Science Quarterly*, **1**, 63–85.

Peng, M.W. (2000), *Business Strategies in Transition Economies*, Thousand Oaks, CA: Sage.

Pettigrew, A.M. (1973), *The Politics of Organizational Decision Making*, London: Tavistock.

Pettigrew, A.M. (1985), *The Awakening Giant*, Oxford: Blackwell.

Pfeffer, J. (1992), *Managing with Power*, Boston, MA: Harvard Business School Press.

Pfeffer, J. and G.R. Salancik (1978), *The External Control of Organizations: A Resource Dependence Perspective*, New York: Harper and Row.

Porter, M.E. (1990), *The Competitive Advantage of Nations*, New York: Free Press.

Porter, M. and C. Linde (1995), 'Green and competitive: ending the stalemate', *Harvard Business Review*, September–October, 120–34.

Powell, W.W. and P.J. DiMaggio (eds) (1991), *The New Institutionalism in Organizational Analysis*, Chicago, IL: University of Chicago Press.

Rodrigues, S.B. and J. Child (2008), *Corporate Co-evolution: A Political Perspective*, Chichester: Wiley.

Scherer, F.M. (1980), *Industrial Market Structure and Economic Performance* (2nd edition), Chicago: Rand McNally.

Schumpeter, J. (1934), *The Theory of Economic Development*, Cambridge, MA: Harvard University Press.

Scott, W.R. (1995), *Institutions and Organizations,* Thousand Oaks, CA: Sage.

Scott, W.R. and J. Meyer (eds) (1983), *Organizational Environments: Ritual and Rationality*, Beverley Hills, CA: Sage.

Selznick, P. (1949), *TVA and the Grass Roots*, Berkeley: University of California Press.

Shorter Oxford English Dictionary (5th edition) (2003), Oxford: Oxford University Press.

Silverman, D. (1978), *The Theory of Organisations: A Sociological Framework*, London: Open University Press.

Simons, T. and I. Paul (1997), 'Organization and ideology: Kibbutzim and hired labor, 1951–1965', *Administrative Science Quarterly*, **42**, 784–814.

Stinchcombe, A.L. (1965), 'Social structure and organizations', in J.G. March (ed.) *Handbook of Organizations*, Chicago: Rand McNally, pp. 142–193.

Veblen, T. (1919), *The Place of Science in Modern Civilization and Other Essays*, New York: Huebsch.

Weber, M. (1964), *The Theory of Social and Economic Organization*, New York: Free Press.

Weitz, B.A. and S.D. Jap (1995), 'Relationship marketing and distribution channels', *Journal of the Academy of Marketing Science*, **23**, 305–20.

White, M.C., D.B. Martin, D.V. Brazeal and W.H. Friedman (1997), 'The evolution of organizations: suggestions from complexity theory about the interplay between natural selection and adaptation', *Human Relations*, **50**, 1383–1401.

Witt, U. (2008), 'What is specific about evolutionary economics?', *Journal of Evolutionary Economics*, **18**, 547–75.

3.   Research design and methodology

A QUALITATIVE LONGITUDINAL APPROACH

The investigation reported in this book is a longitudinal case study covering the co-evolution of a major international joint venture company in China's port sector from its foundation in 1993 to the end of 2009. The objective of the study is to understand how the company and its environment evolved in relation to one another. It looks closely at how the company's management developed its strategies in light of the specific environmental conditions affecting the joint venture, including its attempts to influence the evolution of its environment.

In order to achieve this research objective, a qualitative methodology is appropriate. We seek to understand the relational framework that developed between YICT and external agencies, the intentions of the principal actors, and the key events and processes which took place within that relationship and as a consequence of it. These aims require a methodology of inquiry that can follow the unfolding of events over a period of time with sufficient sensitivity to the intentions, actions and relationships that drove the events forward.

Our methodological approach was informed by previous studies that shared similar aims to our own: particularly those of Pettigrew (1985a), Johnson (1987), Burgelman (2002), Dieleman and Sachs (2008), and Rodrigues and Child (2008). One of these shared aims is to provide comprehensive and perceptive accounts of how a firm evolves as a process that is shaped by its history and leadership, and which unfolds within a relevant context. In light of the debate concerning environmental selection versus managerial intentionality, these studies have also been concerned to explore the role of strategic intent as a driver of organizational change and evolution. In conducting research consistent with this aim, they share the following methodological features:

1.   A relationship based on mutual trust and confidence was established between the investigators and the organizational members on whom they rely for access to detailed information on, and interpretation of, events. This relationship was initially established with the

organization's leader and was maintained over the extended period of time during which the study was undertaken. For example, Burgelman's (2002) detailed study of how strategy-making shaped the evolution of Intel would not have been possible without 12 years of collaboration with Andy Grove, the company's CEO. This collaboration included Grove and Burgelman jointly teaching an MBA elective course at the Stanford Business School and Burgelman having a close and continuing involvement with Intel over those years, allowing him to observe and record its processes of strategic change. The study presented in this book would not have been possible without a 10-year association between John Child and Kenneth Tse, YICT's CEO from 1993 to 2009, which led to a series of Master's research projects into various aspects of YICT's development, Tse's own PhD on the subject, and his appointment as a Senior Research Fellow of Birmingham University. At approximately the same time, Suzana Rodrigues and John Child (2008) were developing their book on corporate co-evolution. This was informed by the long-term association that Rodrigues had with the Telemig Company in Brazil, and the book laid the groundwork for the political perspective adopted in the present study (Rodrigues and Child, 2008).

This kind of close and sustained collaboration between academics and organizational leaders is unfortunately all too rare. It does, of course, run the risk of compromising objectivity because of biased interpretations, and later in this chapter we describe how we responded to this challenge. Nevertheless, the depth and quality of information and understanding that such collaboration offers by opening windows deep into an organization, as well as into its relations with external parties, makes for a huge qualitative advance over the general run of studies on management and organization.

2. A second methodological characteristic shared by the studies mentioned is that as far as possible they investigate organizational change and evolution as it takes place. This means that they are longitudinal not just regarding the period of time they cover but also in the way they track events. To some extent at least, they follow changes and events in real-time or are able to access accounts of them at a point in time not far removed from their occurrence. These accounts are provided by direct participants in the changes and events, and they are also substantiated by documents and records. This combines the use of documentary sources typical of historians with the use of conversations and interviews typical of social researchers. For example, the study of Telemig's

co-evolution covered the company's total lifespan from 1973 to 2000. Rodrigues, the principal researcher, conducted three rounds of data collection from 1986 to 1990, from 1997 to 2000, and from 2001 to 2004 respectively. Sources of data included a total of 192 interviews together with archival materials such as autobiographies of the company's founders, company reports and the newspaper published by the company's trade union (Rodrigues and Child, 2008: Chapter 3).

3. Thirdly, in attempting a careful construction of case studies, researchers became aware of the limitations of each of the multiple sources they used. For instance, Dieleman and Sachs (2008) set out the advantages and limitations of the sources they used in the study of how the Salim Group co-evolved with its environment in Indonesia. Their table is reproduced as Table 3.1. The combined use of several sources and triangulation between them can help to provide some assurance about the validity of the data being used as well as a balanced account of the interpretations and coverage offered by each source where these differ.

A longitudinal case study was deemed to be the most appropriate research design in light of the investigation's aims and methodology. We therefore followed the guidelines for such studies developed by Yin (1993; 1994), Eisenhardt (1989) and Pettigrew (1985a; 1985b). Yin's (1994) classification of case studies as exploratory, descriptive and explanatory is a useful starting point for defining their scope. The present study has all three characteristics. It is exploratory in that there is little previous work on the dynamics of corporate co-evolution, let alone on how this might take place in China. It is descriptive in that it seeks to tell the story of what took place. It is explanatory in that we shall derive a model from the case study that offers an explanation of how political processes shape corporate co-evolution.

In his two books on case study methodology and its applications, Yin (1993; 1994) provided practical guidelines for designing an approach as well as working protocols for case studies. Following those guidelines and protocols ensures that the tradition of scientific enquiry is maintained. In addition, the research was informed by Pettigrew's (1985b; 1990) advocacy of 'contextualism'. According to Pettigrew, contextualism is appropriate for analyzing organizations over a period of time, with multiple levels and units of analysis, applying different perspectives on how the various contexts of those organizations interact, shape and define the content and processes of organizational change. As an approach to studying organizations, contextualism is compatible with the

Table 3.1   Advantages and limitations of different sources

Sources	Advantages	Limitations
Annual reports and corporate documentation	Comprehensive corporate information; financial data	Limited to legal obligations for disclosure; limited to public companies
Media sources	Information from wide range of sources including specialized media	Focus on 'news value'; sources remain unknown; possible limits to free press
Interviews	In-depth information comparing divergent views	Respondents want to speak 'off the record'; potential bias
Secondary sources	Different perspectives; prior analysis is available	Comes with interpretation of authors

Source: Dieleman and Sachs (2008: Table IV)

co-evolutionary perspective adopted in this study. To a large extent, they each complement the other in presenting a more holistic picture than that which is offered by other approaches, one that is sensitive to interactions across levels and units of analysis.

Two specific considerations describe the suitability of a qualitative methodology for this study. The first is that the purpose of the enquiry and the nature of the subject-matter lend themselves to qualitative analysis. The second lies in the recognition that qualitative approaches are capable of achieving a high level of rigour and validity. These considerations are now discussed in turn.

The Purpose of the Enquiry and the Nature of the Subject-Matter

The study of management in an emerging economy shares many of the same characteristics of anthropology in that it is studying the behaviours of strategizing, cooperating, planning, motivation and control in a cultural and institutional environment that is less familiar to western scholars.[1] As a social environment with its own distinctive characteristics, China represents a rich opportunity for field research. The country, having suffered a decade of turmoil during the Cultural Revolution, began opening to the west only some 30 years ago and has since been confronted with numerous foreign ideas and practices. The international joint venture [IJV] has been a major form of enterprise organization for foreign investment in China, and is therefore at the forefront of such changes. Frequently, the Chinese partners who had little knowledge of how international companies operate found themselves suddenly dealing with international executives. These encounters were economically challenging and culturally startling to them. Executives in Sino-foreign IJVs can operate from two very different worlds with widely divergent orientations.

To study these new experiences and to try to put forward explanations about how they function requires in-depth quality exposure and understanding in order to reach 'thick descriptions' (Geertz, 1973) of the what, how and why in circumstances specific to the actors involved. The researcher has to get into the world of the partners in the joint ventures, and into what they experience, not just from an analytical and economic perspective, but also from a personal, psychological and sociological perspective. The current literature on IJVs contains many studies of a positivist nature relying on surveys. Such studies identify factors and map out relationships between variables on a cross-sectional basis. For example, Luo (1997) correlated variables of strategy and investment with IJV performance. This kind of research design is oriented towards testing hypotheses about the predictors of variance in the phenomena of interest. It falls within the category of what Mohr (1982) termed 'variance analysis'.

Although commonly applied in management and organization research, the variance approach is subject to certain limitations. One is that it does not readily provide insights into the dynamics of specific cases, which can be a loss both for theory development and for deriving practical implications. There has been relatively little in-depth investigation into the processes whereby management actions have evolved over a period of time and the influence they have on the performance and environment of an IJV. It is therefore of interest that Mohr (1982) identifies what he called 'process design' as an alternative approach. This is oriented towards the discovery and understanding of the processes and events which underlie patterns of association between variables and/or changes over time. It normally requires a sacrifice of scope in research design – in the sense of sample size – in order to enhance depth and insight.

Indeed, in an article titled '"Messy research", methodological predispositions, and theory development in international joint ventures', Parkhe (1993) argued the need for more in-depth descriptions and understanding in international joint venture studies. Having reviewed the most significant studies of the time, he concluded that the 'current norms of the field seem strongly biased toward large sample multivariate statistical studies ... Qualitative studies do appear in the journals but they are the exception. ... These hard data sources are unlikely to capture the soft core concepts ... ' (Parkhe, 1993: 230). These comments continue to be valid today. Consequently, the theory of IJVs remains fragmented and immature, and its further development could benefit from in-depth, rich descriptions of their social reality.

Accepting Parkhe's argument, the present study aims to contribute in a distinctive way to academic understanding and practical use, and it can achieve this contribution via a qualitative approach. The study provides an in-depth case history of how a firm evolved within an environment that was also evolving, taking into account the managerial actions that helped drive that evolution. Stake (1995) argues that a case study should be studied for 'its intrinsic' as well as 'its instrumental value'. Since the YICT case concerns a significant project in an important industry, an in-depth study of how it evolved with its environment promises to provide a contribution to knowledge of intrinsic value. Adopting a co-evolutionary perspective, we hope that a contribution to theory building will result from a detailed understanding and description of the interactions and processes that took place over a longitudinal timespan. Furthermore, since the case arguably exhibits some very significant characteristics of how IJVs can function in China as a major emerging economy, the conclusions derived from it should contribute to a better understanding of IJVs located in such economies in general.

Methodological Rigour and Validity

The second consideration supporting the suitability of a qualitative methodology is that, despite frequently expressed doubts, qualitative approaches are capable of achieving a high level of rigour and validity. The case method is now an increasingly accepted form of academic investigation, with its own set of theory and methods (Yin, 1993; 1994; Stake, 1995). However, this acceptance by the academic community depends on the application of certain protocols. As described later in this chapter, the study of YICT's co-evolution was conducted with full awareness of the accepted protocols for case-based research. Case studies also have to contribute to theoretical development, otherwise they are little more than interesting stories. The previous chapter set out the theoretical perspective that informed this study and we shall return to how it adds to theory in Chapter 9.

One of the merits of a case study lies in the opportunity to access and take into account detailed and varied information gleaned from a range of sources. A benefit of comprehensive access is that it permits the use of several sources at different points in time. By providing multiple avenues to understanding the whole picture, each source can contribute to understanding the picture in its own and partial way. Moreover, data from different sources and points in time can be used to 'triangulate' the information and interpretations they provide and in this way increase the validity of the research findings. In particular, this procedure enables three forms of triangulation (Denzin, 2006):

- *data triangulation* involving different points in time, different units of analysis and different informants;
- *investigator triangulation* involving multiple researchers in an investigation; and
- *methodological triangulation* involving the use of more than one method to gather data, such as interviews, observations, question-naires and documents.

With this in mind, the study we report used a range of sources and methods accessed at different points in time, namely the analysis of documents (Manning and Cullum-Swan, 1994), participant observation (Denzin, 2006) and interviews (Llewellyn, 1993). It also involved multiple researchers.

CONTRIBUTION OF THE SINGLE CASE

The distinctive contribution of case studies is to provide insights for enriching theory-building (Eisenhardt, 1989; Siggelkow, 2007). Starting from the premise that 'knowledge is socially constructed' (Stake, 1994), case researchers are well positioned to help readers gain insights into such construction in that the cases can provide real-life data and information, albeit partial and incomplete at any one point in time. Case studies can therefore lay out the complexities of reality as a basis for inductive theory-building. Indeed, as a research methodology in advancing the understanding of people in action – the whys and hows – the case study is a powerful tool. Yin (1994: 3) concludes that: 'the case study allows an investigation to retain the holistic and meaningful characteristics of real-life events – such as individual life cycles, organizational and managerial processes, neighborhood change, international relations and the maturation of industries.' Either single or multiple case study designs can be adopted, depending on the research questions, the purpose of the study and other practical considerations such as availability of sites, accessibility and time limitations. This study adopts a single case design. Two key factors have influenced this initial decision: its uniqueness, and accessibility to data and information.

The case of YICT meets two of Yin's criteria for adopting a single case design. Yin (1994) points out that, for a single case research design, the case to be studied should either represent a 'critical case' in testing a well formulated theory or a 'unique' or 'revelatory case' that offers a good opportunity to study certain phenomena otherwise inaccessible to study and research (Yin, 1994: 39–40). The case of YICT is distinctive in terms of belonging to a specific sector and being located in a country with its own very marked characteristics. It could be called a 'unique' case. However, this singularity raises some concerns. One has to ask whether YICT is such an unusual case in such a unique environment as to be able to contribute little to the development of theory on co-evolution. In some respects it is idiosyncratic. Thus, YICT was a greenfield company enjoying powerful parent company backing, and it was established in economic conditions that were strategically propitious. However, this is not a unique situation for the affiliates of large multinationals in rapidly growing emerging economies like China.

One may also ask whether the specific context of the case was too unusual to be useful? It has been suggested that China has such a different business environment that it requires its own theory and cannot contribute to theorizing of a more general nature (Barney and Zhang, 2009). China is different, as the Chinese are the first to claim, but at the same time it presents some important characteristics shared by many other emerging economies. Salient among these is a highly institutional-ized environment, with extensive involvement of government and its agencies in business through heavy regulation and political intervention. High levels of institutionalization are found in other major emerging economies such as Brazil (Rodrigues and Child, 2008), Indonesia (Diele-man and Sachs, 2008) and Russia (Puffer and McCarthy, 2007). While at first sight high government involvement implies a strong external deter-mination of how firms evolve, it also provides channels through which proactive companies possessing valued specialized competencies can endeavour to influence government actions and potentially contribute to the evolution of government policies and practices. The YICT case indicates how such firms can in this way help shape the co-evolutionary process.

Another consideration is that YICT is an infrastructural company and such companies have not been studied as much by management research-ers. Does this mean that they should be considered as out of the mainstream? Actually, infrastructural industries such as transportation, energy, power and water are generally large and of central importance to economies, so they can hardly be dismissed as being of lesser consequence. An indicator of the economic significance of the infrastructure sector is the valuation by the US Bureau of Economic Analysis (Department of Commerce) of the stock of all public non-defence fixed assets at approximately US$8.2 trillion in 2007. This may be compared with the estimated total value of all private non-residential fixed assets, which was US$15.5 trillion (Heintz et al., 2009). While government involvement in the YICT case was undoubtedly heightened because its infrastructural status gave it strategic national importance, this is not unusual – the sector is characterized by a high level of regulation in most countries. In short, although use of the YICT case for theory-building warrants due caution due to its special features, there are comparable situations to which the insights it furnishes into corporate co-evolution may well apply.

The YICT case also has the potential to offer a number of specific 'revelatory' insights:

1. It is an important infrastructure project in South China, with sizeable initial investments and subsequent growth into one of the most important ports in the Asian region. It is situated in Shenzhen, a city adjacent to Hong Kong, run and managed by China as a 'special economic zone', with many special policies of 'openness' to the world. A study of how the ability to operate within this climate of openness encouraged the rapid development of the port can present interesting findings and practical implications for similar development projects.

2. YICT is an equity joint venture between the Shenzhen municipal government and an international group of companies headed by the Hutchison Group, with its charismatic leader, Li Kashing, exercising significant political influence and able to access the Chinese leadership. It is the only Chinese infrastructural project in which the international joint venture partner has been allowed majority ownership and management control. Despite the political sensitivities attached to this unique ownership and control concession, the project has been viewed by the Chinese authorities as an important experiment in port development and customs reform. A detailed account of how these policies and the joint venture structure affected the development of the enterprise will provide insights into the design of future policies and practices.

3. During the period under study, the company grew very rapidly and achieved most of its objectives. In the short space of just five years

the terminal helped Shenzhen container throughput (of which YICT takes up approximately 50 per cent) gain world recognition. As a port, Shenzhen had nothing to show in early 1990s, but with time it ranked second in China and fourth in the world (AAPA, 2009). A study of this growth trajectory would help explain the phenomenon and possibly yield useful insights into deriving critical success factors in port development in emerging economies.

4. YICT's growth was not all smooth sailing, especially during the first three years of its history. In fact, there were very strong sceptics about the business viability of such a port in Shenzhen. In response, YICT's management adopted several initiatives in marketing and relationship development with its customers and stakeholders to promote the port. From 1997, the turnaround was very dramatic. In hindsight, the port's strategy was 'crafted' out of necessity, rather than planned (Mintzberg, 1987; 1989). A study of the turnaround could be revealing to other project managers in a similar situation. A detailed description of the 'crafting' process may lend support to the view that indeed strategy formulation is more art than science.

5. In terms of managing its environment, YICT initially faced tough controls from its 'institutionalized' environments. Through years of intense effort, as described in the following chapters, management was able to bring about significant and positive changes so as to create some strategic space for itself and to achieve improved operational performance. A study of how the strategies of both the company and relevant external organizations 'co-evolved' in an institutionalized setting can provide useful insights into managing external relations and the processes of 'co-evolution'.

In summary, while the YICT case might be limited to a specific location and a specific industry, it is rich in both content and the range of issues it can address. It has the potential to inform and enhance our understanding of IJV management, specifically in the strategy formulation process and with regard to the co-evolutionary process of a company and its environment.

The other important factor influencing the choice of YICT as a single case study was the favourable access to data and information that was available. Chapter 1 noted that it is generally very difficult to obtain valid information about the processes through which a firm interacts with other organizations in its environment. There are often severe restrictions on access to appropriate informants and relevant documentary sources. Gaining adequate insights into what goes on may depend largely on finding participants in the process who are interested in collaborating with scholars. This has been true of YICT, whose former chief executive Kenneth Tse has a belief in the value of business and management research. The study presented in this book is a collaboration between two scholars and Kenneth. The unique opportunity the three authors had to examine the process of the company's evolution comprehensively, in detail and over its total lifespan offers a privileged insight into a case that is intrinsically revealing for reasons already mentioned.

RESEARCH DESIGN

'A research design is an action plan for getting from here to there, where here may be defined as the initial set of questions to be answered, and there is some set of conclusions (answers) about these questions' (Yin, 1994: 19). Yin identifies the components of such an action plan as being:

- a study's research questions;
- its initial assumptions;
- its unit(s) of analysis;
- the logic linking the data to the propositions;
- the criteria for interpreting the findings.

Research Questions

The primary questions addressed in this book ask: (1) 'to what extent did YICT and its environment co-evolve?'; and (2) 'insofar as the company and its environment did co-evolve, what were the processes through which this took place?' There is also an important subsidiary question, which addresses a continuing debate among scholars, namely 'was the evolution of the organization (YICT) primarily due to developments in its environment or to strategic actions taken by its leadership?'

Initial Assumptions

The theoretical base and framework underlying these research questions have been discussed in Chapter 2. Drawing on this foundation, the research was guided from its outset by the following assumptions:

The kind of situation in which YICT operates (shared ownership and an emerging economy context) is likely to pose very special challenges because of the inherent constraints it imposes. It is a theoretical task to explain the nature of such challenges, and also one of considerable practical significance. For, without a full awareness of the implications of a different business environment, it is a common error to adopt a company's proven business model hoping that it will bring about successes. The first general assumption with which we started was therefore that emerging economies are likely to present new, and sometimes unfamiliar, circumstances for the operation of companies investing in them and that knowing how these circumstances can be addressed is of strategic importance. We were aware that China represented, in a rather extreme form, the combination of significant business opportunities deriving from rapid economic growth combined with the challenging institutional environment that is found in many emerging economies. The requirement for local participation, as exemplified by YICT's joint venture status, is also found in many emerging economies especially in nationally strategic sectors. Taken together, these features implied that YICT would have opportunities to grow but that it would be a managerial challenge to realize such opportunities.

The second assumption is that becoming aware of the uniqueness of the environment is a continuous process of learning through trial and error. It involves taking various initiatives and then reviewing the outcomes, with senior management taking a long-term view of the situation by investing resources in understanding and dealing with environmental features such as the role played by government and governmental agencies. Initiatives designed to handle environmental conditions are first taken on an intuitive basis rather than as rationally planned strategies. They may at quite an early stage be expressed as a 'vision', but initially that vision will be quite general and a great deal of work will subsequently be required to effect its detailed implementation. Over time, through a process of learning and crafting, a company can arrive at confirmed policies which become cornerstones in its strategy (Mintzberg, 1987). If the previous assumption regarding the special nature of emerging economies is correct, this learning process can be accelerated for companies engaging with such economies by applying insights from experiences such as YICT's.

Both macro (national) and meso (sector) environments underwent significant and rapid changes during the period studied. YICT's management adopted a proactive stance in strategy development aimed at influencing the development paths of its sector which in turn required it to exert influence at the national level. This leads to the assumption that corporate management can have an impact on co-evolution and that managerial intentionality therefore matters. In other words, that 'strategic choice' is a significant factor in the co-evolution between environments and strategies (Child, 1997).

The fourth general assumption guiding the study is that corporate co-evolution proceeds through an interaction between external actors and company leadership. This interaction is seen to take place with a *relational framework* which itself is a social construction that requires initiatives and time to evolve. Both parties may take actions intended to influence the other and they may do so in a spirit of opposition or of cooperation. These considerations warrant an approach to the subject that is sensitive to the *politics* of interaction and co-influence between companies and their environments.

A political perspective represents an addition to the theories upon which co-evolutionary studies normally build (Lewin and Volberda, 1999). Its employment in this book is therefore consistent with 'theoretical triangulation' – the application of more than one theoretical perspective. Theoretical triangulation is recommended as a procedure intended to reduce the risk of distortion in the interpretation of research findings (Denzin, 2006). A classic example of theoretical triangulation is Allison's (1971) application of three contrasting theories to the events of the Cuban Missile Crisis and the contrasting interpretations to which they gave rise. Insofar as the co-evolutionary perspective is multidisciplinary, as indicated in Chapter 2, its application to our study already incorporates some theoretical triangulation. However, we also adopt and develop a distinctively political orientation and it is therefore incumbent on us to remain aware of alternative explanations for what have we found. We were, for example, aware that a 'rival theory' (Yin, 1994) could have been advanced to account for YICT's evolution. Its argument would be based on the following propositions:

1. YICT is but a copy of Hong Kong International Terminals (HIT), the original Hutchison-owned port developer based in Hong Kong, which had already accumulated considerable port expertise. With the operational know-how and marketing power of the largest terminal operator in the world, HIT transferred these capabilities to YICT. So the evolution of YICT simply rode on the back of the success of HIT. This argument would see YICT's evolution as path-dependent in the sense that it was shaped primarily by the legacy it inherited from its dominant parent company (Schreyögg and Sydow, 2010).

2. The success of YICT was also due to the shift of manufacturing from Hong Kong to South China. The business was already in place and growing rapidly. YICT just happened to be better located than other ports in a place that was closer to the market and also enjoyed lower costs. The history of YICT's development provides a good

example of 'value migration' from a high cost operating area to a low cost area. Managerial intentionality did not therefore play a significant role. Due to the available cargo base growing so rapidly, the market became so large that it could fill all the ports in the region to capacity in no time at all. So YICT would have evolved successfully with or without any significant strategic activities on the part of the key players. This argument in effect regards the evolution of YICT as being due primarily to the unfettered growth of its market.

These alternative explanations (legacy and a rapidly growing market) give primacy to the influence of the external factors on the organization, implying that the actions of the company and its leadership were relatively passive and of limited consequence. By contrast, the interpretation we develop attaches much greater significance to management's intentionality, learning and proactivity. These contrasting explanations for how corporate co-evolution takes place refer to environmental (or situational) determinism and strategic choice respectively, as reviewed in Chapter 2. Later in this chapter we describe a procedure we used – that of consulting a 'devil's advocate' – to help ensure that we did not ignore explanations that differ from our own.

Units of Analysis

The focal unit of analysis is YICT, a joint venture in which Hutchison Port Holdings has the majority equity share and appoints most senior managers. In this respect, YICT can be regarded as a subsidiary of HPH. This means that we have to pay close attention to the relationship between the main parent company and YICT, including how the parent's strategies affect those of the subsidiary and vice versa. Another important relationship is that between YICT and its Chinese minority owner which is an affiliate of the Shenzhen city government. The city authorities are therefore significant actors, while YICT's co-evolution with its wider environment also brings in central Chinese government authorities as important players. Since this book is concerned with corporate co-evolution, its focal unit of analysis is the system of relationships between the company, its stakeholders and relevant external actors. However, insofar as most of the initiatives within this set of relationships came from the company's management, YICT itself will often be the focus of attention.

The Logic Linking the Data to the Propositions

The logic linking the data to be presented with our initial assumptions is that relations between companies and entities in their environments do not occur in a mechanistic fashion. Rather, they are products of human decision and social action. A mechanistic view might, for instance, state that market growth gives rise to enhanced company productivity because of economies of scale. A more realistic view allows for human decision. It would state that while market growth presents opportunities for enhanced company performance, whether that result actually occurs depends on the quality of investment decisions and other strategic choices made by corporate leaders. In other words, the ways environments and firms change in relation to one another cannot be assumed to be automatic. The logic linking data to propositions that informs this book is therefore one of examining events, how key actors interpreted them, and the part that such actors played in shaping them, including how they exercised influence in the process.

The Criteria for Interpreting the Findings

A number of criteria for interpreting and discussing what we shall find in our study of YICT's co-evolution follow from the summarized logic. These are:

- How changes in the both the macro and meso environments during the period 1990–2009 corresponded with strategic initiatives at the firm level during the same period – so as to establish the possibility of a pattern of influence.
- Evidence of how apparently co-evolutionary changes actually came about, in order to more precisely pinpoint the respective roles that company and external actors played in shaping and driving them.
- The inherent logic of the interpretation we shall offer for these events, assessing this in part by reference to parallel insights offered by relevant bodies of knowledge, especially political science.

DATA SOURCES

The information we use is primarily derived from interviewees and documents. It falls into two broad categories. The first is information on events of an evolutionary nature, which enables us to examine their sequence and the main actors involved. This information provides an insight into the connections between events, decisions and actors. The second category is the commentary and interpretation of these events and the motives or rationales behind them, which was offered by interviewees and documents such as internal memoranda.

In applying this information, we pursued 'process analysis' in contrast to 'variance analysis' (Mohr, 1982), in that our aim is to trace an evolutionary sequence and to understand the ability of actors to influence the key events within that sequence. Given that the concept of evolution necessarily refers to a process over time, we accepted Langley's (1999: 692) view that 'understanding patterns in events is ... key to developing "process" theory'. In using the case information at our disposal in order to make a theoretical contribution, we also took to heart Langley's insistence that 'we should not have to be shy about mobilizing both inductive (data-driven) and deductive (theory-driven) approaches itera-tively or simultaneously as inspiration guides us' (Langley, 1999: 708). Chapters 4 to 7 provide the inductive component of this process, while in Chapters 8 and 9 we shall apply the theoretical perspective set out in Chapter 2 to our data and also develop its political aspects further.

Our sources, the foci for our questioning and our checks for validity are listed in Table 3.2. The intention of using multiple sources was to incorporate a degree of triangulation. The interview questioning was standardized only to the extent that each respondent was asked to recall and comment on the main events in YICT's history. Most respondents played some part in these events, but since this varied we tailored our questions accordingly. Dr Leanne Chung, who is a lecturer in human resource management at the Cardiff Business School, participated in the project as an independent researcher. She conducted semi-structured interviews with all the key executives within YICT. The same executives were subsequently interviewed by Kenneth Tse using the same schedule of questions. Both Kenneth and Leanne are fluent in Cantonese, Man-darin and English. All the interviews were tape recorded. These were fully transcribed and then analyzed separately by the two interviewers who then met for several days to concur and discuss the significant events and themes that the interviewees had mentioned with the intention of identifying linking patterns among them. All three authors of this book then shared in the interpretation of the data.

This book draws primarily from this synthesis of the interviews, with the documents consulted serving mainly to confirm events such as the nature and substance of negotiations, and the content of formal agree-ments. Internal documents also provide evidence of YICT's strategic intentions and the views expressed by Chinese government agencies especially at times when change was being negotiated. The key sources of information on specific events and issues to be mentioned are given in the endnotes. Given the secret and sensitive nature of key discussions we could not access these directly but rather relied on reports provided to us via interviews and evidence from documents. However, it was possible neither to access purely internal Chinese government documents, nor to interview some senior actors, such as the HPH Chairman, Li Kashing.

The challenge and process of analyzing data varied. The identification and ordering of events and initiatives in the co-evolution process was relatively straightforward. However, the interpretation of intentions behind them required a comparison of interview statements and agreement between the researchers. Co-evolutionary connections were inferred from evidence on relevant processes and the actors involved in them. An example would be the firm's initiative to fund a study group, whose findings then fed into government reports, which in turn provided the substantive grounds for new practices by government agencies. This latter area of analysis mainly relies on the researchers' interpretations and is therefore the most tentative.

Kenneth Tse was actively involved in the research. Kenneth, as YICT's General Manager, was the actor primarily engaged both in the company's strategic development and in its relational framework with external organizations. His insights and contacts were invaluable. At the same time, however, we wished to take steps to minimize the potential downside of Kenneth's involvement in terms of interpretive bias. It was therefore desirable to adopt a methodological procedure that would permit an assessment of any systematic bias due to the General Manager's two roles in the study as an investigator and a principal actor. The intention was for such a procedure, accompanied by extensive triangulation with documentary evidence, to provide an independent check on possible systematic bias in any interviews conducted by the General Manager with members of his own staff. This was the reason why Leanne Chung participated in the project as an independent researcher. She conducted semi-structured interviews with all the key executives within YICT and conducted interviews before those carried out by Kenneth. In the event, responses to the two interviewers proved to be highly consistent, the main exception being that interviewees tended to take more time to explain the background to their answers when interviewed by Leanne. Kenneth offers his own reflections on his dual role as a participant and researcher in the Appendix at the end of the book.

As a further check on interpretation, we used triangulation with 'devil's advocates' (Eisenhardt, 1989: 534). Once preliminary drafts of the case study were completed, an experienced practising manager was

Table 3.2   Summary of research methods and sources

Source	Specification of sources	Focus of questioning and search	Validity checks
Sixty interviews conducted by one of the authors and a research assistant (both bilingual) between 2004 and 2006. Two on-site visits by the other authors to the Yantian port for informal discussions with 10 executives partly in connection with supervision of Master's projects. Three formal interviews conducted in 2009 by the first author with the General Manager of YICT [CEO] covering key events in the history of the company from its foundation in 1993 until mid-2009.	Key external interviewees: Former Party Secretary of YICT's Chinese joint venture partner; officials of the Ministry of Communications and Transportation [MOC]; former customs officers <u>Key internal interviewees:</u> General Manager, company executives and advisors or consultants to the company	Identification of key events in the history of YICT's relations with external parties, including its Chinese joint venture partner The dynamics of the relational framework: • Who were the key internal and external actors in the company's co-evolution • Identification of their role in this process and actions they took • How sources of power available to internal and external actors were used	Comparison of notes between the authors and the research assistant as to the sequence of events, and identification of actors' roles in the co-evolutionary process Triangulation with documentary evidence and on-site discussions. Use of independent expert on China's port sector as 'devil's advocate' to challenge authors' interpretations. Also feedback from presentations at academic seminars.

Source	Specification of sources	Focus of questioning and search	Validity checks
Documents (all documents deriving from the company were in English; other documents were translated)	YICT joint venture contracts of 1993, 1996 and 2000; reports commissioned by the company on feasibility, planning and strategy; management reports from the General Manager to the YICT board; management reports from the Chinese deputy General Manager to his directors; significant memos and letters between YICT and government departments (including the Shenzhen government); Memoranda of Understanding with various government agencies; reports on port management commissioned by the MOC; research reports from consultants; and YICT's press files.	Understanding of the company's strategy, and performance through time. Identification of the relational framework, key main actors and their role in the company's evolution.	Comparison of documents on the company's strategy; identification of key actors and their position in the port system, relationships with external agents.
Twenty-one Master's dissertations at the University of Birmingham completed 2005–2009	Some of these dissertations comprised studies on the company's evolution, its principal strategies, its relationships with customers, suppliers and government officials. Others investigated the company's policies for HR and government relations. The investigations for these dissertations were conducted on site and each typically involved 20–25 interviews plus a great deal of informal interaction.	Understanding how the company's strategy evolved through time, and the external relationships that were involved.	The material in these dissertations was reviewed in comparison with the data already obtained from interviews and document analysis.

invited to review the story critically as an independent third party. He provided detailed feedback in the form of challenging our identification of emerging ideas into themes and our suggestions of causality between company strategy and organizational success. Moreover, the analysis we developed from the case study, set out in Chapters 8 and 9, was presented and opened up to critical comment from numerous devil's advocates at various conferences and seminars.[2] These inputs have all helped us to articulate our interpretations and arguments more coherently, and to recognize that alternative views are possible.

NOTES

1. Many anthropologists would claim that the objective of their subject is to provide sensitive insights into the structures and life patterns of societies which they compare with a view to arriving at general propositions. The method of study typically employed is ethnographic in that the lives and behaviours of people are described accurately and sensitively based on first-hand encounters. Ethnography, however, is not *per se* concerned with arriving at general propositions or theoretical statements (Ingold, 2008). The study reported in this book shares some characteristics of anthropology in that it embraces an ethnographic approach, while at the same time seeking to advance theory so as to stimulate further research of a comparative nature.
2. We are particularly grateful for comments received from participants during seminars at the Rotterdam School of Management, the Fukua School of Business, Duke University and the 2010 Organization Science Winter Conference.

REFERENCES

AAPA (2009), *Containerization International*, US: American Association of Port Authorities.

Allison, G.T. (1971), *Essence of Decision: Explaining the Cuban Missile Crisis*, Boston, MA: Little, Brown.

Barney, J.B. and S. Zhang (2009), 'The future of Chinese management research: a theory of Chinese management versus a Chinese theory of management', *Management and Organization Review*, **5**, 15–28.

Burgelman, R.A. (2002), *Strategy is Destiny: How Strategy-Making Shapes a Company's Future*, New York: Free Press.

Child, J. (1997), 'Strategic choice in the analysis of action, structure, organizations and environment: retrospect and prospect', *Organization Studies*, **18**, 43–76.

Denzin, N. (2006), *Sociological Methods: A Sourcebook* (5th edition), Piscataway, NJ: Aldine Transaction.

Dieleman, M. and W.M. Sachs (2008), 'Coevolution of institutions and corporations in emerging economies: how the Salim Group morphed into an institution of Suharto's crony regime', *Journal of Management Studies*, **45**, 1274–1300.

Eisenhardt, K.M. (1989), 'Building theories from case study research', *Academy of Management Review*, **14**, 532–50.

Geertz, C. (1973), 'Thick description: toward an interpretative theory of culture', in C. Geertz (ed.), *The Interpretation of Culture: Selected Essays*, New York: Basic Books, pp. 3–32.

Heintz, J., R. Pollin and H. Garrett-Peltier (2009), *How Infrastructure Investments Support the US Economy*, Amherst, MA: Political Economy Research Institute, University of Massachusetts.

Ingold, T. (2008), 'Anthropology is *not* ethnography', Radcliffe-Brown Lecture in Social Anthropology, *Proceedings of the British Academy*, **154**, 69–92.

Johnson, G. (1987), *Strategic Change and the Management Process*, Oxford: Blackwell.

Langley, A. (1999), 'Strategies for theorizing from process data', *Academy of Management Review*, **24**, 691–710.

Lewin, A.Y. and H.W. Volberda (1999), 'Prolegomena on coevolution: a framework for research on strategy and new organizational forms', *Organization Science*, **10**, 519–34.

Llewellyn, S. (1993), 'Working in hermeneutic circles in accounting research: some implications and applications', *Management Accounting Research*, **4**, 1–3.

Luo, Y. (1997), 'Partner selection and venturing success: the case of joint ventures with firms in the People's Republic of China', *Organization Science*, **8**, 648–63.

Manning, P. and B. Cullum-Swan (1994), 'Narrative, content, and semiotic analysis', in N.K. Denzin and Y.S. Lincoln (eds), *Handbook of Qualitative Research*, London: Sage, pp. 463–77.

Mintzberg, H. (1987), 'Crafting Strategy', *Harvard Business Review*, July–August, 66–77.

Mintzberg, H. (1989), *Mintzberg on Management: Inside Our Strange World of Organizations*, New York: Free Press.

Mohr, L.B. (1982), *Explaining Organizational Behavior*, San Francisco: Jossey-Bass.

Parkhe, A. (1993), 'Messy research, methodological predispositions and theory development in international joint ventures', *Academy of Management Review*, **18**, 227–68.

Peng, M.W. (2000), *Business Strategies in Transition Economies*, Thousand Oaks, CA: Sage.

Pettigrew, A.M. (1985a), *The Awakening Giant: Continuity and Change in ICI*, Oxford: Blackwell.

Pettigrew, A.M. (1985b), 'Contextualist research: a natural way to link theory and practice', in E.E. Lawler (ed.), *Doing Research That is Useful in Theory and Practice*, San Francisco: Jossey Bass, 222–74.

Pettigrew, A.M. (1990), 'Longitudinal field research on change: theory and practice', *Organization Science*, **1**, 267–317.

Puffer, S. and D. McCarthy (2007), 'Can Russia's state managed network capitalism be competitive? Institutional pull versus institutional push', *Journal of World Business*, **42**, 1–13.

Rodrigues, S.B. and J. Child (2003), 'Co-evolution in an institutionalized environment', *Journal of Management Studies*, **40**, 2137–62.

Rodrigues, S.B. and J. Child (2008), *Corporate Co-evolution: A Political Perspective*, Chichester: Wiley.

Schreyögg, G. and J. Sydow (eds) (2010), *The Hidden Dynamics of Path Dependence: Institutions and Organizations*, New York: Palgrave Macmillan.

Siggelkow, N. (2007), 'Persuasion with case studies', *Academy of Management Journal*, **50**, 20–24.

Stake, R.E. (1994), 'Case studies', in N.K. Denzin and Y.S. Lincoln (eds), *Handbook of Qualitative Research*, London: Sage, pp. 236–47.

Stake, R.E. (1995), *The Art of Case Study Research*, London: Sage.

Yin, R.K. (1993), *Applications of Case Study Research*, London: Sage.

Yin, R.K. (1994), *Case Study Research: Design and Methods*, London: Sage.

PART II

Environment, evolution and managerial
initiative

4. Yantian port and its changing environment

The four chapters in Part II of this book present the story of Yantian International Container Terminals from its inception in the early 1990s to 2009. After an introduction to the Yantian port and its operating company YICT, this chapter describes the changing macro and meso environments in which the port was founded and grew. Chapter 5 provides a chronology of the port's development. Chapters 6 and 7 focus on the management initiatives that provided major impetus to the firm's evolution and support for its outstanding performance. Chapter 6 looks at innovations in management practice, while Chapter 7 focuses on the policy of active relationship management that played an important part in developing the firm's relational framework with external parties.

PUTTING YANTIAN ON THE MAP

Just under two hours by car from Hong Kong's central business district sits one of the largest container ports in China and in the world. Its name – Yantian – literally means 'salt fields'. One of China's latest additions to the impressive list of firsts in the world, Yantian International Container Terminals (YICT) was only established in 1993 but within a short span of 15 years, it put Yantian's name on the map of world trade and in the annals of the container transportation industry.

Travelling along a six lane superhighway, visitors to Shenzhen's eastern beaches cannot help but notice the port's gigantic site of some 300 hectares (equivalent to 550 acres or 50 football pitches). The elevated highway takes you to the middle levels, away from the hustle and bustle of the operations, offering the observers a neat and tidy view. Beyond the port, only a short distance away, one sees a beautiful hilly landscape along the border coastline between Shenzhen (one of China's special economic zones) and Hong Kong (China's special administrative region). Hong Kong's country parks form the coastline on the other side of the Dapeng Bay, a natural deep harbour, well sheltered from the Pacific

Ocean, which as an environmentally protected site is home to Chinese white dolphins.

The eastern side of Shenzhen has been earmarked as a tourist destination, with fine beaches and embellished with several championship golf courses. Many tourists on their way there stop at lookout points to watch the cranes, all painted blue, that tower towards the sky in rows along Yantian port's quays, with gigantic ships berthed neatly one by one. Rising 30 metres from the ground, 60 large steel moving structures have arms that stretch out to the vessels. They carry 'boxes' (containers) and stow them into the cells in the ships or download them onto waiting trailers. The cranes, each made of hundreds of tons of solid steel, are constantly on the move. On a busy day, through a 24 hour operating cycle, at least 10 ocean-going ships of various sizes come in and out of the place, with over ten thousand boxes moving in and out of the compound on trucks. Over the years the terminal has grown through four phases to 15 berths. The existing berths, mostly built for ships that require a minimum of 15 metres draft, are capable of handling the largest ocean-going vessels plying the high seas today. The ships, ranging from 200 to 400 metres in length, are stocked full of steel boxes of various sizes with names denoting different national affiliations around the world.

As the Chinese saying goes, cargoes should move like spinning wheels, a sign of prosperity. Today, over 80 per cent of world trade is carried by sea-going vessels. Since China's reform and opening from the end of 1978, external trade has played a very important part in the country's modernization process. By 2009, China had become the world's largest exporter and the second largest importer by value (People's Bank of China, 2011; WTO, 2011). Its foreign trade has been contributing over 50 per cent to its GDP in recent years. Its bilateral trade with the US grew to US$457 billion in 2010, and it was America's single largest trading partner. Likewise, China's trade with the European Union has reached staggering heights, to a value of 395 billion euros in 2010. China has become the EU's second largest trading partner, occupying second position in exports and first position in imports. China mainly exports products of a light industrial nature. Ships departing from the Chinese coast carry with them consumer products like shoes, garments, toys, television sets and other electronic products, which quickly find their way into American and European homes.

The popular press is full of stories about 'China's economic miracle' and most agree that what China has achieved to date is indeed impressive. It has now become the world's second largest economy behind the United States. With steady increases in foreign trade and inward foreign direct investment [FDI], China has become an international economic power house whose rapid growth has been fuelled by both international cargo flows and monetary movements. In 2004, China became the recipient of the largest amount of FDI in the world and it has since remained among the top FDI recipients (MOFCOM, 2012).

It all started with the country's change of economic direction in late 1978. Shifting from a focus on heavy industrial production to light industrial manufacturing, China has achieved tremendous economic progress. It has offered its cheap but reliable labour force as part of the global network of designers and marketers based in developed countries. Aptly called 'the factory of the world', China produces goods that fill up supermarkets in the west, being goods high in 'value for money'. China is a prime example of an emerging economy achieving prosperity through export-led growth.

An export oriented economy requires not only manufacturing facilities; it also requires the proper infrastructure to move the finished industrial products to their final destinations. Containerization was invented in the United States in the 1950s. With the adoption of common standards by the world's leading shipping lines, the container industry significantly reduced the cost of transportation in world trade. The consumer only pays the equivalent of a taxi fare from the supermarket to her suburban home to move a television set across the Pacific Ocean. Light industrial production is best suited to container trade and it has pushed China towards becoming a big player in containerization and transportation especially in Southern China where Yantian is located. With scarcely a significant container port in the early 1990s, China thrived in the intervening years to become a giant in the game. In 2007, the country's ports handled a total of just over one hundred million TEUs and that made China the largest handler of container boxes anywhere in the world.[1]

The following chapter will detail YICT's achievements during this period. The singularity of the company's policies stands out and this serves to remind us that while firms located within the same sector and region operate within the same general context, each of them can take its own initiatives and develop its own approach towards that context which contribute to its success. Nevertheless, it is reasonable to ask whether the successful evolution of Yantian International Container Terminals was also substantially assisted by the explosion of container trade with China, which in turn was a consequence of the country's sustained high level of economic growth. This possibility has two important implications. One is that, even if YICT developed ways of relating to its environment that contributed to its commercial success, its economically favourable context may have contributed even more. Secondly, it could be that the climate of successful growth itself provided a particularly favourable ground for co-evolution to proceed.

We return to these questions in Chapters 8 and 9, but they justify taking a closer look at the context in which YICT developed. This concerns the macro environment of China as a political and economic system and the meso environment of Shenzhen and the regional port industry. These facets of the environment are now considered in turn.

YICT'S MACRO ENVIRONMENT

A Transition Economy

An economy in incremental transition from a command to a market order passes through a stage in which both the old and the new modes coexist. In the Chinese economy, while collective and private ownership were gaining ground, state-owned enterprises [SOEs] were still dominant in many industries, especially in strategic areas such as infrastructure. Although enterprises were given an apparently free hand to manage their affairs, the controlling influence of the bureaucracy was never far away. Peng (2000: 19) notes the business activities in which the state tends to assert control in transition economies: 'establishment of a firm, liquidation of a firm, management of production, allocation and distribution of products and materials, decisions on pricing, investment, technology, and foreign trade, appointment, promotion, and dismissal of managers as well as allocation and management of labour'. In all these areas, China was attempting to reform but reforms in SOEs conflicted with the embedded interests of people in power and often got stuck. Chinese laws specify what enterprises can do, and anything outside the specifications is subject to local interpretation (Krug and Hendrischke, 2007). Approvals for development, business expansion, pricing and labour management had to be secured before proceeding. While new thinking about reform and opening was being promoted, old habits and traditional thinking resisting the new ways could be strong at certain times.

Among the phrases that found high currency in speeches and documents about the reform are: *'shi shi qiu shi'* – seeking truth from facts and *'jie fang si xiang'* – liberation of thinking. These phrases expressed encouragement of change and experimentation. In the course of constant changes, rules were being made as the environments evolved, often after the events. *'Shi dian'* or running pilots were a way to try out new ideas in a certain controlled area before full implementation. As the top echelon of Chinese leadership encouraged experimentation, political leaders at various levels had to underwrite or endorse change efforts that could be aligned with the main thrust of economic development. For a while, between June 1989 and early 1992, most of these experiments took a back seat, and China's path to reform seemed to have stagnated. It took paramount leader Deng Xiaoping, then almost 90 years of age, to make his final South Tour to give the reforms another boost. Change again became the most accepted way of managing. The negative aspect was that players within the system sometimes wondered if any consistency existed at all, as the bureaucracy became unpredictable with policies passing down from top to bottom, leaving a lot of room for officials at the level of implementation to interpret and often manoeuvre for their individual benefit.

China's business environment evolved in stages in response to the results of reforms and changes in the previous stages (Child, 1994; Nolan, 1995; Peng, 2000; Warner et al., 2005). Each stage demonstrated different dynamics that affected firm level strategy formulation. Behind them was 'The fundamental theme of China's reform ... the transition from a centrally planned economy to a market economy', as Wu Jinglian states in his definitive work on Chinese economic reform (Wu, 2005: 43). Wu, himself one of the key economists exerting a strong influence on government policies during the reform process, traces the evolution of China's reform strategy back to 1958. He identifies three major stages: (1) 1958 to 1978 – administrative decentralization with government transferring power to lower levels; (2) 1979 to 1993 – incremental reform of 'outside the system' to 'inside the system', focusing on non-state sectors; (3) 1994 to present day – overall advance with key break-throughs. Wu sees the steps beginning in 1958 to delegate power to lower levels as a way to understanding the 'incrementalism' of the process.

In a more detailed description, Zhou has classified the reform process into the following stages and breakthroughs (Zhou, 2006: 106): 1978–84, reforms concentrated in rural agricultural areas; 1985–88, reforms extended into urban centres; 1989–91, economic austerity and retrench-ment; 1992 onwards, wide ranging reforms resumed, steady economic growth and real development ensued; 2001, China's WTO accession which signalled China's determination to join the international system and to accept its rules.

Chinese reform was characterized by gradualism and incrementalism, both in policy and in its implementation. Pragmatism reigned. This was partly due to the fact that the institutional and cultural traditions of hard-line communism never entirely faded away. There was a continuing struggle between the reformists and the conservatives during the reform process. The reformists were in favour of relaxing controls, reducing the role of the central bureaucracy, and allowing market forces to stimulate economic development, while the conservative faction would try to hold them back using traditional Maoist or Marxist Leninist arguments.

Principles of Reform

Overall, the Chinese reform followed a number of principles. First, a policy of 'gradualism' was adopted in China in contrast to 'shock therapy' in Russia. In the late 1970s and 1980s, Russia and China both faced considerable challenges of economic development. Both were ready to reform, but the two countries chose very different paths. Gorbachev, the Soviet leader, led the country to 'perestroika' followed by the 'shock therapy' policies of the Yeltsin era, while Deng Xiaoping chose to open up and reform the country in a gradual manner (Nolan, 1995). The Russian programme brought in political changes before economic reforms, which resulted in the dissolution of the former USSR; while in China political changes were controlled through the dominant and pervasive leadership of the Communist Party under Deng. Opening up the economy to market forces and international influences was pursued incrementally, through a gradual transition from 'delegating more power to lower levels' in agricultural and enterprise reforms, to reforms in ownership (equity reforms using stock markets), price reforms and finally WTO accession. These two contrasting reform programmes led to very different results in economic performance, as evidenced by different GDP growth rates and a large number of indicators such as food production, levels of poverty and of consumption. Nolan argues that 'the main reason for the difference in outcome is the difference in the policies chosen' (1995: 3).

Second, a principle of the Chinese economic reform was 'incremental-ism'. The Chinese leadership was very concerned that any attempts to change did not disturb the overall economic functioning of the country as a whole. Its emphasis on stability was grounded in the need to manage a vast country. So it favoured running pilots and experiments to gather sufficient experience before undertaking full scale country-wide implementation. In both its agricultural and industrial reform, the central government encouraged experiments in various localities before proceeding to national adoption. In opening up the country to the outside world, several cities (Shenzhen, Zhuhai, Shantou, Xiamen) were selected as 'special economic zones' to try out the new policies in the early 1980s before Shanghai opened up the Pudong area in the 1990s. When attracting foreign investments, China prioritized certain industries using a select list. In foreign trade, the country was gradually opened to the outside world, a process which accelerated with its accession to the WTO in 2001.

Third, the movement of the reform was from the coast to inland. The Chinese reform programme started in coastal provinces such as Guangdong and Fujian partly because of the more outward tradition of these provinces and partly because of their relative economic readiness. Families in the coastal provinces have for a long time seen millions of their male members work outside of China in overseas countries in support of their families at home. The overseas Chinese migrated to many places including Indonesia, Thailand, Malaysia, Singapore, Taiwan and Hong Kong. This diaspora gave rise to a successful system of Chinese capitalism which itself has served as a support to Mainland reform: for example in encouraging the authorities to relax restrictions on private business (Redding, 1990; Redding and Witt, 2007). At the start of the reform in the early 1980s, investments from overseas Chinese accounted for over 50 per cent of the total inflow and their contribution of direct investment remains very significant.

Fourth, the old and new co-existed during the process of change. While the country was experimenting with new policies and new organizations, a large part of the country continued to be run along traditional lines. A 'Dual Track System' of new and old ran parallel to each other, sometimes creating tensions and problems. For example, during the early 1980s, while liberal price setting policies were being implemented in various locations, the central government and some provincial governments continued to exercise tight price controls over raw materials, which led to 'rampant rent seeking activities' (Wu, 2005: 73) and corruption. While certain sectors of the economy might complain about unfair treatment, the Chinese leadership always tried to maintain firm control of the tempo of change through macro-economic controls. At the same time, Deng Xiaoping has often been quoted as saying: 'It is all right to have some people becoming better off first', so justifying some imbalance in the development process and some uneven results especially in income distribution.

China's 'Opening' to the World

Another application of incrementalism in the Chinese reform strategy was the use of inward foreign direct investment [FDI] and 'special economic zones' [SEZs] for opening to and integrating with the international economy. The reformers recognized that foreign investment could bring necessary capital, but more importantly could bring technology and management expertise. In September 1978, Deng Xiaoping pointed out that 'actively developing relations, including economic and cultural exchanges, with other countries on the basis of the Five Principles of Peaceful Coexistence' would 'enable us to make use of the capital from foreign countries and of their advanced technology and experience in business management' (Deng, 1996: 294). The reformers also were ingenious in starting their experiments in coastal areas as springboards to wider development.

In the third plenum of the eleventh central committee of the Chinese Communist Party in 1978, foreign investment laws were enacted concerning contracts, taxation, foreign exchange and other matters. These set out in broad terms the way that China wanted to deal with the 'international capitalists' that they had previously rejected. Elaboration of the legal framework continued during the following decades. The first Law on Chinese-Foreign Equity Joint Ventures appeared in 1979, with follow-up laws and regulations in 1983, 1990 and 2001. Similarly detailed rules for wholly foreign owned enterprises [WFOE] were promulgated in 1986 and 1990 and for contractual joint ventures in 1988 and 1995. The Company Law was established in 1993, and the Foreign Trade Law and Tax Law were announced in 1994 and 1996 respectively.

Attracted by the economic benefits of cheap land and labour, as well as the huge Chinese market, multinational companies from the west, Hong Kong and other Asian countries poured in. Initially, the efforts were led by Hong Kong and Taiwan based companies who as overseas Chinese had a tradition of bringing back to their motherland the fruits of business success outside the country. They tested the water and established 'beachhead units' in the coastal areas. Over time, these foreign investments grew in size and complexity. During the past 20 years, China has attracted over 500 000 foreign enterprises of various shapes and sizes to invest in China. The stock of inward FDI in China reached US$579 billion in 2010 (UNCTAD, 2011). According to figures from China's Ministry of Commerce, foreign-invested companies accounted for 55.9 per cent of China's exports in 2009, which is considerably more than from any other category of company. As already noted, by 2009 China had become the world's largest exporter and the second largest importer by value (WTO, 2010).

Apart from establishing a legal and regulatory framework, the country also designed various policies supporting foreign participation in economic activities, such as encouraging investment into specific industries and projects through special tax incentives, land use incentives and labour concessions (Huang, 1998; 2003). Within this context, a growing number of MNCs moved from first to second generation investors, who were no longer content with establishing a beachhead in a single product or in one region of China. According to two surveys conducted by McKinsey (Shaw and Meier, 1993; Meier et al., 1995), these second generation MNCs were committed to pursuing ambitious investment programmes, building world-scale businesses and securing dominant, nationwide market positions. The McKinsey studies noted that many MNCs in China were coming to adopt the perspective of long-term investors and they highlighted relevant management actions for the MNCs who wished to penetrate the Chinese market.

The McKinsey findings were supported by Luo and O'Connor's study (1998). They concluded that foreign investors appeared to follow an evolutionary approach in incrementally increasing their resource and financial commitments to local operations, and in gradually heightening their proactiveness and risk-taking in the Chinese market. Big names such as Motorola, Atlantic Richfield, Coca-Cola, Ford Motor, Amoco, United Tech, Pepsico, Lucent Technologies, General Electric, Hewlett Packard, IBM and Volkswagen have maintained on-going commitments to the Chinese market with ever increasing stakes.

A decisive step for China's integration into the outside world and global economics was its accession to the World Trade Organization in November 2001. As early as 1986, China applied to restore its status as a founding member of the GATT, signifying its intentions to integrate itself into the world economic system. Accession to WTO meant acceptance of the rules of globalization in trade with the world. Since 2001, China has lowered its tariffs down to 9.5 per cent in 2009 (compared to 56 per cent back in 1982), abolished non-tariff quotas and restrictions, reduced its protection of strategic industries, accelerated its development of the market mechanism, lifted some restrictions on foreign investment and overall created a more favourable environment for international business integration. WTO accession also meant changes in the rules of competition domestically. In the industries specified by the terms and conditions of WTO entry, relaxation of controls took place albeit gradually to allow international players to gain entry and sometimes to spread their influence. Overall, the environment became more supportive of international business practices.

The combination of rapid growth, opening of the economy and increasing scope to introduce international business standards encouraged large-scale investment by multinationals like Hutchison-Whampoa, YICT's main investor.

YICT'S MESO ENVIRONMENT

The specific environment in which YICT operated established the conditions which most immediately informed the company's strategy. This environment was that of the Shenzhen SEZ, adjacent to an existing Hong Kong port of international standing, and located in a fast developing region of China.

Development of the Shenzhen SEZ

In line with the principle of gradualism in reform and opening, the leaders of the reform movement conceived the idea of SEZs in Shenzhen, Zhuhai, Shantao and Xiamen in April 1979. These experimental areas breathed new life as 'pilots' (*si dian*) or experimental fields for new ideas and an open agenda for reform. They provided a safe place in which to experiment and, when the experiments proved to be successful, the experience informed their dissemination to other parts of the country.

During a tour of the Guangdong coastal area in the late 1970s, provincial leaders Wu Nanshan and Ding Shusheng were appalled at its backwardness and discussed the suggestion of designating land for export processing activities. They had in mind coastal locations such as Shantou, Shenzhen and Zhuhai because they had a history of opening up to the outside world, were close to colonies like Hong Kong and Macau, and their people had, long before the reforms, been travelling outside China in search of better fortunes. The particular connections these locations had with Hong Kong and overseas Chinese meant that they were suitable to be chosen as experimental fields for opening up. In Beijing, this bold suggestion met with a warm reception by the paramount leader Deng Xiaoping who commented: 'We can cut out an area and name it a "special zone"'. The Communist Party used to run special zones during the revolutionary era in Shanxi. As Liao recalls in his account of early developments in Shenzhen, the government took the view that 'the Central Government has no money, but can offer you freedom to try new policies. You must fight to win in this blood-smeared path to reform' (Liao, 1999: 7). The use of Deng's military analogy was an indication of how difficult Deng perceived the tasks ahead and the level of opposition likely to face the reformers.

With Deng's endorsement, Deputy Prime Minister Ku Mu led a delegation comprising various ministries and conducted a feasibility study on the formation of SEZs. In May 1980, the State Council and the People's Congress formally announced the formation of four SEZs in Shantou, Zhuhai and Shenzhen all in Guangdong Province, plus Xiamen in Fujian Province. In August 1980, the Economic Regulations of the Guangdong Province SEZs were promulgated. These rules and regulations were to form the basic policies and laws of the special zones.

Shenzhen used to be a sleepy village of 30 000 inhabitants bordering Hong Kong, and was only recognized as a railway stop by Hong Kong travellers on their way from Hong Kong to Guangzhou. It had scarcely any industry prior to becoming a special economic zone. Before and during the Cultural Revolution, Shenzhen was known to the world as a gathering place for thousands of illegal immigrants who risked their lives to cross over to Hong Kong.

The mission for the Shenzhen SEZ was to become China's 'window to the world' and an 'experimental field for reform'. From the start, the SEZ was given significant policy concessions like autonomy to seek foreign investments, especially from Hong Kong, Macau, Taiwan and other overseas Chinese communities; authority to approve projects with investment sums under RMB 100 million; special concessions on land use rights; special terms and concessions for commercial banks to make project loans; special tax concessions – foreign investors were granted five years of tax-free terms plus 50 per cent tax concessions for the succeeding five years; and the right of local government to keep a large portion of its revenues.

So the SEZ went ahead and experimented. According to one official history of the city, the development of the Shenzhen SEZ can be divided into four stages (Liao, 1999). During the first stage from 1979 to 1986, led by veteran revolutionary leaders, the SEZ focused on carving out a niche for its survival and development. The focus of attention was on laying the foundations in infrastructure with money from the banking sector and promoting to international investors the benefits of compensation trade, as well as direct investments into Shenzhen. Hong Kong businessmen were the primary targets. Hong Kong industrialists were offered special land and tax incentives to move their production facilities across the border. Initial success was evident in the first few years since labour costs in Shenzhen were one-tenth those of Hong Kong. In this period, Shenzhen's GDP grew 15.5 times and export trade grew eightfold.

The second stage (1986–1990) was one of takeoff. This was a period of significant fluctuations in the reform process in China punctuated by inflation, macro-economic control, price reforms and political incidents causing the downfall of Party Secretaries Hu Yaobang and Zhao Ziyang. Shenzhen experienced these ups and downs to a lesser degree, being some distance away from the political centre and having established itself as mainly an externally oriented economy in the previous years of reform and opening. The SEZ's leaders introduced further reforms during this period, including reforms in company equity structure within the SOE system; modern company management principles separating political and economic control, with executive powers delegated to board chairmen and general managers; establishment of the Shenzhen Stock Exchange in December 1990 – the first of its kind in China; establishment of a modern banking system to detach commercial banks from the Finance Administration of the government; establishment of the Land Auction System; development of the First Free Trade Zone in Shataukok; plus social security reform, civil service reform, and special assistance offered to key infrastructure projects. In these five years, Shenzhen's GDP grew by 300 per cent and external trade increased by 487 per cent.

The third stage covers the years from 1990 to 1995. Shenzhen's development slowed after the 4 June Tiananmen Square incident. It took Deng's 1992 South Tour to reinvigorate the process again. The main effect of Deng's visit was to resolve the decade-long debate of whether SEZs were 'capitalistic' or 'socialistic' in nature. Deng in his forthright manner put a stop to the political debate and the reforms were given a strong boost. The following initiatives were again launched in earnest: further opening up to the world by allowing special approval procedures to be conducted in Shenzhen; further civil service reforms, with a civil service examination system established; refinement of the modern enterprise system (for instance, further separation of government and enterprise management); government policies towards building of industry groups; social security reforms to attract a more educated workforce to emigrate to Shenzhen; special policies to encourage development of high technology industry; and announcement of special priority for port and airport development, with development projects being initiated such as the signing of the Yantian Port Agreement with Hutchison-Whampoa. In these five years, Shenzhen's GDP grew by 485 per cent and external trade increased by 585 per cent.

The fourth stage of Shenzhen's development took place in the years after 1996. Urged by then premier Li Peng to find a new competitive edge for the SEZ, the city leaders switched their developmental focus from speed to quality in this period, naming it the 'second founding'. Shenzhen was famous for its speed in construction and in the execution of projects, but, as its development progressed, the SEZ became conscious of its need to pay attention to quality in both production and service. A new theme was the development of high technology industry, especially electronics, as a key pillar of the city's economy. The electronics sector grew at 60 per cent per annum and by 2000 accounted for 31 per cent of Shenzhen's industrial GDP. Other measures included developing service industries further and organizing industrial groups; empowering the national assets management company to allow a higher degree of enterprise autonomy; attracting more FDI with 'National Treatment'; adding infrastructure in bonded zones and through rail and highway developments; and beginning to establish Shenzhen as a city where 'quality of life' and culture play an important part.

In 2005, Shenzhen became home to 10 million people and it celebrated its 25th anniversary as an SEZ, listing some of its accomplishments such as a GDP increase at an average rate of 28 per cent per annum, and attaining a per capita income of US$7100, the highest of all Chinese cities. The SEZ can also boast of its status as the country's leading city in terms of exports and imports, as well as being home to the fourth largest container terminal in the world. The particular relevance of the Shenzhen SEZ as the immediate environment in which YICT evolved lies in its combination of: (1) a culture of experimentation and modernization; (2) rapid growth (which was also characteristic of the port's wider hinterland in Guangdong Province); and (3) the switch over time in Shenzhen government thinking from quantitative to qualitative development which favoured striving for 'world-class' best practice.

The Port Industry in Hong Kong

While the business of shipping has an ancient history, the containerization industry only began in 1956 with Malcolm McLean's invention of standard steel box units to transport cargo from trains and trucks onto ships. With its high efficiency and economy, containerization spread very fast around the world in the ensuing decades, and Hong Kong caught on to the revolution in a timely manner. In the early 1960s, the Hong Kong and Whampoa Dock Company, a predecessor of Hong Kong International Terminals, found it necessary to expand its facilities rapidly to cope with the surge in imports and exports in and out of Hong Kong. The company started its operations originally from a small dockyard in Hunghom and North Point and soon was reclaiming land for its much bigger and dedicated container facilities in Kwai Chung (Rodwell, 1989).

Then a major entrepôt between China and the west, Hong Kong's trade volume grew exponentially after the Second World War, capturing the growth of traffic from China to the outside world. Hong Kong thrived on light industrial consumer production and exported mainly to the United States and Europe. Trade from the Mainland was of similar goods, which largely came through the Hong Kong port either overland or through ships along the river and the coast. These exports were well suited to the containerized mode of transportation. Geographically Hong Kong was strategically situated on the east-west ocean-going routes, making it a natural stop for carriers to pick up cargo along these routes. Hong Kong was then a British colony, declared a 'free port' by the Treaty of Nanking in 1842. This status made the Hong Kong port an excellent convenience for international trade, while most Chinese ports were underdeveloped. In fact, Hong Kong became the only port in the greater China area available to handle the growth of industrialization in the region. In 1984, Hong Kong came in third place in the world container league with 2.11 million TEUs throughput, behind Rotterdam and New York. By 1987 Hong Kong's port had become number one in the world with an annual throughput of 4 million TEUs (Rodwell, 1989).

The model of infrastructure development in Hong Kong was one of partnership between government and private business. The Hong Kong government had long upheld its non-interventionist policy in maintaining a free economy. It had left the private sector to invest in infrastructure. With the development of container facilities, the Hong Kong government invited private companies to compete in government-organized open bids for land and development rights in building and operating the port in Kwai Chung. Throughout all of its port developments from Terminal 1 to Terminal 9, the Hong Kong government kept its laissez-faire promise, offering development rights to the highest bidder.

In the 1990s, the main operators were Hong Kong International Terminals (HIT), a Hutchison subsidiary,[2] with around 50 per cent of the total business; Sealand Orient Limited (a subsidiary of the US corporation); Modern Terminals (a Wharf subsidiary); and a COSCO-HIT joint venture. These operators effectively operated the Hong Kong port as an oligopoly with tacit understandings amongst themselves over customer and pricing arrangements. Cheng and Wong described this system as one of 'oligopolistic interdependence' (Cheng and Wong, 1997). 'The terminal operators all claim that they engage in fierce competition with one another for customers. However, there are simply too few players for them not to have any explicit or implicit understanding about the avoidance of head-on competition. It would be unbelievable indeed if they failed to recognize their close interdependence to adjust their competitive strategies accordingly' (Cheng and Wong, 1997: 91). With the development of new facilities governed by the 'trigger point' mechanism (an arrangement that only requires a port operator to build new facilities when the existing ones are operating at 70 per cent capacity), the supply of terminal facilities was effectively controlled, and, with the Chinese economy growing so rapidly, the Hong Kong port found itself in an enviable position of demand chasing supply.

The imbalance was so acute that serious competitors found themselves using an outdated mode of operations, the so-called 'mid stream' system, which was no longer found anywhere else in ports. Instead of being handled at terminals, ships and cargoes were handled at 'stream' – with barges going to and fro between ships and small berths using derricks to move boxes from barges to ships and vice versa. This mode of operations was started initially to supplement the big terminals, an admittedly stopgap measure and an outmoded way of operating. However, because of excessive demand, this special practice continued to survive. At its peak in 1995, mid stream operations handled over 3 million TEUs or 23.3 per cent of Hong Kong port's traffic in that year.

In terms of performance and productivity, it was well recognized that the Hong Kong port was one of the best in the world. Using various metrics such as production per berth, productivity per metre of berth or per hectare of land, the operators all performed at a satisfactory level, often above world standards. However, Hong Kong also had some of the highest prices and costs in the world, being more expensive than Singapore, Taiwan, Germany and the United Kingdom (Cheng and Wong, 1997: 22).

In the first half of the 1990s, the industry recognized that there were several issues confronting the Hong Kong port. Should additional capacity be built to cope with increasing demand? Did the 'trigger point' mechanism serve the territory's interest optimally? To what extent did oligopolistic pricing amongst the operators affect port development positively or negatively? How should the Hong Kong port respond to its potential competitors like Yantian, Chiwan and Shekou?

The Hong Kong government established the Port Development Board in April 1990 to advise the government on port planning and port strategic development.[3] In its Port Cargo Forecasts for 2000/2001, the Board foresaw a healthy growth rate for Hong Kong's container business – 4.5 per cent per annum over the period 1999 to 2020 – fuelled by high export growth from Mainland China. The Hong Kong SAR government's *Port Development Strategy Review 2001* noted that Hong Kong's total container throughput was forecast to increase to 31.1 million TEUs by 2011 and 40.5 million TEUs in 2020. This represented a projected average annual growth rate of 5.1 per cent and 3.1 per cent respectively during the first and second decades of the planning period, from a base of 16.2 million TEUs in 1999.[4] In assessing Hong Kong port's competitiveness, the Board noted that Hong Kong had higher terminal handling charges and high road haulage costs to and from Mainland China. It also described Shenzhen ports like Yantian, Chiwan and Shekou as major competitors.

To handle the growing volume of trade, investors were ready with investment money partly funded by internal sources and partly by the thriving financial sector which had plenty of cash for developmental purposes. This was mainly private capital, with very little government involvement except in some basic groundwork in laying out the site and development of simple road networks. However, the Hong Kong government did establish a context for such huge investments to become possible. The 'trigger point' mechanism ensured that there would be no serious competition brought about by overcapacity.

While containerization in Hong Kong grew significantly in the 1980s and early 1990s, a quiet revolution in the demand side had been taking place. Attracted by low labour costs, a good supply of industrial land and an open door policy driven by Deng Xiaoping, Hong Kong entrepreneurs began moving their production facilities inland (HKTDC, 2000). They created the successful business model of 'production in the backyard and marketing in the front'. With over a hundred years of commercial experience in dealing with the west, Hong Kong business people remained responsible for marketing and sales with their partners across the border taking care of quality production on the mainland. The trend started in the 1970s and gained momentum in the 1980s and 1990s, so much so that almost the entire Hong Kong industrial base moved across the Chinese border to settle in the Pearl River Delta in a matter of two decades between the 1970s and 1990s. However, until the 1990s, most of these light industrial products produced at the Guangdong province found their way to buyers abroad via the Hong Kong port.

The Hong Kong port had therefore become very efficient, albeit relatively costly. Sometimes around the annual export peaks in the late 1980s and early 1990s, traffic through the port built up to such a level that congestion appeared. The road network leading to the Hong Kong port could hardly cope with compound annual growth rates of over 20 per cent. Traffic jams became a constant feature around the port, and ships were made to wait for long hours at anchorage.

As a result, the highly profitable port operators began to look for opportunities outside Hong Kong. In fact, entrepreneurial firms like Hutchison Port Holdings (HPH) achieved a rapid expansion of its networks worldwide in a matter of 10 years during the 1990s. At the same time, motivated by a need to lower operating cost, port users began a serious study of alternatives in the vicinity. These were the conditions conducive to the birth of new developments across the border in Shenzhen, including the founding and growth of Yantian port.

The Early Days of Port Development in Shenzhen

While development of the Hong Kong port was very much in the hands of private interests, the development of Chinese ports just across the border was highly regulated. Just emerging out of the command economy in the early 1990s, China Merchants, a Chinese national company under the Ministry of Communications and Transportation, took the first step in Shekou at the tip of a peninsula in west Shenzhen.[5] Shekou Container Terminals received their first ships in 1991.

The idea of having a major port in the SEZ of Shenzhen was conceived almost at the same time as the establishment of the zone. The SEZ, designed to be a 'window to the world' (Liao, 1999: 9), required ways and means of opening up to the world. In its early years, the SEZ had little to show in terms of infrastructure facilities for external trade. Its leaders realized that ports serving ships and airplanes were key to achieving a high level of external connection. A strategy of 'taking off with two wings' – development of both sea and airports – gradually took shape in the early 1980s. That strategy helped spearhead the development of Yantian port. According to Li Hao, Party Secretary and Mayor of Shenzhen between 1986 and 1993:

> In the sixties, I worked in the National Economic Commission which was responsible for the nation's infrastructure development. I was therefore very familiar with the need for good ports. In the seventies, Premier Zhou En-lai showed a lot of interest in port development, and in 1976, Zhou suggested the building of 100 modern ports for China. At that time, our facilities were so backward that ships visiting China were made to wait for weeks to offload and load cargo. That considerably inhibited foreign trade.[6]

In the early 1990s, the Chinese port sector had a highly institutionalized environment characterized by heavy government involvement and control. First, operators and investors required state approvals to develop the coastline into container facilities. Planning reigned supreme and investors had to go through a dense bureaucratic jungle to reach decision-makers for permission. Then, at the operational level, shipping lines had to obtain permissions to operate services, often from the local government branches of ministries as well as from the same ministries in the national capital. Furthermore, to ensure proper tax collection and prevent smuggling, the ports had to be staffed with customs administration authorities who were charged with responsibilities and power to inspect cargoes going in and out. Since ports are by definition at the nation's frontiers, the Frontier Inspectorate was put in charge of overseeing people moving in and out. They had a special mission in those days to prevent the smuggling of people to Hong Kong, which was very prevalent in the 1960s and 1970s. Other regulatory authorities were also present. For example, the Quarantine Inspectorate's job was to screen the goods coming into China for communicable diseases and other health hazards which appeared from time to time.

The regulators had their different administrations reporting vertically from the local authority to the provincial authority with direct super-vision from the national command centre in Beijing. Each of these regulators published different laws, rules and regulations, often vague and subject to interpretations, that formed an outer layer of the 'service package' for port users. They worked different hours and had work cultures that could contrast markedly to those of the service providers. Sometimes, they conflicted amongst themselves in the execution of their individual duties.

In sharp contrast to the Hong Kong free port, ports in Shenzhen as well as other ports in China in the early years only attracted very few users. International shipping lines showed their preference for high-quality service and concentrated on Hong Kong, making it for many years the world's busiest port. Users had little choice but to move their cargo across the Hong Kong-Shenzhen border on trucks to and from Kwai Chung. In the Shenzhen ports, the throughput handled was minimal and shipping services frequency was insufficient to create the critical mass necessary for takeoff.

The rules for government involvement in China's port industry were not totally clear as they evolved during the course of the country's economic reform. The port industry used to be a highly regulated environment – for example, pricing had to be approved, safety had to be controlled, and standards had to be monitored. At the time of rapid change in the 1990s, many of these regulations became less restrictive. Yet they still presented a major obstacle to a port functioning as freely as it would like and for it to reach world-level standards. Furthermore, in the regulated port environment, the government agencies of Customs, Quarantine, Frontier Inspectorate and others occupied key positions in the service offering. Chinese ports suffered in efficiency and effectiveness because of outdated practices in these areas.

Almost all joint venture port operating companies had local partners which were quasi-government organizations with divided loyalties. They also displayed a mixture of the old and the new. On the one hand they were concerned to remain viable and prosperous through seeking an economic return, while on the other hand they had to maintain 'political correctness' as a governmental and therefore political organization. To be politically correct, partners are expected to 'fight' for the rights of the

Chinese party rather than necessarily to cooperate. There was a continuing debate about whether to allow foreigners majority ownership in strategic assets. Allowing land to be rented for 50 years raised the argument that the SEZ should not be permitted to go back to the colonial days of 'colonial free zones'. When these port operators began to make money, some officials suspected that capitalist exploitation had gone too far.

In terms of facilitating change, the port operators relied on cooperation from the government agencies. However, those government agencies that formed an integral part of the service environment were also undergoing changes. On the one hand, they were given the task of maintaining the country's rules and regulations; while on the other hand, they were also expected to support experimentation as part of the wind of change. If officers wanted a career in the new economy, they needed to be perceived as progressive reformers. How the rules were interpreted and executed was very much left to the individual on-site officials, which could give rise to both major problems and opportunities. It made it vital to create and maintain a cooperative relationship with such officials.

Nevertheless, in times of transition and change, opportunities abound. In China's port industry from the 1990s onward the demand for container terminal services was substantial. The South China region was growing rapidly and was bursting to export with most of Hong Kong's factories having moved north across the border. Now the need for Hong Kong's port companies such as Hutchison was to develop across-the-border terminal facilities that would operate effectively in a different macro environment.

The Take-off of China's Port Sector

In 2007, the Ministry of Communications celebrated China's handling of 100 million TEUs in November in Tianjin. From a modest beginning, China's container port industry took off in the mid-1990s and has become one of the largest container handling countries today.

In the early 1990s, mainland South China scarcely had a port industry at all. The Shenzhen port in Shekou (on the western side of Shenzhen) was infrequently called on by its customers, with very small throughput numbers. The Guangzhou port at Huangpo was inadequately equipped to handle modern ocean-going vessels. Indeed, China as a whole only had very underdeveloped container facilities in Shanghai and a few other scattered places. Most if not all of the containers of goods produced for export found their way to the Hong Kong ports, making Hong Kong the

The dynamics of corporate co-evolution

busiest and the best in the world. However, in the ensuing two decades, the scene changed drastically, as Table 4.1 shows.

Table 4.1   Container throughput of China ports since 1990

Year	Throughput (million TEUs)	Annual growth (per cent)
1990	1.6	
1991	2.2	39
1992	2.7	27
1993	3.8	38
1994	5.1	32
1995	6.6	30
1996	8.1	22
1997	10.8	33
1998	13.1	22
1999	17.3	32
2000	22.6	30
2001	26.5	17
2002	37.2	40
2003	48.6	30
2004	61.5	26
2005	75.8	24
2006	93.6	23
2007	114.7	23
2008	128.3	11.9
2009	121.0	−5.7
2010	145.0	19.8

Source: Ministry of Communications and Transportation Reports, 1992–2011

SUMMARY

Table 4.2 draws together and summarizes key features in the evolution of China's macro and meso (regional and industry) environments that were relevant to the establishment and evolution of YICT. It categorizes these into three broad time periods. The first up to 1989 is the period during which the foundations were laid in respect of China's economic reform and, more locally, the establishment of the Shenzhen SEZ and the migration of Hong Kong industry to mainland South China. After the post-Tiananmen interlude, the 1990s witnessed the take-off of China's economic reforms, growth and 'opening', and a new awareness of the role that modern ports had to play in supporting the process. The first decade of the present century saw these developments taken further, with a significant stimulus being provided by China's accession to the WTO. At the meso level, demand for container port services grew rapidly and consistently, with the sole exception of 2009 which reflected the recession in developed countries.

Table 4.2   Evolution of the environment and its relevance to YICT

Environmental evolution	Time period		
	1978 to 1989	1990s	2000s
Evolution of the macro environment	* The third plenary session of CCPCC in 1978 – beginning of reform and opening (under Deng Xiaoping's leadership) * Changes in the 'peasant' work system – more freedom to work units and emergence of Township enterprises * SOE Reforms – delegation of authority * Price Reforms * FDIs in China – compensation trade	* Labour reforms – mobility and productivity * FDI – joint venture laws established * Aftermath of June 4 Tiananmen incident * Deng's South China Tour in 1992 * New leadership – Jiang Zemin * Vice Premier Li Lanqing's reforms on port administration in 1996 (see Chapter 8)	* Further reforms and opening – relaxation of investment conditions * World Trade Organization (WTO) accession – reduction of tariffs * Inward FDI – no. 1 in the world by 2002 * Reform of Project Approval Process in 2003
Evolution of the meso environment (Shenzen SEZ & regional port industry)	* Founding of SEZs in Shenzhen – infrastructure development * Development of the Hong Kong Port into the world busiest * Beginning of migration of industry from Hong Kong to the mainland * FDI from Hong Kong and Taiwan to the Pearl River Delta manufacturing base	* Strategy to develop ports as part of the overall Shenzhen SEZ development plan – 'use port development to boost city development' * HK port – efficiency development; founding of Terminals 8 and 9 * HK port – development of international trans-shipment * HK port – shipping lines seeking alternative ports	* SEZ: 'second founding' – industry upgrade to high technology products; more export oriented * Rapid growth in demand for Mainland container port services * HK port further developed into an international trans-shipment hub

NOTES

1. The TEU (20-foot equivalent unit) is a unit of cargo capacity often used to describe the capacity of container ships and container terminals. It is based on the volume of a 20-foot-long (6.1 m) intermodal container, a standard-sized metal box which can be easily transferred between different modes of transportation, such as ships, trains and trucks.
2. HIT reports to Hutchison Port Holdings Limited [HPH], the holding company for Hutchison-Whampoa's ports worldwide.
3. The Port Development Board was renamed the Hong Kong Port and Maritime Board on 1 June 1998.
4. *Port Development Strategy Review 2001*, published by the Port & Maritime Division, Economic Services Bureau, HKSAR Government.
5. This ministry held responsibility for China's port sector; henceforth, referred to as the 'Ministry of Communications'.
6. Interview with Li Hao, August 2004.

REFERENCES

Cheng, K.H. and Y.J. Wong (1997), *Port Infrastructure and Container Terminal Business* (in Chinese), Hong Kong: Commercial Press.

Child, J. (1994), *Management in China during the Age of Reform*, Cambridge: Cambridge University Press.

Deng, X.-P. (1996), *Selected Works of Deng Xiaoping* (in Chinese), Hong Kong: Joint Publishing Hong Kong Limited.

HKTDC (Hong Kong Trade Development Council) (2000), *Investment Environment in the Chinese Mainland: A Survey Report on Hong Kong Companies' View*, Hong Kong: HKTDC, Research Department.

Huang, Y. (1998), *FDI in China: An Asia Perspective*, Singapore: Institute of Southeast Asian Studies.

Huang, Y. (2003), *Selling China: Foreign Direct Investment during the Reform Era*, Cambridge: Cambridge University Press.

Krug, B. and H. Hendrischke (eds) (2007), *The Chinese Economy in the 21st Century: Enterprise and Business Behaviour*, Cheltenham, UK and Northampton, MA: Edward Elgar.

Liao, Y. (1999), *Phylogeny of China's Special Economic Zones* (in Chinese). Shenzhen: Hai Tian Publishing House.

Luo, Y. and N. O'Connor (1998), 'Structural changes to foreign direct investment in China: an evolutionary perspective', *Journal of Applied Management Studies*, **7** (1), 95–109.

Meier, S., J. Perez and J.R. Woetzel (1995), 'Solving the puzzle: MNCs in China', *McKinsey Quarterly*, **2**, 1–11.

MOFCOM (2012), *Statistical Bulletin of China's Outward Foreign Direct Investment*, Beijing: Ministry of Commerce.

Nolan, P. (1995), *China's Rise, Russia's Fall – Politics, Economics and Planning in the Transition from Stalinism*, London: Macmillan.

Peng, M.W. (2000), *Business Strategies in Transition Economies*, London: Sage.

People's Bank of China (2012), 'China's balance of payments statistics', accessed at http://www.safe.gov.cn.

Redding, S.G. (1990), *The Spirit of Chinese Capitalism*, Berlin: de Gruyter.

Redding, G. and M.A. Witt (2007), *The Future of Chinese Capitalism*, Oxford: Oxford University Press.

Rodwell, S. (1989), *Boxes and Barnacles: The Story of Hong Kong International Terminals*, Hong Kong: HIT.

Shaw, S.M. and J. Meier (1993), 'Second generation MNCs in China', *McKinsey Quarterly*, **4**, 19–32.

UNCTAD (2011), *World Investment Report 2011*, Geneva: United Nations Conference on Trade and Development.

Warner, M., V. Edwards, G. Polonsky, D. Pucko and Y. Zhu (2005), *Management in Transitional Economies*, London: Routledge Curzon.

WTO (2011), *International Trade Statistics 2011*, Geneva: World Trade Organization.

Wu, J.L. (2005), *Understanding and Interpreting Chinese Economic Reform*, Ohio: Thomson Higher Education.

Zhou, L. (2006), *China Business – Environment, Momentum, Strategies, Prospects*, Singapore: Prentice Hall.

5. The evolution of a world-class port

The previous chapter described the changes in the political and economic forces at work in China and Shenzhen during the period of reform and opening. These formed the macro and meso environmental backdrop to the story of Yantian International Container Terminals Limited [YICT]. The chapter also introduced the key players in YICT's domain, and those who played a significant part in the company's co-evolution with its environment. These players and their relevance are listed in Table 5.1.

The present chapter describes the initiatives taken by YICT's management within this environment during the first 15 years of the company's history. With the benefit of hindsight, one can detect a coherent strategy emerging from a series of choices. Driven by the vision of a 'world-class port', yet opportunistic in its approach in reacting to the changing environment, the port's management navigated a developmental path to achieve its financial, service and community objectives.

Like most new ventures, the executives in charge started with a broadly conceived idea and their strategies were crafted along the way (Mintzberg, 1978; 1987). A clear pattern only emerged after some time in the process of relating to external forces that were also evolving over time. This interaction encompassed responses on the company's part to developments in its environment as well as initiatives that it took to shape aspects of that environment. The Yantian port case story is therefore one in which corporate strategy co-evolved with environmental conditions.

THE YANTIAN PORT AFTER 15 YEARS

The year 2007 was very important for YICT, the sole terminal operator of the port of Yantian. It was a year that marked some of the most significant breakthroughs for the company. For the full year, the then 250 hectare, 14 berth terminal handled a throughput volume of 10.16 million TEUs, the largest annual throughput of a single terminal in the history of the container handling industry.

Size is but one of Yantian's distinctive characteristics; productivity and service are others. In 2006, the terminal proudly announced that its average crane production rate had reached 35 moves per hour per crane

Table 5.1   Key players in YICT's co-evolution

Key Player	Relevance
The firm (YICT)	
Hutchison Port Holdings [HPH] a member of the Hutchison-Whampao Group. Together with minority foreign investors, HPH initially held 70 per cent of YICT's equity The Yantian Port Group [YPG], owned by Shenzhen City government. Joint venture partner, initially holding 30 per cent of YICT's equity	The chairman of HPH, Li Kashing, is Hong Kong's leading businessman who enjoys huge personal prestige in Mainland China. HPH supplied the Chairman of the YICT Board, the General Manager and a majority of senior executives. It approved forward strategy and provided finance for investments. YPG supplied the Deputy Chairman and Deputy GM. Although YICT is an affiliate of HPH, it is also a competitor to the latter's Hong Kong terminals.
External parties	
China's central government	Instigated economic and political developments at the macro level: opening the Chinese economy and prioritizing economic growth, which created YICT's market. Also initiated a policy of reform, especially post-1992. The National Development and Reform Commission and Ministry of Communications had to approve the feasibility of port development projects.
Central government agencies operating locally, especially Customs, Frontier Inspection, Quarantine	Have the right to stop the flow of cargo through the port. Their level of cooperation and efficiency directly impact on the quality of service the port can offer.
Shenzhen city government. The Party Secretary and Chief Executive of the YPG were particularly significant players	Its approval was required for YICT's development plans. It also provided support in YICT's lobbying of central government.
Major shipping lines. One (Maersk) held 10 per cent of YICT's equity	Maersk, in particular, has been a keen supporter of initiatives taken by YICT to achieve world-class standards and to become a 'mega' port.

on a consistent basis throughout the previous 12 months, an industry record. On 28 December, in a ceremony celebrating this achievement, the General Manager of COSCO South China congratulated YICT on being one of the best operating terminals with which the shipping line had ever done business, anywhere in the world. The Chairman of the Yantian Port Group, the Chinese partner of the international joint venture, expressed satisfaction with the relationship and mutual support that the partners in the venture had established, mentioning that they had cooperated well in developing the port from its Phase 1 to Phase 3E,[1] and in planning further expansion. The terminal took pride in being one of the busiest ports in the world, operating over 80 international services, over half of which were line haul services to the USA and Europe.[2]

In October 2005 after just 11 full years of operation, YICT received a prestigious award from the Global Institute of Logistics, which has 4500 members spread over five continents. The Institute voted YICT 'The Global Terminal of the Year 2005–2006' based on the following criteria: service, productivity and contribution to the improvement of government regulation in the application of technology, scale and coverage of service. Commenting on the award, the Institute's CEO said:

> YICT demonstrates an excellent customer service plus attitude that is evidenced across a wide spectrum of services designed to enhance the competitiveness of the customers they service. YICT has been a proactive innovator in the appropriation of the next generation technology, which anticipates the changing needs and demands placed on the port industry as a whole. Additionally, its management and executives have availed themselves to the global logistics community in a way that we haven't witnessed before and have done much to enhance port operator/shipper relations (Global Institute of Logistics, Press Release, 2005).

In the same year, the company was honoured by the National Port Association of China as 'The Best Terminal Operator' in China, having achieved the highest scores in service and port productivity (National Port Association of China, Press Release 2005).

For many years, Yantian had been the world's number one port in terms of handling China's exports to the USA. By 2008, YICT employed almost 2800 staff, and with the support of over 7000 contractors had become an important employer in the community. It was also held to be one of the most environmentally responsible enterprises in Shenzhen. Table 5.2 records the company's employment growth.

In the period 1993–2010, China's container throughput grew at an average annual rate of 28 per cent (although it slowed and showed a dip in 2009 because of the global financial crisis), and achieved a 100-fold

Table 5.2   YICT employment

Year	Managers	Employees	Total
1994	15	150	165
1995	28	367	395
1996	30	436	466
1997	42	590	632
1998	43	709	752
1999	45	811	856
2000	47	932	979
2001	55	1060	1115
2002	66	1303	1369
2003	83	1833	1916
2004	90	2062	2152
2005	106	2244	2350
2006	106	2472	2578
2007	113	2605	2718
2008	115	2668	2783
2009	99	2472	2571
2010	95	2352	2447

Source: YICT records

increase in volume, which reflected the growing importance of external trade. Not surprisingly, as Table 5.3 shows, we see similar growth rates in throughput numbers for Yantian port and for the Shenzhen ports in total. The development of trade through the Yantian port mirrored the growth of industry in China. The port of Yantian contributed 10 per cent of the country's throughput, but its contributions amounted to more, according to one responsible official from the Ministry of Communications. Apart from handling large volumes and the largest container vessels, YICT led the Chinese port industry in service to customers and productivity as well as creating innovative port developmental paths.[3]

Table 5.3   Throughput growth in Yantian and Shenzhen ports, 1994 to 2010

Year	Yantian port throughput in TEUs	Percentage growth on previous year	Shenzhen ports throughput in TEUs	Percentage growth from the previous year
1994	13 000	–	178 000	–
1995	106 000	737.4	284 000	59.3
1996	354 000	234.4	589 000	107.6
1997	635 000	80.6	1 147 000	94.7
1998	1 038 000	62.6	1 952 000	70.2
1999	1 588 000	53.0	2 986 000	53.0
2000	2 147 000	35.2	3 994 000	33.8
2001	2 752 000	28.2	5 076 000	27.1
2002	4 181 000	51.9	7 618 000	50.1
2003	5 258 000	25.8	10 650 000	39.8
2004	6 260 000	19.0	13 655 000	28.2
2005	7 600 000	21.0	16 600 000	18.6
2006	8 861 000	15.8	18 452 000	14.2
2007	10 016 000	13	21 099 000	14.2
2008	9 683 493	–3.3	21 416 240	1.5
2009	8 579 010	–11.4	18 250 067	–14.7
2010	10 133 964	18	22 509 738	23.3%

Source: Bureau of Communications, Shenzhen Municipal Government, 1992–2011

Chapter 4 showed how China's container industry experienced 'take-off' during the 1990s. The growth of throughput both for Yantian port and all ports in Shenzhen reflected that of South China's GDP and trade. After 1992, the Chinese economy enjoyed over 15 years of uninterrupted double digit growth in GDP, fuelled primarily by South China's export-led economy. Over most of that time, YICT was also growing at a double digit annual rate, from 13 000 TEUs to over 10 million. In June 1996, *World Cargo News* commented:

Will increased port development in southern China shift the emphasis away from Hong Kong? It is a question that is often asked, but the answer is clearly in the negative. The fact is, China needs to develop its southern ports to keep up with the region's fast growing economy, according to Hong Kong Port Development Board Secretary, Tony Clark. 'I am confident that over the next decade, we will see the ports in southern China develop simultaneously with Hong Kong to provide the facilities which are necessary to support the fastest growing economy in the world,' he said (*World Cargo News*, June 1996: 29).

China's export-led growth directly contributed to the growth of the container industry and to YICT's development. As part of the country's infrastructural development, YICT's expansion in turn facilitated the growth of the export-led economy in South China.

THE START-UP (1993–97)

Establishing the Viability of the Concept

As the top leader in Shenzhen, Party Secretary Li Hao was a key architect in the establishment of a port at Yantian. He took a personal interest in the port's strategic positioning as well as ensuring funds and personnel for the project. According to Li, the choice of Yantian was based on the following factors:

1. Yantian has excellent natural conditions for port development – deep water, long coastline, no siltation and small tidal differences.
2. Yantian is situated on the edge of South China's manufacturing centre with abundant cargo sources, which were generating most of the throughput going through Hong Kong at that time.
3. Confidence in South China's economic development to generate future demand for port services. Since the 1980s, a lot of manufacturing activities began migrating from Hong Kong to the Mainland and the trend was predicted to continue for the next 20 years.
4. The newly formed special economic zone (SEZ) had already shown good progress and it needed a deep water port as a window to the world. Situated on the Pearl River estuary, the ports in western Shenzhen could not service big ships and were therefore excluded from line haul trade.[4]

Combining the foresight of a political leader with the solid professional analysis of the engineer, Li commissioned feasibility studies by the nation's best academies and ministries. In positioning the project, Li believed that the new port should play in the international league by international rules. By that he meant international standards of port construction as well as of port management for international trade. Since Shenzhen did not have the funds or the technological expertise, Li's idea was to open up to the outside world for help. In those early years, such ideas were very avant-garde and shared only by a few pioneers.

Li initiated discussions with various ministries in the 1980s and secured the formal support of the Minister of Communications and the State Council. As initial support, the Ministry of Communications pledged a nominal sum of RMB 10 million as start-up money for the project. At the same time, the project received support from a Japanese government loan to the Chinese government for developmental purposes. The Japanese lenders did a full-scale feasibility study in 1985 and agreed to a term loan of RMB 100 million for Phase 1. On 14 December 1987 the foundation stone was laid in a ceremony at Yantian, officiated by the Minister of Communications, Qian Yongchang, and attended by over 500 guests. The construction of a 5 berth deep water berth facility (Phase 1) began. The expectations of 500 000 TEU capacity, modest by today's standards, were aggressive targets at that time.[5] Unfortunately, several of the Phase 1 berths were not constructed to international standards and as a result their use has been limited.

Looking for International Partners

Motivated by the need for project funds, and more importantly by the need for international experience, the search for international partners began in earnest when construction started. It came to a conclusion in October 1993 with the high profile signing of the YICT international joint venture in Beijing. Yantian International Container Terminals Limited, a 70/30 equity joint venture was formed with the Hutchison Group-led international consortium holding 70 per cent equity and the Shenzhen Dong Peng Industrial Company, a Shenzhen government subsidiary, holding the other 30 per cent share.[6]

Things always look clearer with hindsight, but when a virgin site went to the world looking for partners, its prospects could not be clearly forecast. This was a time when China's opening up to the world was still being tested. In the container terminal industry, Hong Kong dominated the scene. The small British colony was the world's busiest port handling most of the traffic from China and South East Asia. As Enright et al. (1997: 122) commented:

For much of the last 150 years, Hong Kong and its economy were defined by its seaport. Hong Kong's rise as a trading post, its annexation by Britain, and its emergence as an entrepot were all based on its natural location and geographic advantages. Today, those natural advantages are still present, but in addition the Hong Kong sea cargo industry has built its strength on expertise, investments, growing demand, aggressive corporate strategies, a cluster of supporting industries and services and favourable institutional arrangements. Hong Kong has become the world's busiest container port, with a throughput in 1995 of 12.6 million TEUs (20 foot equivalent units, a measure of containers) compared with 11 million in Singapore.

Given such a strong neighbour and potential competitor, most people were sceptical about the prospects of a new port to be developed right next door. The early developers went on a mission and contacted investors from Hong Kong and Taiwan. After several rounds of promotional efforts, they managed to generate interest from a few Chinese business groups from Taiwan and Hong Kong. The Evergreen Group from Taiwan showed keen interest, but the political climate in the 1980s was premature for cross-strait investment, especially in infrastructure. The Wharf Group and the Hutchison Group came forward among Hong Kong companies. The two business groups alternated at different times in expressing a serious intention to joint venture. They started a multi-party negotiation with the Dong Peng Industrial Company and the Shenzhen government, which lasted over two years. They went through many rounds of negotiation that involved the chief executives of the companies as well as the approving ministers and senior government leaders.

Several proposals for joint venturing were put forward, with the equity issue being the focus of discussion and subject of intense debate. The Hong Kong partners wanted a majority share and management rights, a request that went against the prevalent port development policy of majority control by the Chinese government. Departure from that policy required top government approval, literally by the Premier himself. It required a bold political move for Beijing to agree to a major infrastructure project being majority owned and managed by an international concern. There was simply no precedent for this. The joint venture agreement for Shanghai International Container Terminals in 1992 only conceded a 50/50 equity arrangement, with the Hutchison Group being the 50 per cent investor and manager of the facilities.

In addition, the two Hong Kong business groups found it difficult to join hands in managing with a third party. There was a suggestion of a 30/30/40 share amongst the three partners. Neither the Wharf Group nor the Hutchison Group showed serious interest in that proposal since it would effectively give the Chinese party control of the company with the international players putting in the much needed capital. Then a 'five year fixed-term management board' was suggested as the model for alternating management rights amongst the partners. The negotiating parties again were not willing to agree to this, as it would be impractical to implement such a structure in a young enterprise. Besides the international investors wanting majority control rights, the negotiation was further complicated by their desire to secure the Shenzhen government's commitment to building supporting facilities and initiating relevant reforms. The international groups asked for commitments such as a rail connection and definite plans for road connections and electricity supplies. They further wanted firm guarantees on port reforms, especially the improvement of customs procedures. Some of these, including customs reforms, were beyond the decision-making scope of the Shenzhen government. So any commitments by the Chinese team had to be endorsed by the national government, that is, permission had to be granted in Beijing.

Very soon, the process became a convoluted sequence of proposals and counter proposals, with some active behind-the-scenes political infighting amongst the involved parties. Finally it took the withdrawal of the Wharf Group and an unexpected offer by the Hutchison Group to conclude the deal. The Wharf Group considered it impractical and low value for the Group to be involved in a multi-party management of a port whose future was in question. It therefore withdrew from the competition. On the other hand, against an original asking price from the Chinese party of RMB 1.8 billion for the project, the Hutchison Group, through a surprise offer by its Chairman Li Kashing, agreed to pay a premium RMB 2.5 billion for the two berths already under construction at Yantian and the developmental rights for subsequent phases.[7] As seen by the Chinese party, Wharf withdrew willingly, and Hutchison paid more than what they asked for. From Hutchison's perspective, it agreed to pay a premium for the current assets but more importantly it secured the majority equity share at 70 per cent, the very first of its kind in China, as well as rights to all future developments of the port at Yantian.[8]

This apparently was a win-win affair, as the partners celebrated its conclusions at the signing ceremony on 5 October 1993. President Jiang Zemin received HPH Chairman Li Kashing, and Prime Minister Li Peng attended the signing ceremony in the Great Hall of the People in Beijing.[9] It was a highly publicized event. By then, the port was almost ready for physical operation and service.

The process of acquiring international partners was an exercise in judgement and tact. The Shenzhen government was careful in mediating between two major Hong Kong business groups in securing a developer for the port and it ended up with a keen developer and more funds for its investments. It also obtained commitments to develop the port in the long term with the 'trigger point' mechanism being stipulated in the contracts (i.e. the next phase of the port would be developed when the current facilities became 70 per cent full). For the Hutchison Group, the right to develop Yantian served several purposes. It gave the Group management rights to a new developmental opportunity in Yantian, a port adjacent to Hong Kong, sometimes regarded as an insurance policy to protect the Hong Kong facilities. As later events unfolded, securing the port by Hutchison proved to be a very important step in its overall China port expansion strategy. Nevertheless, as YICT grew in size and importance to become a serious competitor to its Hong Kong sister port, there emerged some dissenting voices within the industry as well as internally within HPH which suggested that Yantian's success in attracting cargo could adversely impact the growth of the Hong Kong port.

Li Kashing's surprise move was viewed by the Chinese side as a far-sighted strategic move and they received it very well. When interviewed later, government leaders and executives from the Chinese party praised his judgement as 'a stroke of genius'.[10] The rights to subsequent port development proved to be very valuable, as was the support that Hutchison had been able to generate through its high profile negotiations and political lobbying. Such favourable reactions from the Chinese leadership at a time when port development in China was untested helped Hutchison secure access to, and special support from, the government bureaucracies on the need to modernize customs procedures and in securing commitment to building ancillary road and rail networks.[11]

The Early Years (1994–97) – Turning a 'Vicious Cycle' into a 'Virtuous Cycle'

YICT was formed in 1993 as a joint venture between the Shenzhen municipal government and the international consortium headed by the Hong Kong based Hutchison Whampoa Group. YICT's charter was to develop and operate the Yantian port to become an international container terminal, catering to the needs of international shipping lines.

Administratively, from the Shenzhen government perspective, port development was the responsibility of a quasi-government business group known as the Dong Peng Industry Company Limited, which later in January 1995 changed its name to the Yantian Port Group [YPG]. Typical of special economic developments of the time, the company was given little money but freedom and policy flexibility to explore non-traditional ways of port development. The Dong Peng Industry Company/Yantian Port Group was Hutchison's direct partner in the YICT joint venture.

The Yantian Port Group was a quasi-government body, combining two organizations in one – 100 per cent owned by Shenzhen government through an investment company, operating as a business organization at times and a government bureaucracy at others. On the one hand it had its commercial responsibilities, profit and loss pressures, and competitive characteristics. On the other hand, it functioned as a government department when it came to meeting the political and social objectives of the government. This peculiar form of enterprise organization was quite common in China. In an SEZ, its dichotomy was more pronounced because, being a partially open economy, the commercial role of the company was highlighted and created pressure to produce tangible results. The former General Manager of YPG remarked:

> On seconding me from the Chinese port group to the joint venture company YICT, the Party Secretary told me that I should take care of several key aspects of the job: ensure that Yantian grows steadily on its own merits and not as an adjunct to the Hong Kong port; that our assets are protected and that we develop some port development talent for Shenzhen.[12]

The joint venture was 70 per cent owned by an international consortium headed by the Hutchison group.[13] Its right to manage provided it with the freedom to run the port from a purely commercial perspective. Other shareholders included the Maersk Line, one of the world's leading shipping companies, interested in gaining a foothold in China. In 1993, Maersk sold its shares in Hong Kong's Modern Terminals, their Hong Kong base port, and bought a 10 per cent stake in YICT. Other small shareholders were COSCO, representing China's shipping interests, as well as Mitsui and Company and China Resources Limited. The international consortium represented a combination of national and business interests from the shipping and port industries.

As mentioned, the joint venture company's equity structure was unique for an infrastructure project in China in allowing the international party to have the controlling interest. The Board of Directors consisted of ten members, three from the Chinese partner and seven from outside partners. Management was nominated by Hutchison which was also responsible for day-to-day support of the business and operations. The General Manager was seconded from Hutchison and he was expected to work closely with the Deputy Executive General Manager seconded from the Chinese partner in taking overall responsibility for management of the company. Together they were to form the core of YICT's management team. Preparations for operating the business began right after the first Board Meeting in November 1993. The Hong Kong team moved into Shenzhen and began recruiting additional manpower.

The following organization charts show the formal relationships of the joint venture's ownership and the management structure of the joint venture company YICT. For easy reference, HPH shall represent the international partner and YPG the Chinese partner.

The Business Concept and its Re-examination 1993–95

After six months of detailed preparations and high profile public relations, the joint venture company, YICT, opened its doors for business in July 1994. A half page feature article in Hong Kong's leading English newspaper, the *South China Morning Post*, carried the headline: 'Maersk leads the way as YICT tries to attract more lines to new port – Yantian all ready for business'.[14] The first vessel from a shareholder shipping line – Maersk – called at the port on 20 July 1994, nine months after signing the joint venture agreement. It was a pilot voyage carrying some 100 boxes for import and export. With all the fanfare of a maiden voyage and the attention of the host government, the first voyage went very smoothly. People expected good things to happen. The *South China Morning Post* concluded the article by quoting from a report by brokerage HG Asia: 'The demand for container handling services was likely to reach full capacity before the end of 1995'. YICT's optimistic Board endorsed a rosy budget for the next few years. They fully expected the project to take off quickly.[15]

In reality, for the first two years such expectations were not met. The support from Maersk, the only customer for the first year and a half, did not find any responsive chords amongst other potential shipping line customers. Many were approached and showed interest. They came for a visit, conducted some studies but hesitated. The strong interest remained, but without any actual commitment. The losses were heavy, and unexpected. Interest on the initial investment alone accounted for some 300 000 Hong Kong dollars [HKD] a day. Total losses ran into hundreds of millions of HKD for the first two years. It was time to re-examine the company's business concept. In their review of YICT in 1995, the management team wrote:

> What have we learnt from the first full year of operations? We missed budget in 1995, by a wide margin, due largely to a misjudgement of two key aspects of the market environment: (1) that HK customers would experience increasing saturation and inconvenience using HK terminals, so much so that it

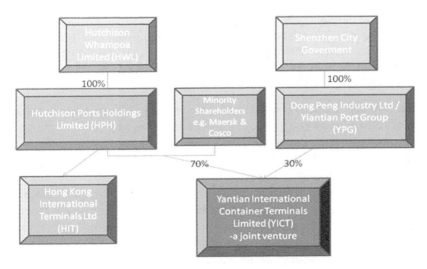

Figure 5.1   Ownership structure of Yantian International Container Terminals Limited

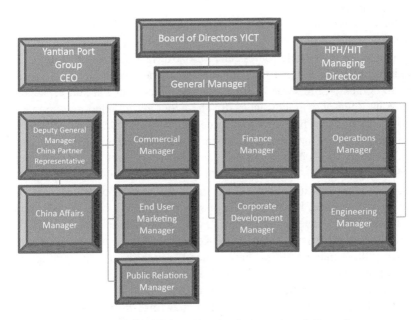

Figure 5.2   Organizational chart Yantian International Container Terminals Limited

would force shipping lines to use other alternatives in South China. (2) that shipping through a Chinese port (i.e. FOB China) would have benefits that outweigh the inconvenience caused by bureaucracy and that the trend would be rapid. We were surprised by the inertia of change as we delved into the complexities of changing from using HK to using Yantian.[16]

The original business concept was a simple one. The Yantian port was very well endowed geographically for becoming an excellent port. It was a natural deep harbour, with a water depth (technically known as draft) of 14 metres alongside the quay deck, which meant that it could berth the world's largest vessels then plying the seas. The port was well equipped with state-of-the-art handling equipment, as well as a computer system and an operating system imported from Hong Kong. Operating management expertise, in the form of over 50 experienced operating staff as well as back-up from Hong Kong, was supplied by Hong Kong International Terminals, the company within the parent group that ran the world's busiest port in Hong Kong. YICT had a good product and all the ingredients for success – physical endowment, equipment and operating expertise – but the market had not responded as planned. For the first two years, the Yantian port was an example of an excellent product waiting for customers.

Business for the new port was expected to come from shipping lines that ran transportation services from port to port around the world. Several of the key trade routes ran from Asia to Europe (the 'Euro-Asia trade') and from Asia to the United States (the 'Pacific trade'). In the Asian context, China was obviously a very important market, especially since its open door policy in 1978. The economy adopted an export-led growth model that had already succeeded in several Asian countries. In the early 1990s, Guangdong province (where the special economic zone of Shenzhen was located) had become one of the most important export processing zones in the world. With a population of 150 million, the province's exports and imports accounted for some 35 per cent of the nation's total trade. It was also the province that attracted a large amount of foreign direct investment, about 50 per cent of China's total. Since the early 1980s, businesses from Hong Kong and Taiwan had been steadily moving their manufacturing bases inland, primarily to Guangdong and Fujian provinces. Often these manufacturing companies had to purchase raw materials from other Asian countries and export the finished products to the United States and Europe. Thus, the fundamental need for good ports in China was self-evident, at least to the planners of the Yantian project.

The economics should also have favoured the new port, at least theoretically. With the manufacturing base being in Guangdong province, route planning to the nearest port should offer an economic advantage. Yantian was located in China itself, close to the manufacturing bases in Shenzhen, Dongguan, Guangzhou and the cities in the Pearl River Delta. Compared to Hong Kong where most of the shipping and port activities took place, Yantian was closer and should be more accessible. The first leg of the journey to the US or Europe for the manufacturers from the Pearl River Delta area cost considerably less for Yantian than Hong Kong. The 31 July 1994 issue of the journal *Cargonews Asia* reported:

> According to a study commissioned by the port operating company, shippers also stand to gain an average of HK$ 2,000 per TEU while moving cargo through Yantian, compared to cross border trucking to Kwai Chung [Hong Kong]. The study is based on sample inland trucking costs between 20 different cargo generating points in south China and Yantian and Kwai Chung. For example, cross border pre-carriage of a forty foot container from Shenzhen to Kwai Chung, a trucking distance of 35 kilometres, costs HK$3,000, while a shipper moving the same box to Yantian will pay only HK$800, a saving of up to HK$2,200. Thus, the overall saving for volume shippers is enormous, the study claims.[17]

Yet the bulk of the cargo continued to cross the border and found its way to Hong Kong, despite these differences in cost.

For a new port to attract business its way, some very significant changes had to take place among the customers. These changes included the economic justification for planning a new itinerary to call at a new port; the availability of cargoes and the ability to access them; the practicality of shipping cargo in and out of a new facility in China; and the confidence that operations would be as smooth and reliable as the arrangements prior to the change. These changes had not yet been made in the perceptions of their decision-makers and advisors.

Inertia had set in. The forces against change were strong. One was the presence of bureaucracy in China, sometimes called the 'China factor', as the management team soon discovered. For ships to come in and out of China, they had to go through a series of formalities in customs and other inspections. Likewise, for cargoes to be exported or imported, the same tiresome procedures applied. These policies and procedures were products of the socialist era, designed years beforehand with the overall perspective of protecting China from foreign exploitation. They were first and foremost control orientated. The execution arm of these policies and procedures consisted of six inspectorates concerned with Customs, Frontier, Quarantine, Commodity, Animal & vegetation, and Commercial matters. Organizationally these units each reported vertically to their respective superiors all the way up to the minister level in the capital. Through the years, these units had developed their own rules and regulations, as well as their own interpretations of them. Together they guarded the entry and exit gates of the country with a barrage of bureaucratic practices. Compounding these was the so-called 'people factor' which referred among other things to corruption and other malpractices. These often led organizations to engage in devious and doubtful deals. At best, they had to engage special personnel to handle the idiosyncratic measures brought about by this system. These were annoying and prohibitive at times, from an ethical perspective. From an economic perspective, they added to the transaction costs of doing business in China.

YICT's General Manager described the phenomenon as the 'vicious cycle of port development in China'.[18] By that he meant that shippers who were part of the decision-making cycle complained about the lack of shipping frequency: for instance, that insufficient services were provided to cater for their shipping needs; while the shipping lines complained about the shippers' preferences for a port not riddled with clearance problems. The new Chinese port had not passed the test of handling the Chinese bureaucracies and therefore had not become the preferred point of departure or entry. Even though a modern port had been constructed in terms of its hardware, the 'software' or operating systems required were not in place. This created a 'vicious cycle', because with very little investment in new facilities during the 1970s and 1980s, the mainland Chinese ports were either not existent or their conditions were dilapidated through lack of use and maintenance. The unattractiveness of the Chinese ports in turn discouraged investment in their modernization.

In addition, there were very efficient alternative facilities in Hong Kong. Hong Kong has since its cession to the United Kingdom in 1842 operated as a free port. Over the years, it had grown to become a major gateway and major entrepôt for China. Its free port status was a very significant advantage for Hong Kong, enabling it to offer a tariff-free flow of cargo in and out.[19] This status enabled Hong Kong to provide a degree of convenience to shippers that could hardly be matched by ports in China's controlled environment.

Hong Kong is located at a strategic point on the trade routes, and is endowed with a natural deep water harbour. Hong Kong thrived and became 'The Pearl of the Orient', a major world-class trading partner. Since the 1970s, Hong Kong had developed a strong light industrial base, fuelling its growth further with domestic imports and exports. The turbulence of the Cultural Revolution added to Hong Kong's prosperity because it was the haven for hot money whenever China or neighbouring countries experienced any political tension. Hong Kong had gained in stature as one of the world's main financial centres, with most global banking institutions represented there. It was therefore able to offer sophisticated services to support trade, such as insurance. Overall, Hong Kong in the early 1990s was Asia's premier transportation centre, and was expected to remain so. One study concluded that Hong Kong would 'unquestionably remain South China's transportation centre, even the most important hub for all of China' (Cheng and Wong, 1997: 170).

It would have appeared reasonable to attribute Yantian's early difficulties to the difference between operating in Hong Kong and the Mainland. A similar development in Hong Kong met with tremendous success in its first year of operations. Terminal Eight run by COSCO-HIT, a joint venture between Hong Kong International Terminals and COSCO, China's national flag carrier, was virtually full in its second year of opening. According to the COSCO-HIT General Manager, 'Hong Kong has an established operation. With COSCO choosing Hong Kong as the transhipment centre in Asia, the port immediately took off with ready cargo diverted from all over China. The free port status also made it easy' (Discussions with COSCO-HIT General Manager, 1999).

This was not the case for the port in Yantian, which was only 30 kilometres away but separated by the Hong Kong-China border. Indeed, for its first 18 months of operations, the only support the company managed to obtain was from Maersk. Other shipping lines hesitated. They liked to continue using existing routes via Hong Kong, even though this might be costing them more. To the shipping industry, the appearance of Yantian as a port vying for attention did not come at the right time. In 1993 and 1994, the carriers were themselves busy regrouping into different consortia. Existing alliances amongst shipping lines were breaking up and new ones were being formed. To put in at an additional port would have simply added a complication. Even though cost savings were hoped for, the alliance members deferred changing their shipping itineraries in favour of more pressing concerns. There was also little pressure to change. Cargo owners preferred the status quo. They wanted certainty in their schedules and would not want to risk dealing with Mainland bureaucratic practices that could create uncertainty. Customs and other inspection practices stood in the way of a Chinese port seeking to attract business. In the monthly management reports to YICT's board of directors for the years 1994–1996, there were repeated mentions of these regulatory problems. For example, the July 1994 report stated:

We ran into serious problems with regard to Frontier Inspections. On one occasion, we were informed by the Frontier Inspection Unit that they would not handle ships berthed at the container berths. Their jurisdiction, they told us, is confined to the 10 000 ton berth only. If that is true, that would mean that we could not operate the terminal at all.

The August 1994 report commented:

As expected, there were some teething problems: (1) Customs inspections – a higher than normal percentage of inspections in some ships (7 out of 26 boxes in Luna Maersk). (2) Unclear procedures – regarding customs clearance and joint inspections. There was more than one unit in customs responsible for control and verifications, as well as different units for joint inspections. There were differences between the shipping line and joint inspection units regarding procedures, and between YICT customs regarding how to accept uncleared export cargo. (3) Insufficient experience in documentation – some delays and box cut-offs because of incomplete documentation on the part of the shippers. (4) Insufficient manning in Customs for 24 hour operations – necessitating overtime requirements, and subsequent issues relating to overtime pay, travelling and schedules.

Again, the November 1994 report noted that:

Whilst there has been a slight improvement in clearance of containers, we are not yet enjoying a situation where all cargo is released before vessel arrival. All vessels are delayed due to this problem and a renewed effort is being placed in tracking down the exact causes of the clearance difficulties.

As a result, the first two years of operations met with unexpected failures. It seemed that the architects of YICT had underestimated the challenges. The company was losing hundreds of millions of HK$. Capital costs were huge, so amortization expenses were over 80 per cent of total outgoings. Cutting operating costs could help only in small ways. There was little management could do to stop the haemorrhage except to go all out for business promotion. A detailed analytical study was conducted within the company concluding that YICT needed a higher volume to breakeven (400 000 TEUs for Phase 1) and the present value of higher revenue generated by lower prices would be higher than a delayed stream of revenue later.[20] Senior management at YICT had always known that the terminal business depended on revenue management and economies of scale. But a cold analysis made it clear that they had more to learn.

Gradually, YICT managers realized that they had to re-examine the business concept. This they did. A period of soul searching ensued, resulting in some critical analysis and development of several strategic initiatives that were to make a significant impact on future developments. 'What were the reasons for the inertia? How had we misunderstood the situation? What could be done to remedy it?' These were the key questions asked in virtually all management meetings within YICT in these early years. There were study team sessions; consultants were employed to research specific areas; sometimes tempers were lost as arguments got heated – it was time to examine fundamental beliefs and assumptions. A process commenced in which YICT's managers had to undertake a fresh interpretation of their company's situation and re-enact it into a new coherent entity that could provide a better guide for action (McKinley, 2011).

Re-examination of the Business Concept and New Initiatives 1995–97

An analysis of reasons for the shippers' lack of support revealed several important factors: timing; lack of incentive to move; government bureaucracy as a constraint; time required to try to prove the viability of the concept; and doubts about the port's ability to manage the 'China risk' factor versus the perceived economic gain from switching from a Hong Kong port call to a China port call.[21] The management team studied these in earnest and undertook a range of initiatives. Among these were launching a shuttle service to supplement the main line haul vessels, marketing directly to cargo owners (the 'end users'), thus bypassing the shipping lines, providing special assistance to users in clearing customs and dealing with other procedures at Yantian port, and lobbying government for support to introduce customs reforms. These initiatives proved later to be important towards both evolving the port and, in some instances, developing norms in the Chinese port industry as a whole. As the General Manager put it a few years later, they released YICT from its initial 'vicious cycle'.[22]

The first of these initiatives – the introduction of a shuttle service – started as an experiment. Having concluded that the new port was competing for business with land transportation to and from the manufacturing bases and the originating port, YICT introduced a shuttle service – a barge connection carrying just 50 to 100 boxes at a time, between Yantian and Hong Kong. The initial idea was to attract some cargo to use the port on a trial basis to prove its service level. While starting a regular service might be a high risk option for shipping lines, the shuttle required little commitment of resources. Shipping lines could deliver the boxes to YICT to be shipped to Hong Kong via small barges on a daily basis and at a cost comparable to trucking the boxes to Hong

Kong. That way, shipping lines could advertise that they were providing a new, albeit indirect service from a South China port at little additional cost to 'end users' – the users of the shipping services. From YICT's standpoint, the shuttle service fulfilled two main purposes: first, to help potential customers prepare for the switch (from using Hong Kong only to using multiple ports in South China) at very low cost; and second, to provide trial operations for potential users to use the new facilities and test out customs procedures. The shuttle service was run on a cost recovery basis, with full support from YICT's Hong Kong parent and partner. Its main purpose was to generate throughput and volume and to help the new port run in.

How did the YICT management come to agree on this idea? The Deputy General Manager explained:

> First of all, we debated hard and long about who our immediate competitors are. In South China, crossing the China/Hong Kong border by land had developed ahead of the emergence of ports, so historically people have got used to land transportation. Changing habits are always difficult. You see, a trucker operating on his own enjoys tremendous flexibility: he can help carry stuff across borders and he can be price sensitive and change immediately. We as terminal operators must find a way to make it easy for people to try the new port at low risk. The shuttle service competes with land transportation efficiently. Of course in pricing we have a constraint: it cannot be more expensive than the trucking cost. The fact that HIT in the last two years had some spare capacity helped. Without HIT offering a low cost, the shuttle service that involves two terminals could be priced out of the question.[23]

Almost unexpectedly, however, exporting through this shuttle service grew fast as more and more shipping lines and end users found this low cost experiment beneficial. Started in 1995, the service quadrupled in size and in frequency within a couple of years. Fairly soon, it became a thrice daily service and became a precursor of the preparation by shipping lines to use the new port. The shipping lines used this as an interim measure to gather the critical mass to justify using Yantian. According to shipping line executives, a new port required 500 boxes per trip load to achieve the right economics. To explore the Chinese market, shipping lines wanted to offer FOB China terms on top of existing FOB Hong Kong terms, and they wanted to do so at low cost before a regular line haul service call at Yantian became economically viable. Shipping lines like COSCO, Hanjin, Yang Ming and Evergreen all followed a similar pattern, using the shuttle service to gather sufficient critical mass before starting a line haul regular call at YICT. How did this experiment turn out to be a strategic move? According to the End User Marketing Manager:

We started this service as an experiment to attract traffic to Yantian, and as our response to realizing that we must compete with land transportation. Little did we know that it would turn out to be a strategic move of some importance. You know when the idea was first raised, I objected to it, but it turned out to be a good idea. Most shipping lines started using the service to test out the system and to gather momentum. For them, it is a cheap way to explore a new market and develop a new service.[24]

The second initiative was to market to the end users of the terminal. The details are described in the following chapter. When launched as a strategic initiative, it was very controversial. Traditional port marketing had always been targeted at direct customers, namely the shipping lines. The logic was simple: they pay your bills and they control the ships and the service itinerary. The shipping line planners and business executives would decide on the ports to call at or skip, based on their understanding of the trade and where cargo is concentrated, balancing the demands with the need for economy and efficiency in route planning. So selling directly to them was more useful and economical. However, an analysis of the value chain revealed that these decisions by shipping lines were heavily influenced by their upstream customers – the port's end users. Conceptually, therefore, YICT Management was confident that the end users held the key to prosperity and to securing a rapid migration of users for the port. But very little was known about how to market to this diverse group.

The third initiative started out as a 'need to do' in overcoming a marketing obstacle. Despite the more favourable economics, shipping lines as well as end users were reluctant to use the new facilities. They complained about a lack of efficiency and reliability in the local customs and bureaucratic procedures. In addition underlying that rationale was the unwillingness of existing operating personnel to change and disrupt the web of long established relationships between shipping executives, customs brokers, truckers and related personnel. However, the marketing team soon discovered that providing help in customs formalities for end users was the key to helping people make the change.

To this end, the YICT management team deployed significant resources. A new department was formed, called the China Affairs Department, and its main function was to provide help for users to clear the customs and related procedures in Yantian. It worked on improving the customs procedures and providing a lot of supportive services to users. With one major toys manufacturer, Mattel, the End User Marketing Department and the China Affairs Department joined hands in providing a customs-related service. Managers and staff from YICT visited over 20 factories in the Pearl River Delta area and explained to the shipping managers concerned firstly the economic benefits and secondly how to handle customs clearance issues. The China Affairs Manager commented:

> We first of all explain the procedures and make sure that people who have to clear customs feel comfortable with contacting Da Peng Customs (The customs office in Yantian). Often, we make introductions and make friends with them. Some people don't want to change: they don't want to upset existing relationships. So a strong commitment from senior management will be necessary to 'force' the change. If the MD is determined to reap the economic benefits and supervise the change with a strong order, our job is to ensure smooth implementation.[25]

During those start-up years, it was common that when a customer agreed to try Yantian, he did so with small numbers of trial shipments. These trial shipments, however small, received a large amount of attention from YICT's senior management who made sure that sufficient handholding efforts ensured smooth implementation. Soon, such efforts found a very warm reception and became hugely rewarding in terms of results, despite the cost of having designated personnel serve customers and work on customs procedures round the clock.

The fourth major initiative was aimed at reforming the government on-site procedures and regulations that created anxieties among customers and threatened the efficient working of the new port. Working with customs procedures on a piecemeal, local procedural level could be tiresome. YICT management was therefore highly motivated to achieve some breakthroughs at the policy and at a relatively senior level. For this, they had to plan and implement a series of strategic moves to create and work through government relationships. Chapter 7 describes these initiatives in detail. They led to an important development in November 1995 when a Memorandum of Understanding (MOU) was signed by the Customs Administration and YICT to streamline transit and clearance procedures at Yantian port.

The MOU was an instrument to document an understanding that YICT had reached with the customs authorities in terms of their mutual obligations in handling special clearance procedures. This was a special device that the customs office in China adopted to allow for flexibility in its policies. In this particular case, the MOU allowed YICT to guarantee import and export cargoes that travelled 'under bond' from the point of cargo origin to Yantian port without the need for repeated inspections. For this privilege, YICT pledged a bond of 6 million HKD to guarantee that goods travelling under bond did reach final destinations without being tampered with. In effect, the MOU and the bond system allowed

Yantian port users the flexibility to import and export more easily than other ports in the region, namely its competitors in west Shenzhen. Instead of requiring an 'Import Connection Letter' and the complicated procedures associated with clearance at the final destination, cargo travelling under bond would henceforth be cleared immediately at Da Peng Customs for transit to inland destinations. This greatly facilitated imports into China. In the other direction, the MOU also specified 'simplified export clearance' procedures at related customs offices all over Guangdong province, facilitating export moves out of Yantian.

The signing of the MOU was a breakthrough not only for the specific aim of facilitating traffic through the port, but also for the landmark event of designating Yantian as the official pilot site for customs reform initiatives in the future. As a sign of its significance, China's Commissioner of Customs Administration attended the signing ceremony in Shenzhen in November 1995. He brought with him all the key Customs Administration personnel in Beijing, including the national Director-General of Customs Clearance, together with his counterparts in Guangdong and nearby regions. At the local government level, the occasion was attended by the Party Secretary of Shenzhen and the Mayor with all their main departmental heads. All eyes were on Yantian and the government, both at national and local levels, who were now publicly committed to ensuring the success of the experiment and therefore the port.

The public relations effect of signing the MOU sent strong signals to the shipping community that things were beginning to change. People who were experienced with China understood that business there depended on government support to prosper. In Yantian, such support had now become very visible.

Another significant move by YICT's management that proved to be useful in breaking the 'vicious cycle' had to do with the pricing of terminal services. In the initial price negotiations with shipping lines, Yantian set a price at a 25 per cent discount to the Hong Kong tariff. This price level was decided in the expectation that the new terminal would be able to provide similar operational service levels, and the discount was offered to attract shippers to make the change. Another premise was that the Hong Kong port was becoming increasingly congested. However, in view of the 'China factor' and the inertia of change, this discount turned out to be insufficient to attract customers to Yantian.

In his report to the Board at the end of 1995, the General Manager commented:

> We were surprised by the inertia of change as we delved into the complexities of changing from using Hong Kong to using Yantian. We discovered that even

though our active marketing efforts successfully created a positive image, proactive switching by shipping lines did not take place as expected ... most shipping lines did not see an immediate incentive to switch' (General Manager's report to the YICT Board, 'Review of 1995 – what have we learnt from the first full year of operations?: 2).

To provide a greater incentive therefore, YICT management decided to drop the YICT tariff by around 20 per cent across the board. They started with the Maersk line which enjoyed the 'most favoured nation' clause, namely that as a shareholder it would always enjoy the lowest rates at YICT. Then a host of other shipping lines were offered similar rates at a 35–40 per cent discount to Hong Kong rates. Offered at the right time, this created an additional incentive for them to move.

These multiple initiatives were launched between 1995 and 1997, and they brought very significant results to the port. From 1995 to 1998, the number of services at the port increased by eight to ten every year and by 1998 the port achieved a throughput of over 1 million TEUs, a landmark that brought it into the world's big league. It had begun to move into a 'virtuous cycle'.

The rapid growth in Yantian after 1995 was instrumental in stimulating similar growth in other Shenzhen ports. Together, the Shenzhen ports gained national recognition, climbing from the eighth position in China in 1996 to second in China by 1997 after Shanghai. This growth also brought Shenzhen ports to fourth position in the world, after Singapore, Hong Kong and Shanghai. The Shenzhen ports have retained these rankings ever since.

From a shipping operator's perspective, the throughput growth was the result of the changes made by a few major shipping consortia. It reflected their initiative to capture the opportunities in South China. Long held captive by the Hong Kong port's high tariff rates, carriers had been looking for alternatives to handling their increasing volumes coming out from their customers' demands for sourcing activities in South China. Therefore, once the pioneers like Maersk proved the viability of these alternatives, others followed. Indeed later adopters were concerned that they would suffer a cost disadvantage if they delayed the move too late. In 1996, the New World Alliance, recently reorganized to consist of American President Lines, Overseas Orient Container Lines, Hyundai, and Mitsui lines, extended their shipping services to Yantian. Later in the same year, the Grand Alliance, consisting of five major shipping companies (P&O/Nedloyd, NYK, Hapag Lloyd, MISC and OOCL) also dipped their toes into the water and started a Pacific service at Yantian. In 1997, they doubled their activity and services and others followed. The

Asian giant Evergreen and the Korean Hanjin both followed suit. In 1999, the port counted 18 of the world's top shipping lines as its clients. By 2005, all major shipping lines, including the world's top 20, had become YICT clients.

YICT made its first operating profit in 1997. Since then it almost doubled that profit every three years. Reaching a cumulative net profit in 1999 (for instance, having repaid for its previous operating losses), the company reached a respectable 10 per cent return in its sixth year of operations. For an infrastructure project of this size, this was considered exceptional.

The turnaround in the Yantian port's business in 1995 and 1996 appeared dramatic at the time to those closely concerned. With hindsight, it could be concluded that the port was riding on the growth of Sino-US and Sino-European trade. Nonetheless, without the reforms agreed in 1995 and various management initiatives undertaken, it would undoubtedly have taken appreciably longer to open the door to this success.

HANDLING THE CHALLENGES OF GROWTH (1997–2002)

Achieving Economy of Scale – Building Phase 2 Facilities in Time

Preparation to build the next phase began even while the port was struggling for survival. Executives at the HPH and at YICT well understood the need to plan for the future and to build for economy of scale. It was part and parcel of the initial contract that as soon as throughput of the existing terminal reached 70 per cent of its design capacity the investors would be obliged to initiate the next phase of development. This was the 'trigger point' mechanism. The international party wished to have this provision to ensure economic prudence in the port's development, while the Chinese party wanted it to ensure that the Hong Kong consortium would not hold back on any appropriate development for Yantian port in favour of protecting the Hong Kong port's interest.

In fact, the Hong Kong investors always envisaged a steady expansion of the port. Shortly after YICT's formation, its General Manager formulated the company's Mission as: 'To become the China's first world-class port: world-class in terms of economic contributions, service and people development' (YICT Strategic Plan, 1995). That this aspiration required continuing investment was made clear in YICT's Corporate Plan:

To become world-class, the port needed the basic facilities to handle the growing traffic. We also needed deeper berths and larger cranes for the bigger ships ... More than 5000 TEU ships are coming into service. They cost more to operate. They also demand ports with deeper water. Driven by competition to offer faster transit times and the need to call at fewer ports, shipping lines will find Yantian preferable to all other Shenzhen ports (YICT Strategic Plan, 1996–2000: 6).

So there was little disagreement as to the need to expand; the difficult call lay in its timing. In this aspect, HPH's leadership was instrumental. As the major shareholder, it was responsible for reading the trend and determining when the next phase of expansion should start. Other minority shareholders of course needed to be convinced with a business case. However, Hutchison had a good track record of balancing economic prudence and strategic foresight in its business decisions. Its decision to go ahead with Phase 2 of the port was made ahead of the agreed schedule, which pleasantly surprised the Chinese partners and the Shenzhen government.

In December 1995, the decision was taken to invest HK$4.7 billion to construct a 3 berth 56 hectare terminal, known as Phase 2 of Yantian. This was at a time when signs of recovery had only just begun to show themselves, and long before the trend of steady growth had become evident. In 1995 full year throughput was only just over 100 000 TEUs, 20 per cent of design capacity and 10 per cent of actual capacity. The new investment was a large one for the time and it was almost double that of Phase 1. Phase 2 had a design capacity of 1.5 million TEUs and a draft of 15.5 metres to cater for larger vessels. It was to be built to international construction standards, which raised the costs of investment considerably. Construction of Phase 2 began in December 1996 and took three years. When it was completed in May 2000, it added substantial handling capacity (2 million TEUs) to the port, making it a significant facility for the region.

As things turned out, the expansion was well timed, as the newly developed facilities were quickly utilized by the growing number of customers and port users who found Yantian a viable alternative to the Hong Kong terminals. Annual compound throughput growth averaged 46 per cent in the five-year period between 1997 and 2002, and this created a huge rise in demand for good container terminal facilities. The port's expansion never seemed to catch up with demand.

Commenting in 2004 on the strategic moves made by YICT in its early years, the Deputy General Manager, who was seconded from the Chinese partner, said:

We have had 10 years of success behind us, but it was not apparent in the beginning. I was doubtful whether the "World Class Dream" could be realized. I think there were several success factors, and one of them was the strategic foresight and decisiveness of the leaders. When the "foreign management" first arrived, they changed existing things around and long before there were full justifications, they purchased three additional quay cranes (the terminal had only three cranes then) and doubled the operating capacity. In deciding on Phase 2, they took the same bold moves – before the demand was evident, they decided to launch Phase 2, a HK$4.7 billion dollar initiative. I doubt if the Chinese party acting in isolation would ever make those decisions. My conclusion is: left alone, the Chinese party might still be able to make YICT work, but the speed of development would have been much slower (Comments by the Deputy General Manager, YICT Management Seminar, 26–27 November 2004).

As the port expanded to handle more volume, its growing scale of operations brought savings in operating and overall costs. Operating cost per box handled was kept reasonably low as overhead costs were spread over a larger volume. The management grew in numbers, but they were conscious of the need to control overhead expenses in case of a rainy day. YICT's Strategy Plans from 1999 to 2005, and management's Monthly Reports to the Board of Directors, contain numerous sections on how cost control and the economy of scale were resulting in lower overall operating cost year by year.

Managing Internal Relationships to Achieve Efficiency

To cope with growth, the company had to manage its internal resources and relationships to achieve efficiency and effectiveness. Operating in a developing country with little experience in container port development and operations, the company aimed high from the start. In 1995, the General Manager began promulgating the concept of providing 'world-class' services at Yantian. Throughout the years, the company kept experimenting with marketing processes, service improvement programmes and people management and development initiatives. For these developments, the company borrowed heavily from experience of its parent – Hong Kong International Terminals [HIT] – as well as leading companies in other industries. HIT has been operating in one of the world's leading ports for over 25 years as well as being part of the global HPH group. Over these years, HIT had built sophisticated processes and computer systems in running efficient terminals. Leapfrogging on HIT's experience, YICT was able to cut short its learning curve and its operating efficiency improved quickly and significantly to a level comparable to most international ports.

During the years of growth, the YICT organization grew rapidly. As was seen from Table 5.2, its workforce grew at 25–30 per cent annually for quite a few years, and inducting them into the organization and getting them trained up was a major challenge. In this regard, YICT directed considerable effort towards people development, first as a business need and second because it was the company's vision to become world-class in people development. It introduced a series of technical training as well as people development programmes designed to produce manpower of a quality and quantity that matched the growth needs. Those investments over the years helped the company develop a positive culture of staff growth and learning, as well as assisting it to become customer oriented.[26]

As the terminal kept growing at a 46 per cent annual compound rate, new challenges emerged after 2001. Its capacity growth fell behind that of demand for services. An unexpected surge in demand in 2002 took the company by surprise. As the General Manager commented:

> Right after 9/11, I went around to my customers asking them to predict the growth trend for the coming year. They were so pessimistic and would only talk about a flat rate. I was considered crazy to predict a 15 per cent growth. However, in 2002, the throughput went up from 2.7m TEUs to 4.2m TEUs, a 52 per cent growth in a single year. And we had major problems. The port was congested (General Manager's Presentation to the YICT Board of Directors, 2004).

The YICT management had no choice but to mobilize all the necessary resources to expand the facilities, increase manpower and raise productivity. Coping with growth became the only focus in the years between 2001 and 2003. The executive committee met twice monthly and the most important agenda item was 'How are we coping? How are we implementing the various plans aimed at alleviating congestion and raising productivity?' In an interview with the Operations Manager, he was very conscious of the need to design and manage a different mode of organization as the company grew in size, particularly as the external environment was requiring a different style of management. He commented:

> As the terminal becomes bigger, organization for production has of necessity become more complex. Instead of giving strict orders to the troops, we have to build an organization that is capable of handling the size and complexity that is demanded by the business. We have to delegate to the lower level of management a lot more. We have to do a lot more training to standardize procedures and to increase efficiency.[27]

A large number of conventional and some unconventional measures were taken. Among these were an accelerated building programme for Phase 3 (a 4 berth 90 hectare facility), productivity campaigns using the Six Sigma programme, new incentive schemes for the labour force, continuous technical and management training, special task forces to handle the external environment including traffic in the vicinity of the port, employing special police to manage the traffic flow, special coordination with the Hong Kong sister port to manage the windows for berthing, special working arrangements with customs on cargo clearance, and introduction of the next generation computer system – nGen – which was capable of handling the increasing volume.[28]

All in all, those were extremely busy times, and the high energy focus of the management team produced excellent results. In 2003, with only 5 berths in Phases 1 and 2, the terminal handled 5.25 million TEUs. That created an industry record of handling over 1 million TEU throughput per berth. This was aided by a jump in productivity. Measured in terms of number of boxes handled per crane per hour of operations, YICT reached the high number of 35 moves per hour in 2004 and achieved a consistent average rate above 35 moves per crane hour in the following year. That effectively made the terminal one of the most productive in the world.

Managing External Relationships to Achieve Competitive Advantage

Because of the infrastructural nature of the business, YICT faced a range of regulators who were actually heavily involved in day-to-day operations of the enterprise. One of these regulators was the Customs office which controlled the declaration and clearance of cargo in and out of the port. The Frontier Inspection unit was responsible for controlling the port as a border of the sovereign state against unauthorized personnel leaving or coming into the territory. The Quarantine unit's mission was to protect the country from undesirable communicable diseases carried by cargoes coming into the port, and passing through it.[29]

These regulators were physically stationed on the port premises and they formed an overlay on all of the terminal's operating processes. As the port was a customs controlled area, the place was under strict surveillance for smuggling and tax evasion. Frontier Inspectors were on the lookout for illegal migrants trying to get out of the country, and they mounted 24 hour patrols. The Quarantine specialists were always present to examine suspicious cargoes in case these brought undesirable materials into the country. Indeed, such regulatory forces formed part of the service package of the terminal, whether desired by management or otherwise. They posed significant external constraints to be reckoned with.

To handle this particular situation, the company set up a special China Affairs Department, with the specific objective of facilitating the smooth flow of cargo and its clearance. At its peak, the department employed over 30 people and operated around the clock to enhance the port's services to its customers.

As will be detailed in Chapter 7, the company expended significant time and resources on managing relationships with both local and central levels of the Chinese government. Of necessity, the chief executive spearheaded these efforts supported by the HPH Chairman, Li Kashing. He organized an Advisory Group attached to the General Manager's office. This think tank of retired government advisors and former bureaucrats discussed tactics with him on how best to manage current challenges in government relationships as well as planning future developments. When it came to lobbying for support and applying for approvals in new expansion projects, this group took on the task of obtaining relevant information and securing the correct approvals in a timely fashion.

The Deputy General Manager, who represented the Chinese partner, summed up the contribution that its active approach towards its institutional environment made to the company's evolution:

> In a developing country like China, understanding the complexities of working within the Chinese bureaucracy helped us shorten the approval cycle and helped us execute the strategies with finesse.[30]

PHASE 3 AND ITS NEGOTIATION (1999–2002)

Against a background of strong economic growth in the South China region, expansion was a natural strategic objective for the company. Although careful study was given to the details of further investment and its timing, management was not always able to match its investment to demand. Sometimes, the company had to play catch-up, as in 2002–03. The need for the company to play catch-up in 2002–03 arose in part from HPH's reaction to YICT's rapid growth following its success in attracting business through the marketing initiatives it had undertaken in the mid-1990s. This success created some short-term tension in its relations with HPH. When the migration of cargo from Hong Kong to South China became more pronounced between 1996 and 2000, some within HPH saw this as a 'cannibalization effect' between YICT and HIT. There were also fears within HPH at the time that the rapid expansion of Yantian port at the expense of Hong Kong would dilute the group's earnings as a whole because YICT was only partially owned by HPH. These concerns led to a temporary slowing down of investment in Yantian's physical expansion.

At the same time, it was not easy to match supply and demand in planning the development of its terminal facilities. In a rapidly growing economy, previous experience only helped to a limited extent. Since achieving the breakthrough in 1997–98, Yantian's growth trajectory was steep, sometimes with unpredictable gradients. The most notable example was the surprise 52 per cent growth of throughput in 2002. Having enjoyed a steady increase of throughput at roughly half a million TEUs every year for four years between 1998 and 2001, the sudden surge of 1.5 million TEUs in one year came as a surprise. The market moved in an unpredictable manner following the 9/11 incident in the US. The management responded in various ways to the upsurge and one of the key tasks was to expand capacity as quickly as possible. Mostly, plans were made ahead of demand, trying to build in a contingency for delays in obtaining approval and other obstacles to implementation. As the General Manager stated in 2004: 'Timing for growth has never been an easy business, and we have not been able to get it right most of the time. For the last 10 years, our forecasts have always been off by a margin, sometimes in a significant way' (Presentation of the General Manager to the Management Team at the 10th Anniversary Celebration, November 2004).

Accordingly, through the YICT management team, the HPH submitted a proposal to the Shenzhen municipal government to develop the next phase of development in March 1999.[31] According to the proposal, Phase 3 was to be built as a 10-berth facility covering some 240 hectares of land to be reclaimed in an area adjacent to the existing terminal. The new terminal, enjoying the same natural deep harbour conditions as the current berths, was to be designed to handle 'mega vessels' of over 10 000 TEUs capacity. When fully developed, it could increase the handling capacity of YICT's facilities by another 8 million TEUs, doubling its existing capacity. The project, also encompassing the development of adjacent infrastructure like interchanges and road and rail networks, would cost over HK$20 billion. It was an ambitious project that when completed would create at Yantian a 'mega port' equivalent to the largest in the world, at par or even exceeding the scale of the European Combined Terminals in Rotterdam, or the Long Beach and Los

Angeles ports in the USA. HPH proposed to be the owner as well as developer and operator of the new facility.[32]

The Chinese partner had its own dreams and aspirations. Within YPG, the faction opposed to the majority foreign ownership of the joint venture never ceased to air its dissenting voice.[33] The people taking this view accepted that an international joint venture was useful in getting the port started on its journey of internationalization, and that the international partner had contributed to bringing in carriers and customers, as well as establishing international level operations. However, they argued that in the later stages of development it would be appropriate for local management to 'regain' control and be in charge of construction and operations. They advocated that local management had the skills and willpower to succeed in managing a world-class port. They organized study delegations to the Dalian, Qingdao and Shanghai ports who upon their return expressed renewed confidence that Chinese management was performing well in developing these projects. This was more than an economic argument. It had strong political overtones. In a socialist country that had undertaken reform and opening for less than 20 years, the nation-building argument had strong appeal.

The proposed project became the subject of a turbulent negotiation. One of the major challenges of securing the rights to Phase 3 lay in a conflict with the Chinese partner for majority equity control. Now that the port was becoming successful, some strong dissenting voices in the Chinese party emerged. They asked: 'Why can't we develop the port ourselves? Why can't we take the majority share?' Since the very beginning, these voices had been present among those opposed to the joint venture, some even among the managers of the Chinese partner organization. The Special Advisor to the General Manager explained:

> There are always different schools of thought in working with "foreigners" in an international joint venture. Some reform oriented bureaucrats see working with the international partner a way to leapfrog developments, a way to get into the commercial relationships with customers really quickly, a way to learn how to make the operations efficient and effective. These people agree that to develop fast, they must let go of control. However, the other side – the more conservative faction – always believes that it is a matter of national pride to be in control of strategic facilities like ports. They believe that the Chinese managers are every bit as good as the foreigners or the Hong Kong employees who picked up management skills from the West.[34]

These nationalistic sentiments reflected certain contradictions that people faced during China's period of transition. On the one hand, it was the official policy of the country to be open to the outside world and to learn from this opening. On the other hand, old ways of thinking die hard. Letting go of control of a company in exchange for development had its price, often a personal one of finding oneself in less important positions. Being in control, of course, meant also economic benefits. When a person headed up a major construction project, he or she commanded large resources and budgets that could easily be turned into substantial personal benefits. In economic and social terms, this was a very significant motivator to be in charge of resources. On paper, the Chinese government paid their management poorly, when compared to the joint venture's foreign counterparts. However, when in a senior managerial position, incumbents could spend considerable sums on living, education and travel benefits that they could make available to a wider circle beyond themselves and their families. At the very least in terms of 'face', one gained more respect from the community and the family.[35]

Therefore, for a variety of reasons, economic and otherwise, in the initial stages of negotiations, the Chinese party started by demanding a majority ownership (60 per cent) of Phase 3. They also argued for management control. Their position signified a will to take on the management challenge by the Chinese partners themselves and indicated an assertion of the intention to regain control. While it was politically the right thing to do, it had economic implications. To the international partner in the joint venture, these posed a major threat. The founding phases of the port had required the international partner to expend huge energy and resources to achieve success. Now that Phases 1 and 2 were proving to be financially successful, it was natural that they wanted to continue along the same path, which, as they saw it, meant maintaining a majority equity share and, more importantly, maintaining management control over the further development of the port.

The ensuing negotiations were far from straightforward. When the YICT General Manager representing the international investors met with the YPG Chairman for a discussion of the Phase 3 development, the relationship was professional and cordial, but also distant. Both parties accepted the need for Phase 3 and agreed that initial works should start as soon as practicable. On the technical aspects, the two teams also agreed on the rough layout and preliminary design of the terminal. That was where agreement ended. The equity issue was a central difficulty, with political undertones present during all discussions and negotiations. There were also the connected side issues of the land price, and prices for support infrastructure like the adjacent roads and the connecting railway, subsequent development rights, project control responsibilities, and a long list of other concerns. From start to finish, the negotiations took three years to complete. To understand the process better we need to trace some of the organizational and political background of the Chinese partner.

Concurrent with the growth and development of the port there were some significant changes in the Chinese partner. Having worked hard at building the initial phase of the port and having successfully brought in an international partner and investor, the Yantian Port Group had not forgotten their original mission of building a 'Large International Transhipment Hub'.[36] With cash coming in as a result of Yantian's commercial success, YPG sat on some significant resources. They invested in many areas like warehouses and trucking and even overseas in unrelated projects like a forest development in South East Asia. In 1997, they successfully floated part of their shares in the Shenzhen stock market and formed the Yantian Port Holdings Company Limited [YPH] to take charge of port related businesses like trucking, the Wutongshan tunnel, and warehousing in the Yantian free trade zone. The floatation was handled successfully, largely on the back of the successful port operation and the Hutchison affiliation.

Internally, with the secondment of its previous General Manager to become the Deputy General Manager of the joint venture company in 1994, the Chinese partner was headed by a party official who espoused more of a bureaucratic and political rather than professional attitude towards managing the company. He directed the company in a very autocratic manner. As with many other state-owned enterprises, the Yantian Port Group lacked checks and balances on its power. Corruption set in, and by 2000 the CEO and his financial deputy were arrested for 'misappropriation' of funds. Funds amounting to $200 million were not properly accounted for. He was later sentenced to five years' imprisonment.

Within the Yantian Port Group, a major management reshuffle took place in 1998 due to the corruption case. A new chief from Beijing came on board in 1998 and he recruited his new team of executives through a public examination and secondment process from other state-owned enterprises. In 1999, YPG's management team was young and energetic, ready to make a difference to the Group and to the territory. The atmosphere became tense. Driven by the need to be politically correct, the incoming CEO was not as free as his predecessors to make the concessions necessary to work with the international party. Furthermore, it was still national policy for all ports to be managed and majority owned by Chinese enterprises. That understandably became his starting position in the negotiations.

The Chinese partner also explored other ways in which it might regain control. For example, it examined the possibility of having the port authority develop the infrastructure and arrange a leasing arrangement for the operating companies. There were also suggestions that other interested parties could invest in Phase 3 and beyond, either in parallel or in competition with Hutchison. It is true that the initial joint venture contract provided Hutchison with the 'first right of refusal' in subsequent development of the port, but this right could only be activated when the Chinese party went out to seek partners for such further development. The terms of the contract were not clear concerning the possibility that the Chinese party were to develop the port as a sole proprietor.

Opinion within the Chinese party was divided. The supporters of the joint venture idea advocated a continuation of the current set up mainly for economic and developmental reasons. They saw concrete developments since the joint venture was formed and were satisfied that the IJV was delivering on both economic and social fronts. On the other hand, people holding the opposite view attacked supporters of the joint venture as 'betraying' fundamental national interests in allowing the international consortium to dominate the port's development and management, accusing YICT of causing a 'dilution of national assets'. In a letter to a senior government minister on 14 September 1999, six past YPG employees argued against further development of the port by international investors, claiming strong dissatisfaction amongst the port group staff over the proposed arrangements.[37] They appealed to the minister to rule against international control of 'strategic assets' like ports and railways. The apparent purpose of the letter was to express concern among a small number of disillusioned employees who saw their economic interests hampered, and future careers threatened, because of the situation at YICT. These forces lobbied for local management control and put pressure on the Chinese negotiators to stand firm or bargain hard in the next round of talks on development.

To respond to these challenges, the YICT General Manager together with his advisors undertook a number of initiatives aimed at political figures in Shenzhen and people of influence in various central government ministries. They launched a series of lobbying campaigns aiming at developing a positive image of the international partner in port development. The target audience ranged from political figures in Shenzhen to decision-makers and people of influence in various central government ministries. These were timed so as to achieve an impact in the right place and at the right time. Their focus was often on issues of 'foreign' participation in China's development and its benefits. The YICT team accessed some of the more sympathetic key actors within the Chinese partner organization to persuade them to the view that the rapid development of the port could only be possible with an international partner contributing the necessary resources. Hutchison's name and international reputation was leveraged significantly.

A second initiative was framed in terms of cost benefit analysis. Even though politically concerned Mainland executives care less about economics than do business people, they also understood that at the end of the day numbers speak louder than words. To advance a defensible argument, YICT contracted consulting companies and advisory groups to conduct feasibility studies on various aspects of the port's development. A number of consultants were involved, including the Fourth Engineering Consultancy Company and Shenzhen's National Economic Development Consultants, as well as many individual consultants who sometimes served as 'go-betweens' and lobbyists. The YICT management was therefore able to put various scenarios of competition and cooperation on the negotiation table, together with their financial results. They contrasted the scenario under 'monopolistic' pricing if YICT remained the only port operator in eastern Shenzhen with a competitive scenario of having both YICT and a rival Chinese port in the same location. The calculations also took into account the cost of civil construction and maintenance of infrastructure like the navigational channel, and they addressed how competition might affect the price of land for port development.

The compromise that was eventually reached had a number of key provisions. The first was that the Chinese partner would own a higher percentage (35 per cent) of the Phase 3 development, with the international party keeping majority control with 65 per cent of the equity. Second, the international joint venture paid an above-market price for the land and accepted that the Chinese partner contributed in kind (for instance, with land). Third, in addition to sharing part of the civil construction responsibilities, the joint venture (YICT) assumed responsibility for developing the infrastructure including a series of road improvements and flyovers near the port, to the tune of RMB 250 million. Fourth, as part of the deal, the joint venture also purchased the shares of the money-losing company that owned the rail link to the port. The price paid was RMB 350 million, a sum higher than the original development cost of the rail line. Taken together, these compromises significantly raised the cost of developing Phase 3 of the port, but they secured a 'peaceful' coexistence for the partners over the next decade.

A Memorandum of Understanding Phase 3 was signed between the two parties on 5 April 2000 to coincide with an official visit from the HPH Chairman Li Kashing to the Yantian Port Group. In the MOU, key terms were agreed including a revised percentage of equity to the Chinese party of 35 per cent and to the international consortium of 65 per cent. The 35/65 split (versus 27/73 in Phases 1 and 2 – YPG sold 3 per cent to the international partner in 1994) meant that YPG's share representing Chinese interests advanced by 8 per cent while majority control and management remained with the international investors. The package agreement included land, supporting infrastructure, and the rail operations. Adding civil construction costs meant that the whole investment on Phase 3 (part A involving 6 berths and 90 hectares) amounted to RMB 11.4 billion. A profit sharing arrangement based on resource contribution was also agreed for Phases 1, 2 and 3A, such that on a daily management basis all resources were to be shared.

The development of the Phase 3 6-berth facility went ahead at speed. The first, Berth 9, was delivered in 2005, in good time to handle the growing volume of traffic. With Phase 3, YICT achieved a larger scale of operations which afforded economies of scale. It was also able to expand the range of services it offered.

A port can achieve considerable economies of scale because a high percentage of its cost is sunk in the initial investment. Most of the capital cost of opening for business lies in building infrastructure and civil works, as well as equipping the terminal. Operating costs, namely labour, fuel and power, and the running cost of everyday operations, are relatively small, accounting for approximately 15 per cent to 20 per cent of total costs. With the initial investment spread over a larger throughput, average cost per production unit comes down. At Yantian, per unit cost came down significantly after 2000 and was then maintained at a relatively low level. With growing scale, the company could also investigate possibilities of further improvements and productivity gains. The key productivity indicator – crane moves per hour – rose from an ordinary 25 to a world leading record of 35 in the three years, 2002–2005.

Growth also enabled YICT to achieve economies of scope. It expanded into other related and supporting activities like warehousing, the tug boat business, and container repair business to increase its attractiveness to clients and to gain market share. Of particular interest was the company's venture into inter-modal transportation via a rail service. The Ping Yan Railway Company was acquired as an outcome of the Phase 3 negotiation, almost as a compensating condition offered to the Yantian Port Group to buy its money losing asset. However, the rail connection later became a key part of YICT's client acquisition and differentiation strategy. Instead of competing head-on with the western Shenzhen ports in building a feeder connection, YICT saw the rail connection as a way to penetrate China's inland provinces. Over the years, YICT built up a network of clients who produced light industrial products for the US and European markets. These manufacturers were facing increasing pressures from US and European buyers for lower costs. One of the ways to meet that challenge was to seek lower cost production opportunities by moving north or further inland away from the coastal cities. However, transportation was a limiting factor as the factories moved further inland. The rail network could prove to be a useful solution. It was a strategy that YICT actively pursued as it acquired scale after 2004.

With nine deep water berths and further new berths on the way, YICT had become a facility where shipping consortia could concentrate their ship deployment and cargo canvassing efforts. To be economical, carriers had to develop load centres to ensure that all their ships coming in and out of the hubs carry a high level of loads. A loading factor of 90 per cent would mean high profits and anything below 60 per cent would mean losses, depending on ship deployment and other economics at work. In line with this trend towards concentration was the appearance of so-called 'mega vessels'. These are ships that can handle 10,000 TEUs or more when fully loaded. The journal *Containerization International* reported in August 2005 that over 150 mega vessels were on order and were expected to come into service in the years to 2008. These vessels placed very demanding requirements on ports. Indeed, the incapacity of many ports to service these vessels because of limited draft and other constraints would become a limiting factor.

Aware of this trend, YICT in 2005 articulated a mega vessel strategy, which was to become the preferred hub for mega vessels.[38] This strategy had four main components:

1. Build the required infrastructure in a timely manner. It was planned to build a further six deep water berths from 2006 to 2009, known as Phase 3 Expansion [Phase 3E].[39] These berths were to be dredged to 16 metres alongside to cater for the sixth generation mega vessels (up to 15 000 TEU capacity).
2. Improve service processes and people skills to achieve a super efficient service environment to handle these vessels at a consistent 35 moves/crane hour. The company would employ process techniques like Motorola's Six Sigma and develop new computer systems like nGen to sustain this process level.
3. Improve customs processes and intensify marketing efforts to build a load centre – YICT would employ dedicated resources to work on customs improvement pilots so that the processes would be smooth enough to handle heavy loads in a short span of time. It would also intensify its marketing efforts with end users to secure its preference and influence over the shipping line's choice of Yantian as a load centre.

4. Establish a customer oriented and flexible organization to support growth – here the emphasis was on becoming more 'customer oriented' through training, coaching and culture building. YICT embarked on a serious campaign to 'build core values – create customer value, build responsible teams and establish mutual respect'.

The signing of the Phase 3 contract almost precluded competition in the next phase of the port's development. YICT had become so dominant in the Yantian port area that it would be very difficult for another company to become a serious competitor there. It also strengthened YICT's political influence with the central government. For it demonstrated that HPH and the Chinese partner had developed a good working relationship and had become collaborators in development. This perception, fostered by both HPH and YICT, helped smooth the way for its negotiations of Phase 3 Expansion, another 6-berth facility on the adjoining end of the peninsula. Negotiations for the project started in 2004 and were concentrated mainly on the price of land and other supporting facilities. By comparison with the earlier Phase 3 agreement it was a simpler deal, even though the sum of money involved amounted to over HK$10 billion, one of the largest investments in the history of port development in China. The agreements were signed in 2005 and construction started immediately. The central government saw no problems in approving the 'expansion' to an existing large facility as they also now recognized the significance of having a world-class port of international repute.

All in all, therefore, these advantages afforded by its growing scale helped YICT position itself as the leading port operator in China. With throughput achieving double digit growth despite a large base, and productivity and service levels publicly recognized by the industry, Yantian port was well on its way to becoming what its original founders had designed it to be – a 'world-class' international port in China. In May 2000, Hutchison Chairman Li Kashing wrote that the mission of the port was to 'become the largest and the best port operator in the world' (YICT company records, May 2000). With subsequent port development (up to 24 berths when fully developed) in place and improvements in technology and service being planned in 2006 and beyond, its executives were manifestly pursuing a 'world-class' mission. The achievements of 2007, therefore, did not come as a surprise.

Having reached a high point in 2007 with the 10 million TEU mark, YICT took a hit in throughput during the 2008–09 financial tsunami, as China's exports to both America and Europe suffered a downturn. However, with the strong foundations built in its formative years, the terminal regained some of its lost ground. In 2010 YICT again became one of the few terminals in the world with over 10 million TEU annual throughput.

NOTES

1. Actually the fourth phase of the port's development; the reason for this unusual numbering is explained later.
2. 'Line haul' services involve the movement of freight between major international ports.
3. Based on comments made by the Deputy Minister of Communications responsible for port development during a regular visit by YICT's General Manager to Beijing, December 2007.
4. Interview with Li Hao, August 2004.
5. *20th Anniversary Report of Shenzhen Yantian Port Group Company*, 2005.
6. Renamed the Yantian Port Group in 1995.
7. This initial construction came to be known as 'Phase 1'.
8. Interviews with the former Party Secretary of Shenzhen, Li Hao; the former General Manager of the Yantian Port Group; the Yantian Port Group Administration Manager; and the Executive Director from Hutchison responsible for the Yantian negotiations.
9. It was rare for China's top two leaders to be personally involved in a business event of this kind together.
10. Interviews with Shenzhen government former Party Secretary and Chief of Bureau of Communications, 2005.
11. Interview with former Shenzhen Party Secretary Li Hao, August 2004.
12. Interview with former GM of Yantian Port Group, 2004.
13. Hutchison's worldwide port operations were brought together into Hutchison Port Holdings [HPH] in 1994. The consortium led by Hutchison acquired a further 3 per cent share from the Chinese partner in 1994. Thus for Yantian port's Phases 1 and 2 the shareholding in YICT became 73 per cent held by the international consortium and 27 per cent held by YPG. The shareholding for Phase 3 and beyond was changed following negotiations to 65 per cent held by the international consortium and 35 per cent held by YPG.
14. *South China Morning Post*, 8 July 1994: p. 1 Shipping and Freight section.
15. Management presentation to the Board of Directors in 1995; YICT Plans, 1995.
16. Management Report to Hutchison Port Holdings, October 1995.
17. *Cargonews Asia*, 31 July 1994: 12.
18. Presentation to an industry seminar in September 2000.
19. The only exceptions were four items: cosmetics, tobacco products, liquors and armaments.
20. YICT report to the Board of Directors, May 1995 and McKinsey's Report to YICT, 1995.
21. Management Report to the YICT Board, October 1995.
22. General Manager's presentation to an industry roundtable, August 1999. The ideas for marketing directly to cargo owners and launching a shuttle service first came from the Chinese partner.
23. Interview with the YICT Deputy General Manager, July 2005.
24. Interview with the YICT End User Marketing Manager, July 2004.
25. Interview with China Affairs Manager, July 2004.

26. It is relevant here to note that the General Manager had previously worked for eight years as partner in an international management development and training consultancy.
27. Interview with the Operations Manager, July 2004.
28. Interview with the Operations Manager, July 2004; various company records, including the General Manager's Monthly Reports to the Board of Directors.
29. Before their consolidation in 1996, there had been six inspectorates operating in Chinese ports, as noted earlier. This consolidation followed one of the recommendations in the 1996 Li Lanqing Report (see Chapter 7), and it resulted in better coordination between the units.
30. Interview with Deputy General Manager, July 2005.
31. Proposal to the Shenzhen municipal government on Phase 3 Development, 5 March 1999.
32. A mega port is one capable of taking the latest generation of huge 'mega' container ships.
33. A detailed account of the Phase 3 negotiations from the Chinese partner's perspective is given by the YPG Chairman in his book, *My Memorable Days at Yantian Port* (Zheng, 2009).
34. Interview with Special Advisor to the General Manager, July 2005.
35. This phenomenon reflects the persistence of fief-like informal social networks in China (Boisot and Child, 1996).
36. Yantian Port Introduction Pamphlet published in 1993 by Dong Peng Industrial Company Limited – later renamed Yantian Port Group.
37. Report from the General Manager's Special Corporate Development Advisor, 19 January 2006: 4.
38. YICT strategy document, September 2005.
39. The unusual numbering (3E) of the phase following Phase 3 is partly explained by the fact that four is an unlucky number in traditional Chinese culture. It is also alleged that naming the new project an 'expansion' made it easier to obtain high level approval.

REFERENCES

Boisot, M. and J. Child (1996), 'From fiefs to clans: explaining China's emerging economic order', *Administrative Science Quarterly*, **41** (4), 600–628.

Cheng, K.H. and Y.J. Wong (1997), *Port Infrastructure and Container Terminal Business* (in Chinese), Hong Kong: Commercial Press.

Enright, M.J., E.E. Scott and D. Dodwell (1997), *The Hong Kong Advantage*, Hong Kong: Oxford University Press.

McKinley, W. (2011), 'Organizational contexts for environmental construction and objectification activity', *Journal of Management Studies*, **48**, 804–28.

Mintzberg, H. (1978), 'Patterns in strategy formulation', *Management Science*, **24**, 934–48.

Mintzberg, H. (1987), 'Crafting strategy', *Harvard Business Review*, July–August, 66–75.

Zheng, J. (2009), *My Memorable Days at Yantian Port* (in Chinese), Beijing: Social and Economic Publishers.

6. Innovations in management practice

This chapter records the initiatives taken by YICT's management to introduce new practices in a number of specific areas that reflected its overall strategic intention of becoming a 'world-class port'.[1] These were the managerial actions that fashioned the evolution of the company, as well as that of some aspects of the Chinese port industry as a whole.

The previous two chapters have shown that the growth of Yantian port was closely correlated with the growth of external trade in South China. One could conclude therefore that it was favourable external economic conditions which enabled the port to develop. While this is true, it does not account for the form that development took, which emerged from initiatives taken by the company's management. Nor would it recognize that some of those initiatives also helped to shape the evolution of the company's environment. It will become apparent that many of the initiatives taken at YICT were actually uniquely informed by the special conditions its management had to deal with. Over time, these responses impacted on the port industry in China in more significant ways than anticipated. Taken together, they may be regarded as 'emergent strategies' that led the industry in developing or adopting new practices and standards. Even though designed initially in response to business needs, these initiatives were at the same time informed by the vision of building a world-class port. They helped to propel the organization to become a leader in its field and they brought about a proactive interaction with its environment.

This chapter focuses on the following areas of innovation in practice initiated by YICT management:

1. Espousing a service mentality and developing world-class productivity practices.
2. Adopting a strategic orientation towards port construction and development.
3. Innovating in port marketing.
4. Establishing a favourable ecological system – transportation, intermodal, warehouse and logistics developments – and the 'Green Port' initiative.

In each of these areas, we first report management's strategic intent, then examine the new practices and whenever possible provide an assessment of their effectiveness. The following chapter will then describe a further area of management initiative, that of 'relationship management'. This aimed at creating a relational framework through which HPH and YICT could push back constraints imposed by YICT's Mainland partner and by the agencies of the Chinese government. While the implementation of the other management initiatives all depended on constructive relations with stakeholders, relationship management was particularly important as a condition for the implementation of YICT's strategy. It was through the presence of a continuing and active relational framework that initiatives at the company level came to have a wider impact on practice in the sector as a whole.

SERVICE AND PRODUCTIVITY IMPROVEMENTS

The Service Concept

The concept of service and a customer orientation were underdeveloped in China's port industry in the early 1990s. Due to its capital intensive nature, what the industry recognized as critical success factors were a choice of good location at the right time and the ability to build capacity and handle volume at relatively low cost. Providing service was viewed mostly in terms of the ability to handle volume and throughput using the least resources and at minimum cost from the provider's standpoint. China had also inherited many legacies from the days when it was a planned economy typified by 'shortages' – in other words, by demand exceeding supply. Most ports were operated by government port authorities who ran the enterprises as government departments or state-owned enterprises (SOEs). These enterprises had a socio-political rationale as well as an economic one. The need for efficient service was acknowledged because an undersupply of port services meant a breakdown in the infrastructural chain. Congestion at ports or delays in servicing ships represented a sign of bad planning in the socialist system and as such needed to be avoided. Yet, before the era of reform, such congestion and delays were commonplace in a large number of port locations such as Shanghai and Whampoa. There were many reasons for this, but the inefficiency of the port operators and their lack of a customer orientation were among the more significant factors.

Before opening up to international participation, most SOE port operators were large bodies of employees, some with over 20 000 in number, engaged in production, management of various subsidiaries and functions and a huge web of related services like trucking, forwarding, warehousing, rail operations and non-vessel operating carriers. As SOEs, they took care of their employees from 'cradle to grave' and therefore had to build a large bureaucracy to manage employees' work, life, education and health and related welfare. With such a heavy internal focus, service to customers took a secondary role.

As the affiliate of an international operator, YICT espoused a contrasting mentality and adopted a different mode of operations. From the start, service and productivity were viewed as critical to the success of the Yantian port. This was partly due to the need to attract customers in the South China environment, where the Hong Kong port was already setting a high standard in customer service. Hong Kong International Terminals (HIT), YICT's immediate Hong Kong parent, was well known in the industry as a good example of productivity and service improvements. HIT had been able to handle a significantly higher volume than other terminals of its size because of its productivity initiatives. Building on the successful example of Hong Kong, YICT's management inherited a service orientation without any reservation. For example, service loomed large in discussions at the 1995 YICT management seminar:

> Our number one job is to serve our customers. We must ensure that ships are handled in as accurate and efficient a manner as possible. Remember – ships only want to stay at ports for a minimum of time. Our customers make money when the ships are sailing; in port, they spend money. We therefore have to be as productive as possible to help our customers (General Manager's presentation to the YICT Management Seminar, November 1995).

There were regular mentions of 'operations and service' in YICT's Annual Business Plans over the years, reflecting their key role in the company's strategy. For example, 'Establish a customer oriented culture and quality processes'[2]; 'Ensure service quality with reliable terminal operations and predictable customs environment'[3]; and 'Meeting customer expectations and service demands in a cost effective manner'.[4] The 2000 Business Plan clearly saw innovations in practice as providing the means of achieving service improvements:

> We need to build in a higher level of professionalism in our operations, with business process improvement and benchmarking technologies, plus the appropriate training and strengthening of human resources. An on-going emphasis on customer service will permeate all related activities (YICT 2000 Business Plan).

A similar emphasis was found in the business plans of subsequent years. Customer service and productivity improvement were themes consistently attracting management attention. They became major drivers of the company's evolution, regarded as the translation of its mission to become a 'world-class port' into tangible forms. In the YICT mission statement first published in 1995, service was included as one of the three world-class attributes.[5]

With this strong emphasis coming from the top of the organization, the service concept became part of a management ethos that aspired to define the competitive advantage of the company. Repeated at most of their annual meetings, YICT management created a consistent message that had been cascaded to all levels throughout the organization. Over time, service and productivity became the name of the game and was widely accepted in the organization.

The manager who spearheaded this effort commented:

> We cannot grow our people fast enough to deliver the service demanded by our customers. We talk about 'world class' service, but the workforce is young and inexperienced. We can provide the right incentives. They are most willing and we need to provide leadership in defining what we can do to satisfy our customers. We must put in extra effort to bring all our people up to speed with 'world class' concepts and skills.[6]

The accent on service appeared in slightly different forms over time. During the early years, the company's focus was on raising levels of throughput because that defined success and failure, so the service attention was on clearing vessels and handling problems arising from customs practices. When a terminal handles over a million TEUs, it gets onto the port industry charts in China. By 1998, that goal was realized when annual throughput exceeded a million, bringing the volumes handled in Shenzhen as a whole up to number two in China's port ranking. Thereafter, the port faced a somewhat different challenge – how to cope with growth, as the customers came in much larger numbers than expected. Sometimes, management talked about the 'Ketchup' analogy – it was not easy to get it to flow initially but then it overflows. In the 2001–03 period, the company experienced this challenge. In 2003, the port achieved a throughput of 5.3 million TEUs with only five berths. Each berth on average handled over 1 million TEUs while its design capacity was only half that number and the industry standard was 600 000 TEUs. The challenge now was therefore how to manage productivity.

To cope with such fast growth, YICT launched several productivity improvement programmes. In 2002 it set itself a very high target – to handle 5 million TEUs and to reach 35 moves per crane hour.[7] For that time, these were very aggressive targets. If achieved they would set new standards for the industry not only in China but also worldwide. There were quite a few dissenting voices. Some questioned the need to do so, raising the concern that it might set the competitive train going too fast. Others questioned the practicality of doing so, doubting the ability of the young port to achieve these targets in a sustainable fashion and without incurring a huge marginal cost.

Implementing the Service Concept in YICT

The company adopted a number of specific actions to implement its service concept.

Focusing the organization

Management reviewed the work organization and delegated more decision-making power down to the front line. Rather than allowing different sections in the planning and execution areas to function separately, YICT's operations management played the critical integration role by providing immediate direction and more frontline support in terms of coordination amongst various sections – planning with execution, engineering with frontline operations. The role of 'production manager' was given to the shift managers whose responsibilities were to ensure productivity and service during their shifts and to hand over to the next shift. Every morning, frontline management met to discuss target vessels to achieve breakthroughs in speed and efficiency. These meetings were supported by various functions: commercial, computer planning, ship planning, yard execution, the gatehouse and engineering maintenance, as well as the China Affairs Department which stood ready to handle customs flexibility. On a daily basis, progress was reviewed by senior operations managers who in turn reported the daily production results to the General Manager. The results were announced every morning at eight o'clock and regularly reviewed.

The control tower superintendents and managers were empowered to change the operating flow and use appropriate resources to bring about productivity results. Operating the terminal with over ten berths could be complex with up to ten vessels and thousands of trucks and boxes moving at the same time. Each superintendent in charge of a vessel operating plan was given authority to ensure that the last boxes to be handled met expected time for departures [ETDs] and gross crane rates [GCRs] set for the vessel before operations on it began. He could decide on the number of gangs of longshoremen and trucks to be employed. The control room was also electronically equipped with the state-of-the-art equipment to control production in progress, allowing the people in charge to read those indicators in real-time.

The next generation of computer technology
Management also initiated the development of the next generation of computer technology, known as 'nGen'. A RMB 70 million project spanning over three years, nGen was the new computer system that could enable the port to handle its growing volume with finesse and dexterity. Its architecture was scalable and adaptable to meeting customers' needs for speed of operations – in ship and yard planning and in terminal operations. The investment succeeded a few generations of very efficient computer systems that supported the HPH's operations in Hong Kong and in other ports. The terminal operating management system [TOMS] that won the coveted Computer World's Smithsonian Award in 1997 for Hong Kong International Container Terminals was first transferred from Hong Kong to YICT in 1998. TOMS functioned well in a smaller operating environment but demands on it soon outgrew its capacity. Initiated in 2001, the nGen project was a combination of investment efforts by both HIT and YICT. This meant that a significant level of resource could be invested into computer software with the assurance that when fully developed the system could be amortized over a wide network of ports managed by HPH. With the design capacity to cope with 10 million TEUs, the new system launched in November 2003 became a critical resource for helping YICT to meet the challenge of handling its growing volume. Its sophistication helped increase the speed of planning, improve operating efficiency in yard and ship management, and overall provide a better service to customers.

Training for productivity
Training was another component in the push for higher productivity. The company had since its inception placed considerable emphasis on both technical and management training. A series of technical modules was designed and developed for different job families from the front line to middle management, while Hutchison's regional centre and head office supported the company with senior management development. YICT had both a technical and a management training setup. In technical training, for example, the company used multi-media crane simulators to provide a 'virtual' exposure of trainees to operating the quay and yard cranes. It managed to cut down training time by one-quarter and improve operating accuracy and speed by between 10 and 15 per cent. Other supervisory and management training programmes supported the company's push

towards delegation and teamwork. A series of tailored modules aimed at improving supervision were organized for frontline supervisors. Called 'operations trainee programmes' or 'duty managers' trainee programmes', such training helped the supervising workforce instil a sense of urgency amongst the workforce. They also helped to introduce some professional people management practices.

Use of monetary incentives

To support the drive for higher productivity, YICT used monetary incentives. The company had an incentive scheme that gave not just workers but all employees an incentive to achieve targets. It was necessary for every department to contribute towards achieving the company's service and productivity goals. For example, to make time for repairs, the engineers had to innovate in providing just-in-time repairs and maintenance. They employed what they called the 'Formula One Racing Team' repair concept. Instead of staying in the engineering office waiting for emergency repair orders, a team of engineers were actually on site and on standby mode around the cranes that might require a breakdown service. In this way, they were able to reduce downtime very significantly. In order to rally the whole company around providing efficient service, management designed the incentive component to be as high as 25 per cent of take-home pay for some staff. The key targets were spelt out very clearly. They were: monthly throughput of the terminal, crane productivity as measured by number of moves per crane hour, tractor turnaround time, and accident rate. These targets were broadcast everyday through the internal mail system as well as put up on notice boards and in meeting rooms. In 2005, the emphasis was put on a 'consistent 35 moves per hour', and additional dollars were paid when the company produced 35 moves per hour consistently for six, nine and 12 months. Despite some criticism that the management was tough and unfair in raising targets every time the incentive was reviewed, the incentive scheme did contribute to raising the awareness of the need to produce at high efficiency and it also helped to promote team unity in supporting a key company target.

Improving operating processes with Six Sigma methodology

YICT also made a conscious effort to improve its processes. Process awareness and improvement had always been an element in management thinking in YICT since its early days. In several annual management meetings, the idea of business process engineering was put forward and discussed. In fact, some experiments were carried out during the years 1999 to 2001. For example, '5S', a methodology made popular by

Japan's introduction to standardization of processes, was introduced to YICT. Initially applied in the Engineering Department, the process emphasized standardization of working procedures and work habits. To a certain extent, the 5S programme heralded the intention of the organization to look for process improvements. During the implementation of 5S, some publicity, training and auditing took place but they covered only part of the organization and the methods were mainly introduced at the working level. Senior management support was limited.

These early efforts only brought partial results, and YICT management was not content with them. It was seriously searching for a management technology that would form the foundation of a process improvement that could support YICT's competitiveness in the long run. At the launch of the ensuing process innovation initiative (PII) programme, the General Manager explained:

> We always believe that process superiority and the ability to self improve on the processes are key competitive edges for any organization. We were looking for a process answer until we came across Six Sigma (Presentation by the General Manager at the launch of the PII, 2001).

The introduction of Six Sigma as a process improvement programme was timed against an urgent requirement for the port to be more productive. In 2001, when the terminal had to handle more than its design capacity, the General Manager spearheaded the introduction of Six Sigma for process improvement. Its stated aim was to 'Challenge the 5 million TEU throughput requirement; break the 35 moves per crane hour productivity barrier so that trucks have to queue no longer and ships leave earlier' (PII Goals published in 2002). Six Sigma was chosen to be the main methodology to bring about the changes. A 'Jumpstart Management Workshop' was conducted by a Motorola University Senior Consultant with the executive team, and they mapped out the strategy for implementation. The whole executive team was later trained later as 'green belts' and several 'black belts' were achieved in the next couple of years. An external consultant was also brought in full-time to provide help as 'master black belt'. A steering group headed by the General Manager himself was formed to provide direction and monitor progress. They identified key projects as 'mission critical' and others as 'service excellence' and 'process improvement' projects. In the initial implementation phase, the focus was on examining possibilities of improvement in existing processes and this led to new ways of doing things. Later in the implementation, some issues were the subject of serious examination and process review, including commercial differentiation, product introduction and strategic planning processes.

During the course of four years, over 200 people were trained and 45 projects launched. The projects covered a wide variety of areas ranging from broad strategic issues like designing VIP programmes for carriers and voice of customers management, to specific operational issues like minimizing accident rates and lowering fuel consumption of the RTGCs [rubber tyre gantry cranes]. Some projects came out successfully with specific and measurable results; some with further developed concepts. Most managers participated either as project sponsors, champions or leaders, and over ten 'black belts' were trained. In an effort to build higher commitment, the company mandated 'green belt' learning as a pre-requisite for all staff promotion to management status. The methodology and acronyms like 'DMAIC – define, measure, analyze, implement, control' became synonymous with management itself. It was a stated aim of PII that Six Sigma should become the DNA of the organization.

Developing supportive core values

A further aspect of utilizing its human resources for better results lay in the company's continuous efforts to build a supportive culture. The company first put forward its 'seven core values' in 1999 after a reorganization of the finance department. The core values were 'trust, respect, openness, consideration, teamwork, responsibility, and innovation'. Referred to as ideals of behaviour, these were put forward as drafts for discussion. Management intended them to be the starting points for discussion and to serve as behaviour models, trying to provide some sense of direction to unite the workforce in a changing environment. Management programmes were also built around institutionalizing these values in management practices and performance evaluation. In 2002 and 2003, several week-long campaigns were organized to publicize these efforts. As a reminder to everyone, these values were translated into behaviours. For example, in one of the campaigns, one of the participating teams developed a series of 52 supportive behaviours in easy-to-remember verses. They were printed onto playing cards and distributed widely amongst staff. The public relations people also handed out these nice-looking playing cards to visitors.

However, inculcating such values into the setting of a tradition-bound industry was by no means easy. In 2004, a company-wide 'employee engagement survey' was undertaken. The question about 'core values' provided some interesting feedback. The staff thought that it was very good to espouse the seven key values strategically and indeed, at the company's strategic level, such values were perceived to be supportive of the aims the company was pursuing, namely differentiation and service excellence. However, the survey report provided less favourable results when commenting on 'walking the talk'. Scores were low on implementation especially amongst middle and lower management. In response to this feedback, the YICT management team gathered its thoughts over several more rounds of discussion. It decided to distil the core values down to just three and it planned a series of implementation steps. The new core values were announced by the General Manager in February 2006 in a letter to all staff. They were: 'create customer value; build responsible teams; promote mutual trust' (General Manager's letter to all staff, February 2006). Together with the value statements, a list of positive and negative behaviours describing those values was also put forward. A 360 degree feedback process was designed to provide monitoring of the implementation of the announced behaviours. A series of workshops conducted by the executive team led by the General Manager involved all management personnel in working out details of implementation. In his letter to all staff, the General Manager appealed to all for support to 'make YICT a good place to work'(General Manager's letter to all staff, February 2006). He intended the 'core values' to provide the foundation of this campaign.

Results and assessment
With the constant emphasis on improvement and the various initiatives adopted, YICT achieved a level of operating efficiency that met and sometimes exceeded the industry's recognized standards. Using the industry's most important measurement, GCR – for instance, the number of boxes moved per crane per hour on average, YICT achieved the results shown in Figure 6.1.

While the productivity curve showed a steady improvement from 1995 to 2005, the rise was most marked for the years between 2002 and 2005, coinciding with a surge in throughput handled. The targets set at the launch of the Process Innovation Initiative project in November 2002 were met with 35 moves per hour being achieved consistently in 2005. Regarding the possible objection that these productivity improvements incurred rising costs, a management accounting report indicated that from 2001 to 2005 the operating cost per TEU had been maintained at a low level with only a slight rise over the years. The cost of investment in productivity appeared to have been offset by growth in volume and economy of scale effects.

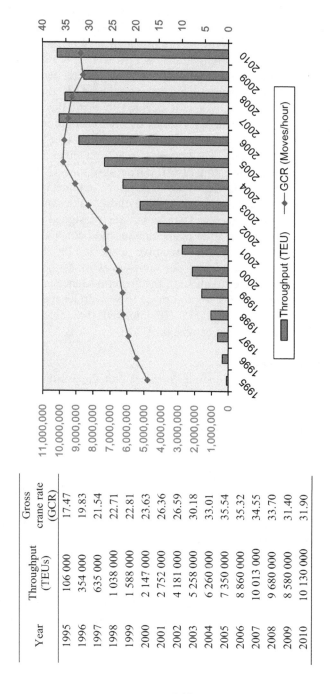

Year	Throughput (TEUs)	Gross crane rate (GCR)
1995	106 000	17.47
1996	354 000	19.83
1997	635 000	21.54
1998	1 038 000	22.71
1999	1 588 000	22.81
2000	2 147 000	23.63
2001	2 752 000	26.36
2002	4 181 000	26.59
2003	5 258 000	30.18
2004	6 260 000	33.01
2005	7 350 000	35.54
2006	8 860 000	35.32
2007	10 013 000	34.55
2008	9 680 000	33.70
2009	8 580 000	31.40
2010	10 130 000	31.90

Figure 6.1 Throughput and productivity at YICT

YICT conducted regular customer satisfaction studies. The 2006 study showed some positive results but also pointed out various areas for improvements:[8]

- Overall YICT scored over 70 points (max 100) in the customer satisfaction index.
- Client service (including responsiveness to client requests, accessibility, understanding client needs and client communications) provided the most positive contributions to customer satisfaction (average 74.3).
- Clients were concerned about berth accessibility and wished that the company could resolve issues more proactively through productivity improvements.
- Carriers were in general satisfied with the proactive attitude YICT took in resolving infrastructural issues: for instance, building more berths and handling the traffic problems.
- Customers indicated that there was room for YICT to improve on regulatory reform initiatives, and achieve a better balance between short-term and long-term customer relations, with particular reference to relationship pricing and charging for items such as tally fees.[9]

Using a similar methodology, another 2006 survey also provided the following results:[10]

- YICT is outperforming the market. It had a TRIM (TNS consultant's performance feedback system) index of 79 (out of 100), driven by a strong rating on overall satisfaction with basic product and service delivery. This score placed it in the top 33 percentile of norms for cargo/logistics providers worldwide. Areas of strength were: information accuracy, vessel productivity, reliability of agreed vessel departure time and staff professionalism.
- However, areas for improvement included flexibility in resolving ad hoc customer issues, follow-up on claims, pilot and tug boat services, depot operations, and repair and maintenance services.

Overall, the implementation of the service concept was producing both tangible and intangible results.

However, while the hard-core business results showed that these efforts were bearing fruit, it was questionable whether the investments in the 'soft' areas were leading to comparable improvements. As with many 'transfer of management practices' initiatives it was much more difficult to ascertain how successful the transfers were. They were intended to improve the organization in the long run and would only have positive results if organization members were committed to them. Since these soft developments could be perceived as elusive, the extent to which they had been accepted and become embedded in the specific YICT context was a question that deserved further study. Under the Birmingham University MSc in International Business Dissertation Abroad Programme, several studies examined various aspects of the functioning of management practices in the context of a developing country using YICT as a case example. They provided some insights into the challenge that YICT's management encountered when pursuing its world-class mission in areas such as creating organizational culture, difficulties of cultural change, transferability of western human resources management practices, use of Six Sigma in improving productivity, and trust, commitment and '*guanxi*' in business to business markets.

For example, Amen's study (2005) investigated Six Sigma implementation in YICT against a Chinese cultural setting. It indicated that that the top down approach had only achieved limited results in YICT:

> It is argued that complete or at least majority buy-in on Six Sigma has still not been achieved throughout the organization ... With the results of Six Sigma in YICT so far, more employees are beginning to appreciate its value to the organization and also to their personal development. Some demonstrate real commitment and enthusiasm in the projects (Amen, 2005: 51).

Apart from pointing out the varying degrees of staff commitment to Six Sigma in YICT, Amen highlighted the need for bottom up initiatives, and for the emergence of a YICT model in using the methodology not just for transactional or cost saving applications but also for transformational applications (for instance, development of people and culture) (Amen, 2005: 51). Nevertheless, the interviews she conducted recognized that the Process Innovation Initiative represented a conscious effort on the part of management to introduce an accepted management technology to improve the operating processes in YICT so that it could meet its growing challenges. 'This reflects the determination and openness of companies in China including YICT to adopt foreign best practices. Six Sigma is the next phase in YICT's and China's quality transformation' (Amen, 2005: 51).

In another study on the same subject, Nhankaniso (2007) tried to match the actual implementation of Six Sigma at YICT with the critical success factors identified by senior management and/or in the management literature. Through interviewing the key managers involved in the process, he identified some areas where lack of alignment was hindering effective implementation. These raised a number of questions: whether Six Sigma should be an end or the means to an end in YICT's pursuit of organizational excellence; the extent to which, and the specific ways in which, top management should be involved; whether the 'green belt' qualification should be an obligatory requirement for promotion to management as a lever to ensure institutionalization of the practices; and the appropriateness of the rewards and penalties being applied (Nhankaniso, 2007: 27–32). Although he noted further difficulties in implementing the processes, Nhankaniso also identified certain critical success factors [CSF] in cases where implementation was achieving the required results. These CSFs were consistent with those found in the management literature. For example, in the Service Delivery and Development Department and the Engineering Department, whose goals were to improve the gross crane rate and shorten the tractor turn time, implementation of Six Sigma was observed to be more complete and the CSFs more evident:

> These departments from the findings show that they have top management involvement and commitment; they have the second layer buy-in; they have a recognition and reward structure; they have part time black belts within their departments, to mention a few of the CSFs identified in YICT. There are many six sigma projects that have been successful within the two departments but the two that YICT clearly identify with Six Sigma was achieved by these departments being the major contributors (Nhankaniso, 2007: 49).

Nhankaniso concluded:

> The success of six sigma in YICT after five years is still not completely clear at the moment, as the success of a business process improvement initiative needs time for the benefits to be clearly noticed (Nhankaniso, 2007: 50).

Amen and Nhankaniso were not alone in pointing out YICT's lack of complete success in implementing the best management practices and ideas. In studying the transferability of international HRM into Mainland China, Garner (2005) found that a direct transfer of HRM practices was not feasible and that significant modifications would be required in their implementation. He observed:

> All YICT managers posited that customization of HR has been an important factor contributing to the marked improved performance of the firm. YICT is an encouraging case for the transfer of IHRM and suggests success can be achieved, but constant persistence is called for and adoption of an integrated perspective is critical (Garner, 2005: 79).

Similarly, attempts to build and institutionalize a set of core values to guide management behaviours and promote a unique YICT culture experienced implementation problems. In the 2004 Employee Engagement Survey conducted by the company, YICT management was given the feedback that the core values remained 'empty talk'. Few of them were seen to apply to everyday managerial behaviour. While the staff in general agreed with senior management's strategies of cultural change and with the principles contained in the core values, they hoped that more managers would 'walk the talk' in their everyday dealings with staff.[11] In studying the change process, Heuermann (2006) interviewed 24 YICT employees and managers and observed the inadequacies of 'western' methods of change in action. He pointed out a number of problems that were all contributing to the limited success of the change effort, including that the local Chinese culture was not being taken into consideration, that some Chinese staff perceived a lack of opportunities, and that a 'glass ceiling' existed for local staff (Heuermann, 2006: 54). These findings were echoed in McHale's study of the YICT brand of organizational culture. She pointed out that, while the proclaimed aim was 'a culture of synthesis', actual practice leaned more towards domination by Hong Kong culture. This gave rise to the danger of 'resentment' by people in the dominated culture, namely the local staff (McHale, 2005: 56).

These revealing studies all contributed to a better understanding of how various parts of the organization were performing against the company's overall strategic objective of becoming a world-class port and the 'preferred mega vessel hub'. While the strategy seemed to be working well judging by the company's sustained business results, the more mixed picture in terms of how well new practices were being accepted and becoming embedded raised a question mark over the sustainability of its successful development.

A STRATEGIC ORIENTATION TOWARDS PORT CONSTRUCTION AND DEVELOPMENT

The perspectives that YICT brought to port construction and development were very different to those of the Mainland authorities and its partner. The latter did not initially share the same concept of a 'world-class' port.

In terms of design capacity and actual operating capacity, the YICT planners borrowed very heavily from international experience and they adopted some stretched targets for the new port. The design capacity for a berth according to the Ministry of Communications was 400 000 TEUs, but in Hong Kong operators had been able to handle up to 1 million per berth when necessary, namely in the Sealand terminal. Many factors were at play, including civil construction standards, size of operating yard, numbers and standards of equipment, and supporting information technology. A synergistic combination of these factors plus high labour productivity and good management would produce what the industry calls the 'operating capacity' of the terminal that could far exceed its design capacity.

Looking at the economics, YICT management was not content to design the new terminal to handle only 400 000 TEUs. They asked for an operating capacity of 800 000 TEUs per berth. To achieve this, the new terminals had to be built to demanding and stringent civil construction standards and equipped with the latest set of cranes and other ancillary support systems. On securing the right to develop Phase 2, YICT decided to insert these standards into the planning stage. The Phase 2 Construction Department adopted British standards in the planning and also used international standard processes for managing the civil engineering. In specifying contract terms with civil contractors, the 'FIDIC' (International Federation of Consulting Engineers) terms were used. They also put in place plans to order the best cranes available in the industry from Japanese and Korean manufacturers. They commissioned the development of a new set of computer systems for the operations. They specified 'a terminal that could last for 50 years without major repairs'.[12] Behind such reasoning lay the aim of becoming world-class in port operations. Another consideration was the company's anticipation that, as soon as the new facilities were completed, the berths would be fully utilized. With full utilization there would be little time for shutdown and major repairs since that could disrupt business significantly. Business that was turned away would benefit competitors so much that it would be very difficult to regain it.

The plan immediately raised some eyebrows because it would mean significantly higher development costs. The Chinese partner was not alone in objecting to it. Since development plans had to be endorsed by expert panels and other personnel from relevant ministries and bureaus, YICT's new management had to fight a difficult battle to convince these conservative parties. This they did with patience and tact, because they knew that without their support it would be very difficult to run things smoothly despite the fact that the majority shareholder was accorded the formal authority to decide these matters. To help gain support, YICT management employed consulting engineers of international repute and sought technical advice from various parts of the world to lend credibility to the plans. They put in a strong organization of engineering staff to supervise the civil construction. They kept strict rules in day-to-day engineering management emphasizing standards and quality adherence. On the question of total cost, management conducted several rounds of discussions with the Chinese partner and their associates concerning the need to provide the best facilities in order to justify a tariff premium of over 25 per cent. With the projection of full utilization, they managed to convince doubters that the terminals could ill afford periodic 'major repairs'. They framed the discussion in terms of the 'average cost in use', indicating that, with amortization over the life span of the project, it would be more economical overall to build a quality facility, to demand a good price and provide a high level of maintenance dollars than to do otherwise.

Behind the fight for control in civil project supervision was a fight for power in allocating benefits to the parties involved. To resolve this, the YICT civil engineering team distinguished 'critical to quality' components from non-critical ones, and apportioned these into different contracts. 'Critical to quality' components included the 'quay deck construction' and the 'container yard and services' components, while 'ground improvement' and 'dredging' were classified as less critical. A compromise was reached allocating the responsibilities amongst the partners accordingly, with the ground improvement and dredging contracts managed by the Chinese party. The purchase of cranes was done centrally by Hutchison technical support at the group level.

As a result, the facilities developed by the joint venture introduced new standards into the Chinese port industry. The terminals at Yantian were constructed with deeper drafts and stronger quay decks, wider and larger container yards paved with state-of-the-art interlocking blocks, and better-than-average cranes able to handle the next generation of ships. As YICT pursued its mega vessel strategy, it continued to head into the future with similar leading edge design considerations in the later Phase 3 and Phase 3E projects. Despite their initial objections over the high costs incurred, some opponents later became supporters. Indeed, the presiding officer of the expert panel, a former senior minister from the Ministry of Communications, spoke glowingly of the new standards. In the 'Design Approval Meeting for Phase 2' in September 2000, he commented:

> I have seen so many terminals in China and I have never seen a terminal built to such standards like your Phase 2 berths. During the initial design meetings, I thought the standards were too high, that it would be too costly. Now when I see the real berths, I like what I see, and YICT management has convinced me that if the berths can be immediately filled with full utilization, you are right that we cannot afford to stop the flow of traffic for repairs. Fifty years

with no major repairs is a noble target and you seem to be able to justify it with "good value in use" (Comments made in the Phase 2 Design Approval Meeting, September 2000 – minutes of meeting).

The standards applied at Yantian soon became those adopted for civil construction in ports like Shanghai's Yangshan, Ningbo, Qingdao and other large Chinese ports all over the country.

Commercially, these investments in quality paid off. With leading edge standards, the facilities stood head and shoulders above those of YICT's competitors in usage and service to users. Apart from looking and feeling different, the facilities enabled a lot of new operating initiatives to function well. At the new gatehouse, for example, the new designs enabled a smoother flow of traffic and better control of security. The wider container yards shortened the time of internal traffic management and cut the tractor turnaround time. More importantly, with the strong quay decks and the latest cranes, YICT could operate the latest generation of vessels with ease, achieving a speed and efficiency envied by its competitors.

In 2004, the Fourth Harbour Engineering Company was awarded the 'Lu Ban Award' by the Ministry of Building and Construction for its work on Yantian's Phase 2. The award, named after the greatest builder in the history of civil construction in China, signified the highest national recognition given to any civil engineering project in the country. In 2007, the company was awarded the same accolade for their quality work in Yantian's Phase 3.

The downside to all these quality installations was that the cost of building successive phases of terminals in YICT rose significantly. Although part of the reason for the cost escalation was land price, the demanding standards required by the company's high-class and preferred mega vessel hub strategic positioning added to the burden. The Phase 3 and Phase 3E projects were secured with heavy cost outlays in civil construction and equipment levels as well as commitments to ensure that supporting infrastructure was in place concurrently with the basic civil works. These cost escalations were not insignificant as an analysis of cost per berth revealed an over 50 per cent escalation from Phase 1 through to Phase 3E, albeit with a higher level of design specification to cater for mega vessels and higher productivity. Together with a heavier upfront outlay of cash, a higher level of investment also meant a greater burden of depreciation in subsequent years.

How and whether the relatively higher cost of construction will later turn out to be a competitive disadvantage when competition gets keener remains to be seen. YICT started with a differentiation strategy and has continued that strategy to the present. The high cost of development might make it difficult for YICT to adjust to another strategy. Its high sunk cost obliges YICT to charge a higher price, which might make it less competitive. However, the large scale of its operation, based on a large market share, has so far enabled YICT to maintain a relatively low unit cost.

INNOVATING IN PORT MARKETING

By 2007, it was clear to industry observers that YICT's profitability was due to a smart strategy well executed. Despite strong competition, it still dominated US and European trade to and from South China, with a 70 per cent share of the former and a 53 per cent share of the latter.[13] These sectors were the most profitable segments of the terminal business. YICT's share of the market in intra-Asia trade and international trans-shipment was minimal, but these were the less profitable segments of the business. With high growth rates at the time in both the US and European markets, it was little wonder that new competitors were striving keenly for a share of the cake. One of the key challenges confronting YICT management was whether and how it might be able to sustain such a leading position in the ensuing few years.

Such domination of the market had not come about by accident. We have seen that it involved a struggle in the early years and required YICT to prove the viability of Yantian port against strong competitors in Hong Kong to an inert group of customers who were too busy regrouping into the New World and Grand Alliances to be concerned with the new alternative port. The Maersk line was the only customer with the foresight to establish a strong base in China ahead of others. In order to survive at this difficult time, YICT's marketing team had to study the port's value chain more carefully and also learn from its local partner's insights into the context in China:

> Carriers come to collect cargo; they do not bring cargo in the first instance; so it's the port's ability to organize and attract cargo that forms the basis of its survival.[14]

The newly formed marketing team conducted a series of market studies in an effort to understand the source of cargo – the who, what and how of cargo generation and their transportation modes. From the detailed information obtained, some key points emerged.[15] A study was conducted to understand the port's end users – who they were and why and how they influenced port choices. The study provided some useful insights:[16]

1. The region's exports were heavily concentrated on light industrial production – toys, clothes, shoes, furniture and electronic goods.
2. They were mainly exports to America and Europe with large buyers like Walmart, Mattel, Hasbro, Toys R Us and other large department stores like Sears in the US and those on the European continent. These purchasing organizations had been increasingly shifting their sourcing to China, especially South China, because of its cheap and reliable production capabilities.
3. Their influence on the choice of ports was in the hands of logistics executives in the domestic buying offices who examined the overall transportation cost picture in light of reliability and service considerations.
4. The transportation mode prevalent at that time was to truck the cargo in full containers or in general cargo trucks to Hong Kong for direct shipment or consolidation in warehouses before getting to the Hong Kong port. Due to Hong Kong's free port status, crossing the border was the only hurdle to overcome. Once over the border, the containers could easily and reliably be handled in the Hong Kong port through a very efficient logistics industry that had developed over the years.
5. Most industrial players might be aware of the benefits of using a Chinese port nearer to the manufacturing sites. However, a concern over customs and other bureaucratic practices in the Chinese ports effectively prevented most people from contemplating the change. The vice presidents of logistics in US MNCs were interested in getting to the cost savings (the difference in trucking cost was US$200–300 per container) but they could not win the argument over their shipping managers and agents concerning the complexities of customs clearance.

These insights forced the YICT marketing team to rethink its marketing strategy. In addition to its attempts to attract shipping carriers to try the new port, YICT initiated some marketing offensives aimed at end users. Now armed with an understanding of the economics of transportation, namely differences in transporting the cargo via the new and existing routes, the YICT marketing team divided themselves into two sub-teams. One team – the End User Marketing Team – targeted the buyers and merchandisers in the US and Europe. The other team focused on the vendors or suppliers of light manufactured goods in South China. In the

US and European markets, the team promoted the economics of saving US$200–300 per container handled at the new Chinese port. In South China, the second team discussed how to speed up customs procedures and achieve reliability of transport schedules and delivery, thus becoming the 'manufacturing centre of choice'.

Very little was known about how to market to the diverse groups of port users. There was simply no prior experience in Hong Kong or around the world in the ports that HPH managed. As the End User Marketing Manager commented:

> We simply depended on trial and error. We were desperate for business. Carriers told us they needed 500 TEUs to justify a new port call, but end users were not confident of the operations and customs formalities, despite the fact that the cost of shipping via a Chinese port meant substantial savings.[17]

Meanwhile, the YICT team was encouraged by the comments of Maersk's Managing Director, Henrik Zeuthen, reported in the *South China Morning Post*:

> Mr Zeuthen said Yantian offered several advantages to consignees compared with Hong Kong. One is that it is close to the cargo. Most of the factories set up by Hong Kong manufacturers after China adopted its open door policy in the late 1970s are located in southern China. Second, since Yantian is not crowded, ships are able to turn around much faster than in Hong Kong, which has become increasingly congested. To promote shipments from Yantian, Maersk sent separate teams of officials to US and to Europe immediately after starting the two services (*South China Morning Post: Freight & Shipping Post* 28 November 1994: 3).

Armed with insights from the research that had been conducted, the newly formed End User Marketing Team targeted the toys industry and department stores sector to promote the use of 'FOB China (Free on Board)' shipping terms going through Yantian. They worked with the end users on pinpointing the economics and cost benefits of using the new port. They drew attention to the saving that could be derived from a lower trucking cost in taking the cargo from the manufacturing base in South China to Yantian as opposed to taking the cargo across the border to Hong Kong.[18]

Customers were telling YICT's marketing people that the ability to achieve reliability through smooth customs procedures was critical to success. This meant both understanding and assisting the customer. As the End User Marketing Manager explained:

We have to understand the customers from all angles. No one wants to change when it is uncertain. If we become their friends, they will tell you what actually stops things from happening. We discovered we needed to do a lot of handholding at the ground level to make the grand strategy work.[19]

To provide a handholding service, therefore, YICT established a service team known as the 'China Affairs Department' to handle customs enquiries and building understanding and relationships between the regulatory authorities and YICT's customers. For instance:

In one case, we contacted and worked with over twenty-five South China vendors on behalf of a toys retailer to convert them to buy FOB China. Through examples and pilot projects, we convinced them and their customer in US that going through Da Peng Customs (the customs office supervising the Yantian port) could be efficient and smooth. We connected them with the customs people and provided a handholding service in case of need to execute the orders.[20]

The practice of marketing to indirect customers was not without controversy. Traditionally port marketing in Hong Kong was focused on immediate customers, the shipping lines. There was little experience of going beyond them. Secondly, the end users were large in number and spread out over several continents, which involved significant costs in marketing to them. Reaching out to the end users and leveraging their influence on the choice of port decision was unexplored territory.

Traditional wisdom indicated that ports should market to their direct customers – the shipping lines only. YICT had made a serious attempt to do this to demonstrate the port's viability. They marketed the port as a strategic choice in the carriers' drive into China.[21] At the time when multinational companies were putting their toes in the water to try out their investment strategy in China, or, according to McKinsey Consultants, pursuing Phase 1 of their China strategy, only far-sighted shipping lines like Maersk explored the importance of using a South China port as their base, while others waited. So the initial marketing appeal of Yantian fell on only a few receptive ears.

End user marketing was tedious, but it soon produced interesting results. It generated some pressure on the carriers from their customers to explore calling at the new port. These end users were eager to push their logistics providers to help them save cost, and the US\$ 200–300 saving per container was an attractive signal. Indeed, the General Manager recalled being confronted by a shipping line executive as 'forcing us to use Yantian', to which he responded by interpreting the activities as 'canvassing cargo' for YICT's immediate customers.[22] Of course, YICT management had to be very careful not to offend their immediate customers. Fairly soon, however, shipping lines conducted studies and discovered that, with operating efficiency, customs facilitation, and end user marketing, the new port was proving itself to be a viable alternative to Hong Kong. Traffic growth gathered momentum from 1996 onwards and the number of shipping calls at Yantian soon doubled every other year.

YICT has not stopped marketing to end users. Following its initial success, YICT management put in additional resources and increased the level of activity to cover more than just the initial group of customers. It launched more organized penetrations of different markets in different locations. Through a conscious effort to listen to customers, the marketing team channelled their voice back to the organization in an effort to improve services as well as create new ones. Over the years, YICT has modified its offerings effectively to cater to the needs of both its immediate customers and its end users in the form of tailored services like the 'HK-Yantian Shuttle', 'Special Christmas Storage Project', 'Speedy Gates for Selected Customers', 'Buyers' Information System', 'End User Special Depots', 'Dedicated Train Services', and 'Special Project Cargo'. Some of these projects were later integrated into the generic service package. Together with the service teams dedicated to helping customers, these special efforts or value added services helped establish the 'YICT Brand'.

There have always been differing views about end user marketing. Dissenters argued that undertaking marketing and promotions to such a diverse group of customers was not the best use of resources and that its usefulness might be limited to the early stage of development when the port was still not known. However, since a port is literally a fixed facility, ways of extending both its hinterland and its range of services represent basic strategic moves to increase its business (Hedges, 2008).

MANAGING THE ECOLOGICAL SYSTEM

'Necessity is the mother of invention', commented the Project Manager of Pingyan Railways, a subsidiary of YICT running the 24 kilometre rail system connecting the port and the national rail system. 'I should have the title of manager of the world's shortest freight railway system!'[23] We shared a laugh as he told the researcher about the positioning of YICT's new acquisition. As part of the Phase 3 package, YICT expanded the port's facilities and acquired a RMB 350 million asset to connect the port with the national rail system. The intention was to increase the port's competitiveness through utilizing yet another means of channelling cargo its way.

> Currently, 95 per cent of cargo using Yantian comes in and out through the trucking system. Thousands of trucks run around in Guangdong province serving a radius of up to 300 kilometres from the port. However, as manufacturers are moving more and more inland, there is a growing demand for inland transportation and we think the rail system will soon be instrumental to facilitating that change. We are expanding our connections to Dalang and our next stop is Shaoguan at the border of Guangdong province.[24]

In addition to their transportation responsibilities, the railway company executives were also charged with developing the warehouse and depot businesses around the port. Even though the size of warehouses and depots run by YICT were relatively small, compared to the other operators, the Railway General Manager saw their significance in broader terms:

> The purpose of our warehouse and depot businesses is not to run profitable businesses per se. Rather, they are there to facilitate end users to utilize the port better – they are part of our attractiveness to users like Sony and Mattel who require more by way of a logistics service than just "lift on lift off" from a port operator.[25]

To enhance the attractiveness of the nearby area to port users, YICT was also engaged in facilitating active dialogue between other warehouse and depot operators and the regulatory authorities. An Assistant General Manager was in charge of a 'social club' of warehouse and logistics operators, with an express purpose of creating a mutually beneficial environment for all operators in the community. Topics discussed included facilitation of traffic in the area in times of crises, and joint lobbying of the authorities for improvements in customs procedures.

Further afield, 24 kilometres northwest of the port, the Hutchison group managed an inland container depot, a warehousing complex of 40 hectares in size. The inland container depot and YICT were connected with a global positioning system [GPS] that enabled customs to track cargo in trucks via satellite technology. Thus the two facilities were integrated as one. This was another effort to integrate the value chain and to build into the chain features that would make it attractive to channel cargo to YICT.

In the community, YICT was active in helping the Shenzhen SEZ to become a logistics centre. One of the areas in which the company was heavily involved was traffic management. In 2002, it contributed RMB 250 million as part of the Phase 3 project to building a set of flyover systems just outside the port. The Mingzhu Exchange later proved to be instrumental in easing traffic jams and is now the main artery for channelling traffic in and out of the port. In 2003, the company supported the employment of 20 traffic policemen at times of heavy traffic flow. Since the port was the main user of the road system in the vicinity, its control centre was electronically linked with the district traffic control centre and the two centres communicate on a very frequent basis. YICT also contributed to installing some of the traffic management equipment in the area. YICT as the largest business operator in Shenzhen has also made investments in software development in Easyport and a community system to connect users for the exchange of information. Easyport was an initiative developed by YICT between 2003 and 2006 to provide information exchanges among port users. To achieve real-time tracking of the whereabouts of cargo in transition and the status of customs clearance, port users needed timely information to make logistics decisions. Such a platform helped the terminal operator communicate with its users and increased the 'stickiness' of end-user customers to the port.

> The rationale behind all this involvement, the General Manager explained, 'is to create an ecological system that attracts users and outcompetes our competitors. We will participate in related businesses not to win in them *per se* but to help create an environment where all players win, and if logistics businesses around the Yantian area become successful we become more successful (General Manager's comments in the YICT Executive Team Seminar, October 2005).

In the same vein, YICT seriously examined the possibility of investing in more warehousing and depot businesses in Yantian and the related areas. As a standing member of the Shenzhen Political Consultative Committee, the General Manager put forward a concept of a 'virtual free port', suggesting the use of information technology to connect all free zone areas and other related areas into a 'virtual free trade zone'. The Shenzhen government reacted favourably to the concept and drafted an application to the central government seeking approval to grant the special powers required.

Another contribution to the local Shenzhen environment was YICT's adoption of a 'Green Port' policy. In January 2007, YICT was presented with an Environmental Protection Certificate from the Shenzhen Pengcheng Waste Reduction Steering Committee for its efforts to reduce waste and protect the environment. At the time, YICT had plans for over 70 environmental projects including the replacement of old equipment with new modern energy-efficient equipment, a reduction in the electrical output of the facility's quay cranes through the modification of circuits and modes of operation, the systematic up-grade of the rubber-tyred gantry cranes whereby diesel-powered engines would be replaced with electric-powered engines, automation of its office space, installation of an automatically controlled central air conditioning unit, a solar-powered heating system, smart and energy-saving street lamps, as well as a programme to heighten the environmental awareness of its staff. In June 2007, YICT signed a Memorandum of Understanding with the Port of Long Beach, California, another leader in environmental port policies, to exchange technical information on their best environmental policies and practices. The aim of the agreement was for the two ports to collaborate on environmental issues such as marine wildlife, air quality, soils and sediments, water quality, sustainability and community engagement. According to YICT's General Manager:

> As a world-class port, we recognize our social responsibility and the importance of safeguarding the environment. By working closely with the "green" Port of Long Beach, we can both implement better long-term, sustainable strategies to ensure environmental protection in all our commercial activities (Port of Long Beach News Release, June 12 2007).

NOTES

1. In addition to sources specifically noted, this chapter draws on YICT company records, some of the Birmingham University Master's dissertation projects conducted in YICT, and many conversations with the company's General Manager.
2. YICT 1994 Business Plan.
3. YICT 1997 Business Plan.
4. YICT 2000 Business Plan.
5. YICT Mission Statement, September 1995.
6. Interview with the Head of Service Delivery and Development, July 2005.
7. Six Sigma launch, 4 November 2002.
8. Colmar Brunton Consultants, YICT Customer Satisfaction Final Report, 16 October 2006.
9. Relationship pricing refers to different pricing for customers usually on the basis of volume. Tally fees are charged by an external agency for tallying service, but often absorbed by the terminal as part of the per box handling fee.
10. TNS consultants, YICT Customer Satisfaction Study Final Report, 28 September 2006.
11. YICT Employee Engagement Survey, October 2004.
12. YICT, Design Specifications for Phase 2.
13. YICT Internal Reports, 2007.
14. Interview with the Deputy General Manager, July 2004.
15. Market Study Reports by the End User Marketing Team, September 1995.
16. End User Market Report, July 1995.

17. Interview with the Deputy General Manager, July 2004.
18. YICT Presentation to end users, End User Marketing Department Report to Management 1995 and other marketing materials.
19. Interview with the End User Marketing Manager, July 2005.
20. Interview with Cargo Sourcing Manager, July 2005.
21. YICT promotional material, 1995.
22. Interviews with the General Manager, End User Marketing Manager, and Deputy General Manager, 2004, 2005.
23. Interview with the Railway General Manager, August 2005.
24. Interview with the Railway General Manager, August 2005.
25. Interview with the Railway General Manager, August 2005.

REFERENCES

Amen, K. (2005), 'Six Sigma in the East', Unpublished Master of Science dissertation, Birmingham Business School, University of Birmingham, UK.

Garner, J.E. (2005), 'The transferability of international HRM into mainland China', Unpublished Master of Science dissertation, Birmingham Business School, University of Birmingham, UK.

Hedges, C. (2008), 'Port development and expansion: within customers logisitics chains and the South-East China region, the case of YICT', Unpublished Master of Science dissertation, Birmingham Business School, University of Birmingham, UK.

Heuermann, D. (2006), 'Cross-cultural influences and their impacts on the application and implementation of a culture change process in mainland China', Unpublished Master of Science dissertation, Birmingham Business School, University of Birmingham, UK.

McHale, B. (2005), 'Impediments to building a strong international organizational culture in China', Unpublished Master of Science dissertation, Birmingham Business School, University of Birmingham, UK.

Nhankaniso, F. (2007), 'Six Sigma and its critical success factors', Unpublished Master of Science dissertation, Birmingham Business School, University of Birmingham, UK.

7. Relationship management – creating a relational framework

YICT's management consciously set out to develop its relational framework with governmental and regulatory authorities through what it called 'relationship management'. It concentrated its efforts on three areas. The first was with the Chinese partner (effectively the Shenzhen SEZ government) to create a good working relationship. The second was with Chinese government ministries in an effort to secure timely approval for port development and expansion. The third area concerned the management of relationships with the governmental regulatory authorities operating in the port. This was aimed at producing an efficient service for the port's customers.

In each of these areas, YICT management orchestrated a programme of developing the company's external relationships in a continuing effort to learn about, adapt to, and influence its specific environment. This was an intentional activity on the part of managers which serves to demonstrate that a relational framework does not simply emerge by chance. During the course of the company's evolution, its managers learned that they had to handle the institutional constraints they faced in a proactive manner which required the fostering of appropriate relationships. At the time when they were first confronted with these constraints, they struggled and tried to achieve results through a common sense approach. A more systematic approach, involving conscious relationship management, evolved only as a result of repeated learning and review.

It is commonly recognized among those concerned with joint ventures based in China that managing relationships or 'guanxi' is a critical success factor. Some have gone as far as inventing a term 'guan xi xue' for the study of relationship management in the Chinese context (Yang, 1994). In an infrastructure project like a large port development, managing relationships becomes particularly critical. Since most if not all the major activities involve various levels and areas of government, having a systematic and structured 'government relationship' programme is essential for the implementation of a comprehensive and considered strategy.

In YICT, the planning and execution of such relationship management has been directed from the most senior level in the organization. The

General Manager, his deputies and senior managers all had relationship responsibilities. They were assisted by full-time 'relationship managers'. All members of the executive team became heavily involved in the execution of relationship management. To provide insights and help, YICT engaged a group of advisors from various sources, often academics and retired government officials. The advisors helped executives understand the changing situation, especially regarding changes of policy or emphasis. They also provided the requisite connections and assisted in the undertaking of lobbying. When issues called for very senior contacts, higher levels within Hutchison became involved in opening doors and pushing for significant breakthroughs. For instance, during the course of applying for exemptions and obtaining approvals to build additional phases of the port, the Hutchison Group Chairman, Li Kashing, and the Group Managing Director, Canning Fok, intervened as required by the rules of protocol in dealing with government.

The need for relationship management in China is frequently mentioned, but the rationale and the skills for it to be effective are little discussed, let alone practised. Often people equate relationship building with buying lunches and dinners, and sending gifts and souvenirs. In YICT, however, these and other activities were carried out with a clear rationale and a well defined purpose. According to the company's Corporate Affairs Manager:

> Relationship building rests on a solid understanding of the working of the government and institutional system. If you want to get something done through the contacts you make, you must understand what drives their decision-making. You must understand what motivates them, what purpose and aspirations they have, what kind of authority they are given and what influences their thinking in choosing between alternatives. In other words, you must be an insider who processes the knowledge and skills of influencing patiently.[1]

Incidentally, this manager had previously worked for many years as research director and advisor to the Mayor of Shenzhen before he joined YICT. He therefore qualified as an insider. On the 'philosophy' of working effectively with government officials, the General Manager commented:

> We noticed that the economy was going through changes and government must be perceived to be leading the changes. At YICT we aim always to be at the forefront of technological advances as well as of the economic reforms so that we can lead the industry to become truly international. With the government we position ourselves to be working closely with them as partners in pursuit of a worthwhile aim together. We must be perceived to be

supportive of the overall economic development aims and programmes. The commercial objectives must be in line with the national development agenda for the officials to be able to lend their support. But we keep a distance and lead with ideas (Memorandum from the General Manager to the YICT Chairman, October 1997).

Equipped with insider knowledge, an emphatic attitude and a guiding concept of leading with ideas, the YICT management team began to chart its course in the muddy waters of managing partners, ministries and government agencies.

MANAGING RELATIONSHIPS WITH THE JOINT VENTURE PARTNER

The relationship between the principal partners in the YICT joint venture went through a sequence of stages: initial coming together, conflict, reaching understanding then working together.

In December 1993, immediately after the first Board Meeting when the General Manager and Deputy Executive General Manager were appointed, establishment of the YICT management team began in earnest. The joint venture contract specified that the General Manager seconded from the international partner took overall responsibility for the company and he would be assisted by the Deputy Executive General Manager seconded from the Chinese party. The YICT General Manager reported to the YICT Board of Directors, with a dotted line to HPH. The Deputy General Manager reported to the YICT General Manager and its Board of Directors, with a dotted line to YPG and the Shenzhen Party Secretary.[2] Once appointed, the General Manager quickly assembled his team of executives – key among them were a British manager responsible for operations, and a commercial director and a finance manager, both from Hong Kong. The Deputy General Manager persuaded four of his colleagues to leave the Chinese port group to join the joint venture. They were to be responsible for 'Chinese related' aspects of running the port, namely managing customs and government relationships as well as canvassing cargo from the hinterland. The small team got started in Shenzhen to prepare for operations and in six months moved to Yantian to establish a base for operations.

In the initial phase of coming together and forming a company to attack the market, the key challenges were to establish trust and a working relationship between the partners, and the main task at hand was to secure business from the market. As the market was only responding in a lukewarm manner to the new facilities, the international partner tried to establish its credibility by demonstrating technical competence in running the operations.[3] It was a difficult period, as both parties were trying to understand one another and establish a working relationship. Even though the team, composed of Hong Kong Chinese managers and a couple of British and Singaporean expatriates, were learning quickly, cultural differences compounded the difficulties associated with two different companies and setups merging into one. While the fact that the international partner had majority control meant that it held the final decision-making power, many differences in habits and practices could give rise to conflict in the day-to-day conduct of the business.

For example, there were differences of opinion as to how to approach the negotiations with the Customs Administration on working hours and simplifying cargo clearance practices. The international managers pressed for clear-cut agreements, while the local managers advised patience and accommodation. However, during the process of negotiation, when problems persisted despite promises being made, it was hard to judge if any progress had been made at all. The Deputy General Manager later described the process as 'circular but a different circle every time'. He continued:

> We need to understand that this was a negotiation over 'power and benefits': the authorities had power and they wanted to trade concessions (i.e. operating improvements), for benefits that help them do a better job in the eyes of their staff and seniors … Everybody wants clear cut progress but this had to come in different doses in exchange for different concessions from the terminal.[4]

It was difficult for the western trained managers to work with a high level of ambiguity, such as when what appeared to be real progress turned out to be part of the bargaining process. There were also differences over who in the company should deal with government authorities, and how. For a short period of time, the General Manager decided to delegate this activity to an outside operator who promised to smooth the relationships in a basket of deals with the authorities, bundled with the operator's warehousing business in Yantian. The Deputy General Manager disagreed, but kept quiet and waited for results to come in. The arrangement did not work out because, while the third party helped maintain a smooth functioning of the current customs operations, when it came to effecting changes, it was ineffective.

Even though the majority owners clarified their formal authority, the international managers were conscious of the need to gain acceptance and exercise influence. Through the HPH network, they were aware of the problems of managing a joint venture port in China. For example, in Shanghai Container Terminals where HPH had a 50/50 equity joint venture and each side sent a manager for every position, getting agreement and achieving change had been troublesome. With that understanding, the YICT team largely composed of international expatriates made special efforts to be culturally sensitive. They were aware that they spoke a different language and were confronted with a different way of getting things done in a 'familiar yet foreign country'. As chief executive and company representative, the General Manager was very conscious of the need to show humility and respect for local managers. He quickly learnt to speak Mandarin Chinese fluently and adopted a 'semi-Chinese' management style in terms of listening before speaking, learning before directing, being open and kind but firm and demanding, paying attention face to face, and showing respect to individuals especially to lower-level employees. Amongst his main colleagues, the Deputy General Manager, who was the Chinese partner's representative, also played a key role. He demonstrated a down-to-earth professional style of working that focused on getting results rather than politicking or fighting for power. The British Operations Manager also played his part in adapting to the local environment. He adopted a friendly attitude and soon spoke a level of Cantonese that endeared him to his colleagues who nicknamed him 'Gweilo Tim'.

The modest and professional attitude displayed by the international management group helped them to project a good image. The Chinese executives initially viewed the relationship with a 'wait-and-see' attitude, but when over time the international team demonstrated a task orientation – namely focusing on getting the job done above all else – they accepted that they might have something to learn from the international management team. As YICT's management got into serious discussions on 'turning the vicious cycle to a virtuous cycle' by searching for answers, and when its experiments incorporated a lot of ideas from the Chinese partner, such as the Hong Kong-Yantian Shuttle and the marketing programme to end users, some real cooperation began to emerge. Both parties felt that they had a lot to learn and the effective answers could only come from integrating western management with a solid analysis of the case embedded in the particular Chinese business environment. The final acceptance by both sides of what each had to offer came when the experiments proved successful. Their success incorporated the best thinking and processes of both joint venture partners. The Hong Kong party brought technology, and operational systems, and a lot of confidence from international carriers. The Mainland Chinese executives brought an excellent understanding of how to approach customs facilitation and local marketing. In retrospect, the fact that two chief executives worked well together in compatible styles was also a key factor in establishing an atmosphere of cooperation that set the scene for subsequent development. Performance and the quality of relationships reinforced each other – being able to work together undoubtedly led to more effective solutions but at the same time success eased tensions and improved the quality of cooperation.

However, while cooperation in the executive team evolved well, it did not totally resolve the differences between the partners. In respect of port development, significant issues remained as to the timing of the next phase of civil construction. The Chinese partner, ultimately represented by the Chairman of the Yantian Port Group and behind him the municipal government in the person of the Vice Mayor, was driven partly by political considerations to push development faster than the circumstances demanded while the international partner desired economic prudence in investment, not least in view of the huge losses being incurred.[5] The two partners used different measurements in assessing capacity and demand. By its very nature, forecasting economic growth and demand for terminal services was difficult. The picture was complicated further when views were taken before studies began. For example, in predicting growth, the Chinese authorities used cargo forecasts based on Guangdong Province, without considering the throughput that would go through Hong Kong. On the other hand, when the Hong Kong government conducted its forecasts, it also ignored the Shenzhen ports. So to the Chinese partner, the future was always rosy, sometimes more so than the numbers justified. The two partners also tended to use different methods of estimating the supply side. The design capacity of 400 000 TEUs per berth was used to argue in favour of early expansion of capacity, while the actual capacity of each berth could become 1 million TEUs. A more reasonable figure would be 800 000 TEUs, as later operations demonstrated.

So, with different motivations and supported by studies that emphasized different aspects of the case, the two parties continued to differ. The Chinese party was of course aware of the formal agreement that building the next phase (Phase 2) would not be required before the 'trigger point' – 70 per cent of design capacity – was reached. But it was unwilling to wait that long. Through high level meetings and exchanges of correspondence, it put pressure on the management team to try new ways to turn around the slow start-up situation and to shorten the port's gestation period. The international partner, however, pointed out that the reforms and changes stipulated in the original agreements had not been realized and that this inhibited progress. For example, in a letter dated 5 June 1996, YICT's Chairman wrote to the Party Secretary, the Mayor and the Executive Vice Mayor of Shenzhen providing a list of 'unfinished' items and requesting urgent attention to customs improvements and infra-structural developments like electricity and communications installations. In the Chinese context, however, it would not be acceptable for these disagreements and arguments to come out in the open. In most if not all communications, the executives on both sides painstakingly ensured that the accent was always on the positive, that appropriate protocols were observed, and that good manners prevailed in meetings and banquets.

The issue over the timing of the next phase of civil construction was finally resolved with the majority shareholder deciding to build ahead of plan and ahead of the 'trigger point' agreement. It judged that the trajectory for growth of business would justify the investment eventually, and that it would be better to take a slightly higher risk of investing earlier than losing out to other competitors. In 1996, the decision to invest HK$4.7 billion into a new development when the terminal was operating only at 25 per cent capacity surprised many observers. As events turned out, that decision worked in favour of the company in an important way. It brought to the port the capacity necessary to cater for the tremendous growth resulting from a migration of cargo from Hong Kong ports to Yantian. While, on the face of things, the international partner made a compromise, it turned out to benefit both parties. That also paved the way for subsequent cooperation between the partners.

Partner Relationships and the Port's Development

Against the background of the Chinese economic reform and growth making significant strides in the late 1990s and China's forthcoming accession to the WTO in 2001, the planners and operators of Yantian port had cause for optimism. The terminal was enjoying strong double digit throughput growth since reaching the 1 million TEU mark in 1998, with the number of shipping services getting increasingly frequent. There had been an annual growth in trade between China and the USA as well as Europe of over 25 per cent for more than five years, and this seemed to be continuing. FDI into China was reaching new heights. The terminal reported its first profitable year in 1997, with significant growth antici-pated. Both the Chinese and the international parties realized that it would be a good time to expand. This led to the Phase 3 and Phase 3 Expansion (Phase 3E) projects.

The importance of these investments for the development of Yantian port cannot be over-stated. Together, they defined a port of mega size and complexity. The Phase 3 negotiations that took place between 1999 and 2002 provide a good example of partner management in action.

Chapter 5 described how the negotiations were protracted and at times turbulent. They lasted for three years. There were numerous rounds of discussions, some formal, others informal; some directly face to face and some through the written word between the two parties at various levels. Behind the scenes, both parties organized a large number of lobbying activities, mounting various exercises in persuasion, power play and political compromising. Here we focus on initiatives taken by YICT's management, backed up by its HPH parent group.

To counter the negative voices on the Chinese side who were arguing for at least a controlling interest in the expanded facility, a small group of lobbyists headed by YICT's General Manager and assisted by his advisors mounted a series of what they called 'public relations campaigns' aimed at specific audiences. For government circles in Shenzhen, they produced reports which showed the benefits of joint venturing, namely the influx of capital, the provision of port development experience, commercial connections and operational management expertise. These reports also showed how Yantian's development benefitted from its association with Hutchison's international network and extensive back-up expertise. More importantly, the international investors demonstrated how the joint venture actually brought financial returns to all the shareholders, majority and minority alike. The timing of this input was significant because it was designed to coincide with YICT's first dividend payment to its shareholders in 2000. To fortify their message, the international investors engaged an independent consultant, the Shenzhen China Development Institute [CDI], to conduct a study on the future development of Yantian port. The CDI, a semi-government research organization, was headed by the former secretary-general of the Shenzhen municipal government. The institute was staffed by academics and researchers who also consulted on development projects. The YICT team cooperated well with CDI in producing a credible report in favour of joint venturing and continuing with the existing arrangements.

YICT management was also active among government circles in Beijing whose opinions really mattered, setting out its arguments and organizing systematic 'persuasion' campaigns. It accessed opinion leaders in ministries like the Ministry of Communications [MOC] and the National Development and Reform Commission [NDRC] as well as leading researchers in the capital's think tanks. In Beijing, arguments for and against reform and opening had not ceased since the 1980s and one could always find supporters of either position. However, reformist views seemed to be able to secure more responses now that the country's political inclination was for more rather than less opening to inter-nationalization, attracting more FDI and continuing with modernization and change.

The YICT story had, of course, to be a credible one to merit attention and support. To articulate the story in the language and context of Chinese reforms, YICT engaged a leading expert in transportation to help develop YICT's strategy development plan for the next five years. His report linked the development of Yantian port to the development agenda of the nation, for instance through the vision of developing 'world-class' facilities for 'mega vessels'.[6] Through the expert's connections, the report was delivered to decision-makers in the MOC and the NDRC in order to pre-empt opposing views. Having completed the report and convinced that Yantian port's development was in the interest of the nation's port industry, the expert helped introduce and present YICT senior managers to policy makers and opinion leaders in the ministries. Think tanks also contributed to the lobbying process. Under the overall policy guideline of attracting more FDI and developing the port as a model for the whole country, arguments could be put forward that a continuation of present policy in the case of Yantian was acceptable. While it was acknowledged that YICT's majority non-Mainland ownership was exceptional, this was argued to be beneficial to the country's development and opening to the world economy, and should therefore be allowed to continue.

The Chinese partner, YPG, held the key as to whether the next phase of cooperation would proceed and if so with whom. The appeal to its leaders would require a considerable and careful interpersonal effort. Organizationally they reported to the Shenzhen municipal government and were therefore highly influenced, indeed directed, by it. In a highly politicized environment, the Shenzhen authorities' stance had to be expressed in terms that accorded with the rationality of the then current policy emphases on national development. Relationship development with the leaders in YPG took place through both formal inter-organizational channels and informal interpersonal meetings. Interperson-ally, all HPH and YICT executives were conscious of the need to show the partners the right level of respect and ensure a high level of personal comfort in day-to-day dealings. The YPG Chairman was invited to meet with HPH's chief executive to discuss future cooperation prospects. YICT's General Manager travelled with him to Europe on a study trip and they became better acquainted as colleagues and friends. The occasion of a visit from an expert Beijing acquaintance to Shenzhen offered the opportunity of providing a favourable third party opinion. These relationship building efforts involved many rounds of formal and informal discussions on the pros and cons of cooperation and competition, and they eventually opened up the possibility of frank dialogues and compromises.

Opinion within YPG was divided. Its Chairman tried to take a balanced view between economic and political considerations. The international investors offered YPG predictions of the consequences to be expected for both competition and cooperation scenarios in the belief that the latter would be seen to be the more attractive option. For example, in a presentation to a senior group of YPG executives, the YICT General Manager discussed the likely downside of 'competition' in specific terms:

> In Yantian, the profitability game hinges on managing revenue and we rely on a relatively monopolistic position at least in the eastern side of Shenzhen to ensure that the revenue stream remains healthy. If Phase 3 has different shareholders than Phases 1 and 2, and is managed separately, then price competition is likely. In an effort to attract customers, Phase 3 management will have to lower prices and YICT Phases 1 and 2 will have to follow. That affects the bottom line immediately. Furthermore, for Phase 3, there is a start up period when revenue income will be below the costs of depreciation because of a heavy up-front outflow of cash. This will create a most undesirable situation for YPG – you will suffer double hits i.e. lower profit from YICT Phase 1 and 2 (less revenue because of competition from Phase 3), while Phase 3, in which you are considering taking a majority stake, will suffer big start-up losses (Presentation to YPG by the YICT General Manager, October 2000).

With YICT contributing more than 70 per cent of YPG's income, this scenario was a cause for alarm within the organization. YPG executives began to take a detailed look at the economic realities. Over time, the Chinese party became convinced that economically it would be more beneficial to it to stay as a minority shareholder of a sole operator, which consequently remained more profitable, rather than creating a new unit with a different kind of ownership. However, it was still important for them to be perceived as having fought the battle hard and coming out winning the game. In the event, the international partner had to make concessions. Gradually, the doubters in YPG changed the tone of their arguments to focus on 'benefits rather than equity; long-term rather than short-term'. This was how the YPG Chairman expressed his view during negotiations, which he repeated when he lobbied for support in both YPG and in Beijing.

The two sides gradually moved towards a compromise. The issue of equity was discussed but was left pending a final decision at the HPH and Shenzhen government levels. The sharing of other infrastructure costs was grouped together with the infrastructure for regulatory authorities, which amounted to some RMB 700 million to 800 million. As part of the package, YPG wanted to dispose of its loss-making rail operations, which YICT would take over as a strategic investment. Then there was the price of land over which both sides had only limited flexibility because the Shenzhen Land Bureau had the right to decide the matter. It took several summit meetings in Hong Kong in the period of August 1999 to April 2000, between HPH's Chairman and CEO representing the international party and the Shenzhen Deputy Mayor and the YPG Chairman representing the Chinese party, to agree on the equity issue and overall transaction price.

Examination of the detailed agreement governing Phase 3 and subsequently Phase 3E points to a consistency in partner relationship management. The international partner's perspective was primarily focused on the market and its long-term implications for the joint venture. When the overall economics justified letting go of certain benefits, the international partner was ready to trade short-term losses for long-term gains, and in this way accommodated the distinct objectives of the Chinese partner. The Phase 3 negotiations could well have developed into a stalemate with both parties demanding majority ownership and control. As the result of an accommodating attitude on the part of the international partner combined with considerable lobbying at various organizational levels, the Chinese partner became convinced that having a less than 50 per cent share of a growing pie was actually the preferable position. The cost benefit analysis supported this conclusion; while on the inter-personal level the Chinese side felt that their points had been listened to and respected, making it possible for them to agree.[7]

Another example of this approach to partner relationship management was the handling of the potentially conflictual Yantian Westport situation. The Yantian Westport was a 7 berth terminal situated at the west side of YICT, adjacent to existing YICT Phases 1 and 2 terminals. Originally designed as a multi-purpose terminal to handle general cargo and container business, Yantian Westport was built and managed by Yantian Port Holdings Limited, a Yantian Port Group subsidiary and a YICT minority shareholder. The question of whether the Westport facilities should compete with YICT had been debated since its inception in 1998. According to the international partner, the Westport should not be in the container business at all, since the Shenzhen government had ceded the exclusive right to operate a container business within the 6 kilometre of coastline to the Hutchison-led consortium on signing of the Yantian master agreement in 1993. However, the management of the Westport was of the opinion that its multi-purpose berths could also operate in the

container business. So a potential conflict arose between the two partners. That it did not become a legal battle was the result of three years of
negotiations amongst the 'relationship managers' of the two parties
involved: YICT and Yantian Port Holdings Limited [YPH], and an
exercise in the art of compromise.

In the beginning of the process, both parties insisted on their rights and
tried to convince the other party to concede. A compromise appeared
unlikely. Meanwhile, motivated by the opportunity to run an independent
and profitable terminal operation, the Chinese party pushed ahead with
the investment and the operation of the facilities. Applying political
pressure, YICT escalated the issue to the Shenzhen government level.
Two main principles were then agreed: (1) that the two operating units
should not end up in 'unhealthy' competition, namely fierce price
competition to the detriment of development of the Shenzhen port as a
whole; (2) that the two units should seek areas of common interests so
that cooperation became possible. Finally, after many rounds of heated
discussions, a compromise emerged dovetailing the different positions:
that the two companies form a two-tier structure for Westport. The
structure was designed so that at the first tier the Chinese party held a
majority share, while the foreign partner held a majority share in the
second tier operating company. In this way, it met the need of the
Chinese party to incorporate the Westport into its annual report, satisfying its shareholders that it was a port operator, while effectively the
second tier company, an operating unit, would run the company day-to-
day. YICT's intention was to avoid head-on competition, especially from
a terminal right next door, and sharing some of the resulting gains
became a relatively easy solution.

Thus, on both the Phase 3 development and the Yantian Westport, the
two partners started off with different positions in 1999/2000 and over
the subsequent years they resolved their differences through acceptable
compromises. When the NDRC approval finally came to Shenzhen in
March 2005, the YPG Chairman celebrated the successful conclusion as a
good example of Shenzhen/Hong Kong cooperation. In the celebration
party, he said:

> Thanks to the direction and support of the government, we at YPG are very
> pleased with the cooperation we have achieved with our partner, the Hutch-
> ison Group. Together, we have created a 'joint economic body' a closely
> knitted body of mutual interests bonded into the future of YICT. Together we
> are moving forward to a more prosperous future (Speech by the Chairman of
> YPG at the Phase 3 Celebration Party, 8 March 2005 – translated from his
> Chinese handwritten note).

The concept of a 'joint economic body' – an entity where both parties shared the economic benefits – vividly described the key role of YICT as a joint venture. YICT's contributions to the Chinese partner's profitability grew to make up over 70 per cent of YPH's income.[8] The increase in the Chinese partner's percentage equity holding had actually contributed to cementing the economic relationship further. As the joint venture grew and became a significant contributor to both parties' profitability, it was in both their interests to ensure that their joint investment bore fruit.

YICT has been regarded as an example of a well managed partner relationship in Shenzhen government circles.[9] In arguing for continuation of the partnership in Phase 3E, the support of the Chairman of the Yantian Port Group was critical, which he gave willingly. The partners were able to compromise on the Westport Project, in the form of an agreement between Yantian Port Holdings and YICT to cooperate rather than compete in a neighbouring facility. The partners also jointly invested in the Yantian Tug Boat Company, with YICT serving as a minority shareholder. These cooperative successes were certainly assisted by smooth relationship management. However, other factors also helped to achieve this outcome. One is the controlling interest enjoyed by the international managers. There were several instances where the dominant position of the international partner helped ease the decision-making process on controversial issues such as in: (1) the initial positioning of the terminal and purchase of additional equipment during the early problematic years; and (2) the decision to develop Phases 2 and 3 earlier than anticipated.

It could also be argued that another positive factor for the relationships between the partners, and hence YICT's evolution, was their shared desire to secure growth. The Chinese partner consistently supported the port's expansion, motivated by political and social considerations to do with the development of Shenzhen. Indeed, initially there was some concern on the local partner's part that the controlling international consortium would not be fully committed to expansion in Yantian so as not to affect the Hong Kong port too adversely. So if the international partner took a positive view of the joint venture's economic future, it would not be difficult to create a consensus over the decision to expand. Majority ownership was not the deciding factor in this case.

In other aspects of management, like marketing and service delivery, human resource development, and culture management, majority ownership did bring about unity of command and singleness of purpose. Leadership could become more evident with a clearly established line of command. Nevertheless, even in the operational sphere the international managers preferred to proceed on the basis of collaboration rather than on the basis of ownership rights. When interviewed, senior managers attributed YICT's performance to a collaborative and customer oriented culture.[10] Indeed, collaboration between the two parties as symbolized by the relationship between the top managers seconded from both partners – the General and Deputy General Manager – was perceived as a key factor in achieving harmony and effectiveness in the joint venture.[11] One could argue that YICT's international joint venture format imposed an organizational constraint that could be turned into an advantage. For it augmented the 'relational framework' between the company and government, which provided a channel for dialogue and promoting understanding.

MANAGING GOVERNMENT RELATIONSHIPS FOR OBTAINING PORT DEVELOPMENT APPROVAL

The securing of approval for port development projects in China is another complex process. Hence a well coordinated strategy of developing the relevant government relationships is critical to getting approvals in time. In YICT, this was dealt with by the Assistant General Manager responsible for development, with the General Manager and his advisors providing help in connecting with the right contacts at the right time. The process was a complex one partly because it had to go through various levels of government bureaucracy, each of which had to be satisfied with the rationale of the investment. The country had inherited the mechanisms of a planned economy when it came to approving investments of a significant size. There were four broad stages in the process: (1) project registration; (2) project feasibility; (3) project design; and (4) project approval.

Each of these stages subdivided into detailed sub-stages at both local government and central levels. First the local government through its planning bureau had to check the project's economic feasibility because the Shenzhen government was a minority shareholder. At this stage, several rounds of expert panels would be held to cross check the economic feasibility report submitted by the investor-appointed consultancy, usually one of the four or five major engineering consultancies of the Ministry of Communications. This check was conducted to determine whether central government would accept the project to be registered. On approval, the Shenzhen Planning Bureau would submit the proposal to the city government for endorsement. There the Mayors would be invited to comment on the size and feasibility of the plans. Once city-level approval was obtained, the proposal was then submitted to Guangdong

Province and Beijing for MOC endorsement before it was passed onto the National Development and Reform Commission [NDRC] for 'verification'.

There were quite a few steps at the 'verification' stage – first economic feasibility, then engineering feasibility, and then whether the proposal complied strictly with national plans, and with foreign investment, industrial and environmental policies. Various sections within the NDRC would have to issue their opinions and comments with regard to their areas of expertise. For example, the section responsible for studying the project's impact on foreign trade would comment on this aspect of port investment on trade and whether it was the right time to approve such additional investment. If deemed necessary, the NDRC would appoint another consultancy body to provide a third party perspective. Before the limits were relaxed in 2005, the local government could only approve projects up to US$30 million in value. Any project above this amount would have to be approved in Beijing. One could easily imagine the number of projects exceeding US$30 million swamping the NDRC in the burgeoning economic environment of China in the 1990s and 2000s. The sheer amount of work and the limited number of officials in the MOC and NDRC would alone account for the delay in approvals. All project owners had to compete for attention to get their projects approved. The approval process sometimes took two years; a significant project often took three to five years.

In such circumstances, understanding the system and getting one's case heard was an art in itself, and an exercise of flexing one's muscles in building and executing relationship management amongst government circles. To navigate in such waters, YICT employed a group of advisors who either came from government ranks or had retired from active service but still maintained some influence in the current hierarchy. Theoretically, getting government approval was the Chinese partner's responsibility. So YICT joined forces with its Chinese partner to lobby actively for support at various levels. The ability to gain access was partly aided by YICT's reputation and that of the Hutchison Group Chairman, but it was also dependent on the skills of the executives involved in the lobbying efforts. With the Chinese government appointing new well-educated personnel to its upper-middle ranks, lobbying took on a different dimension. While YICT's significance was viewed in purely commercial terms by the investors, the perspective in government circles was quite different. It took into account wider political considerations to do with the national interest as well. Sometimes, the question of how development of the Yantian port would impact on Hong Kong was raised as a concern; sometimes the impact of a foreign owned port versus a port developed by local capital was discussed. In addition, with a planning mindset, bureaucrats in central government would question whether there would be an over-supply of facilities should all the port development projects submitted be approved.

Through the years, the YICT government relationship team built and maintained a framework of numerous relationships with various ministries both at the local and central government levels. The relationships were usually developed on a professional basis, aided by the high profile personality of the Group Chairman and the reputation of YICT as China's main hub. While the relationships were first and foremost maintained by personal contacts, the company was conscious of the need to keep government informed, through various means such as newsletters, seminars and conferences. In these ways, it built a reputation over time that, despite its private ownership status, the port's facilities were the best of their kind in China and could be used as a show piece for international visitors. A measure of its success in creating an image that supported its 'world-class' aspirations is that YICT became one of the ports most visited by foreign dignities interested in infrastructure development in China. In terms of representing China in the port industry, YICT had also secured a solid professional recognition that it was the 'best in class' in the industry.

The securing of approval for Phase 3 illustrates the required process of managing relationships to secure governmental approval. The process started in June 2000 after the signing of the MOU between the two parties to the joint venture, which expressed the agreement of the joint venture partners on the ownership issue. Final approval of the project was issued by the NDRC in March 2005. Over that period, several executives from YICT worked full-time on securing approval. They mobilized other resources like consultancies and think tanks in Shenzhen and Beijing to furnish reports and studies to review past developments and project future scenarios. The YPG and the Shenzhen government teams were also very active with full-time staff stationed in Beijing to ensure that the case was heard in a favourable light. Through the various stages and sub-stages of the approval process, detailed preparations were carried out to satisfy the enquiries made by different levels of officialdom. The YICT team headed by the General Manager visited Beijing at least monthly to meet officials from MOC and NDRC and their appointed economic and engineering consultants. 'Expert meetings' were held on different aspects of the proposal like economic feasibility, engineering design and environmental protection, and these were attended by leading experts from all over China. YICT and YPG, as well as the Shenzhen municipal government, sent their representatives as a joint force to present the Yantian case at these meetings. When managed well, these meetings became forums for shaping opinions and for exchanging developmental experiences.

In practice, as much lobbying took place outside the meetings as within them. In pre-meeting work, the lobbying teams provided the experts with information and reports that helped argue the case. They used their networks of acquaintances and influential friends to present an image of professionalism and to ensure that the case for Yantian was presented as a progressive change that was in line with the nation's development focus. In this aspect, YICT's Corporate Development Manager and the group of advisors played a key role. With their background as ex-government policy makers, implementers or advisors, they demonstrated an understanding of insider logic. In his report on Phase 3 development, the Corporate Development Manager remarked:

> It would be over simplistic to understand government relationships as giving gifts and buying lunches. China's FDI policy is a key aspect of Reform and Opening. Progress at every stage during the process must be preceded by clarity of thinking and policy. The Chinese way of thinking wants to dig deep into the rationale behind the development and the new policy. Otherwise the policy will not get full support in implementation. So it is important that people working on government relationships acquire a deep understanding of this and are able to articulate the logic, the underlying ideas and theory driving the project in order to win the respect of the various levels of government people we talk to. We must speak the same language, and indeed sometimes have to approach the problem from a higher perspective in order to persuade and gain acceptance (Corporate Development Manager's Report to YICT Management on Phase 3 Development, 19 January 2006).

So the YICT and YPG teams pursued a quiet campaign through months of working with different levels in government ministries, persuading as many people as they could along the way and gradually winning acceptance. In the process, senior Shenzhen officers like the Mayor and his deputy made an invaluable contribution in opening doors and articulating government perspectives on economic development using international capital and management. Senior Hutchison executives led by the Group Chairman received important visitors from Beijing to Hong Kong and Yantian, including a visit in mid-2000 by the Deputy Prime Minister who oversaw the work of the NDRC. They first obtained the endorsement of the Ministry of Communications as the 'supervisory ministry' before approaching the National Development and Reform Commission for 'verifications'. They convinced the planners that Yantian port development was in the national interest in line with FDI policy. The case of majority ownership was presented as a continuation of an exceptional case approved by the Prime Minister in 1993 and that in the spirit of cooperation all parties were satisfied that continuation of such an arrangement brought the best economic benefit to port development in Shenzhen. It took the joint efforts of the partners and the local government to achieve the necessary breakthrough.

MANAGING RELATIONSHIPS WITH IN-PORT REGULATORY AUTHORITIES

An issue of key importance to both the company and government concerned the practices of the government agencies located within Yantian and other Chinese ports. Due to the fact that they had the right to stop cargos moving in and out of the port, as well as to determine the speed of inspections, these agencies directly affected the port's productivity and the speed of turnaround that could be offered to customers. The ability of YICT to achieve its goal of becoming a 'world-class port' depended on finding ways of changing these agencies' practices. The relationship with the in-port regulatory agencies was therefore a vital one for the company to manage.

Before their consolidation in 1996, there were six government inspectorates operating in Chinese ports. From 1996, these activities were grouped into three agencies: the Customs Administration, the Frontier Inspectorate, and the Quarantine Inspectorate. All reported to central government ministries through a number of levels – city (Shenzhen), province (Guangzhou), and national (Beijing) – although as a special economic zone Shenzhen had direct access to Beijing. There was only limited local coordination between these agencies, despite the fact that officers of each agency in the port could decide which cargo to inspect, and whether to hold it up or even not let it through. Their responsibility was to ensure that regulations were adhered to, not whether a ship could leave or whether cargo was piling up. Their domain was defined as 'providing service while enforcing regulatory control'. They enjoyed considerable power – the city Mayor, even senior ministers, could not countermand their decisions because the agency officers were 'protecting the country' and any attempt to countermand them would raise suspicion about collusion or corruption. Their practices were therefore highly significant for the performance of the port.

The aim of YICT's majority owner, HPH, was that the new port should be treated as China's 'pilot site' for modern port facilities and management. It therefore pressed for a specification of reforms in government port administration as a condition for signing the contract for the joint venture in 1993. As a result and concomitant with the YICT joint venture agreement, China's State Council in October 1993 specified five directives for reforms to simplify customs and port clearance (see this chapter's Appendix). Although the signing of the agreement had received endorsement at the highest level, with both China's President and Prime Minister in attendance, implementation of the directives was initially resisted by the government agencies within Yantian port. For customs officers working in the port, the directives were regarded as statements of intention and were too general to guide implementation let alone to cause deeply entrenched practices to be changed.

Against a background of losses and difficulties in attracting business largely because of shippers' fears that the new port could not overcome Chinese bureaucratic holdups, this resistance to reform by the government agencies at the local level created growing frustration among YICT managers. They then decided to take action at central government level to try to break the deadlock. The first step was to mobilize support by establishing an advisory group of retired senior officials to facilitate their access to the relevant central government offices.

Senior staff from both HPH and YICT personally lobbied in the MOC, the central government ministry in charge of the port sector, as well as in the NDRC, the powerful bureau for national reform and change. As a result, it was agreed that YICT should fund a study group to examine the specific impact of government agencies on the port's performance. The study group consisted of middle-level officials from those government agencies. The study group's report was presented in August 1995.[12] The report requested permission to try out new streamlined customs procedures in Yantian port and to designate Yantian as the pilot site for reform in China's port sector as a whole. It passed up through various ministries and levels in the government system, finally gaining the endorsement of Vice-Premier Li Lanqing. Li Lanqing then passed the report with his positive comments to another Vice Premier, Zhou Jiahua, and to the head of the Customs Administration, Chien Kunlin. At the same time, YICT's General Manager also approached Chien for sympathetic help through the offices of the former Shenzhen Party Secretary, Li Hou, who enjoyed personal contact with Chien. The report eventually secured central government endorsement in the form of an MOU issued in November 1995. It led to the first significant reform of customs procedures in the port and, very importantly, to an official confirmation of the port as the 'pilot site' for national port administration reforms.

In the following year, the central government's Vice-Premier Li Lanqing produced his own document on port reform, the preparation of which HPH had influenced through facilitating several official studies of the best international practices in leading ports such as Hong Kong and Rotterdam. This government report recommended that the government agencies operating within ports should be consolidated into three; that their efficiency should be raised by applying 'scientific' techniques; and that they should adopt international practices. The report further opened up opportunities for YICT management to agree with the three consolidated government agencies (Customs, Frontier Inspectorate, and Quarantine) on the implementation of reforms within its port.

A reform initiative introduced by Premier Zhu Rongi in 1999 also had consequences for practices within the port. This was the containment of staff numbers working in government establishments – a freeze on staff count, and in some areas a reduction. This was applied at both central and local government levels. Most units responded through efforts to squeeze more productivity out of their existing manpower. The governmental in-port regulatory authorities found YICT's support, especially its moves toward automation and computerization, very important in handling the dilemma between expanding business activities and limited resources. For example, the use of technologies like CCTV in patrolling the port area and its vicinity proved to be as efficient as using manpower. With streamlining their procedures and increased use of technology, most regulatory agencies were better able to meet their targets.

Its official recognition as a pilot site for national port reform provided a significant public legitimation for YICT's programme of improvements in efficiency and customer service. Moreover, as the 1990s progressed, China's desire to gain entry to the WTO increasingly motivated reforms to facilitate trade, and this provided stronger central government endorsement for YICT's initiatives. The company was encouraged to formulate new practices and to support them with financial investment, such as in electronic gate control systems, and training. While YICT's management took much of the initiative in introducing reforms in Yantian port, which then disseminated to other ports, the MOUs between YICT and the regulatory agencies suggest that the latter also exerted some influence. These documents identified their mutual obligations in the developments being negotiated regarding, on YICT's part for example, provision of physical facilities such as computers, container X-ray equipment, offices, and telecom facilities, and on the part of the agencies' changes in procedures regarding inspection rates, methods of inspection and clearance and working hours.

Although the macro environment was supportive of an evolution in port practices, YICT with the backing of its parent company played a clearly proactive role within this context. To gain access, the YICT management secured the help of key influential figures within government circles to reach ministry chiefs to conduct lobbying. For example, through the introduction of the former Shenzhen Party Secretary and Mayor, a personal friend of the head of the China Customs Administration, the YICT team met the top customs officers in Beijing and secured the opportunity to explain the importance of customs reforms for port development. That eventually led to the November 1995 signing of the Port Reform MOU in Shenzhen, attended personally by the national Commissioner of Customs Administration. YICT's group of advisors and its China Affairs Department carried out similar work on the firm's behalf in establishing a relational framework with officials at various levels of government. As the YICT Deputy General Manager and representative of the Shenzhen government put it:

> In a developing country like China, understanding the complexities of working within the Chinese bureaucracy helped us shorten the approval cycle and to execute the strategies with finesse.[13]

In the course of a few years, the YICT team developed a full agenda for reform in government agency port practice ranging from simplification of procedures to innovations in controls employing the latest computer technology. The company formulated specific programme objectives, examined existing procedures, and then proposed and drafted new procedures and detailed implementation plans. It also provided material and technological resources for implementation. Such detailed efforts ensured, firstly, that the firm's agenda supported the country's broad reform objectives of growth and development; secondly, that the proposed changes were low risk and implementable; and thirdly, that the frontline officials charged with implementation had a sense of owning the reforms and gaining prestige from them. The company's willingness to provide supporting investment not only made these initiatives possible but also helped to secure legitimacy for them. These changes enabled the young port to handle the volume of trade attracted to use its facilities, which grew at over 30 per cent per annum in some years.

NOTES

1. Interview with YICT Corporate Affairs Manager, July 2005.
2. See Figure 5.2 in Chapter 5 for YICT's senior management structure.
3. The Phase 1 operational facility was already being built at the time that the joint venture contracts were concluded.
4. Interview with the Deputy General Manager, July 2004.

5.   YICT management report to the Chairman of the Board, September 1995.
6.   *YICT's 5 year Strategy – A Report on its Development and Future Prospects*, Beijing: Institute of Logistics Studies, September 2000.
7.   The Chairman of the Yantian Port Group Mr Zheng Jinsan has provided a detailed account of the negotiation and described the Phase 3 contract as a 'win-win' outcome (Zheng, 2009: 169).
8.   Yantian Port Holdings Annual Reports, 2003, 2004, 2005.
9.   Interview with the Shenzhen Director of the Ministry of Communications, September 2005.
10. Interviews with the YICT Operations Manager and Human Resources Manager, 2005.
11. Interview with the Deputy General Manager, July 2005.
12. Report on the YICT start-up situation from the Reform and Development Commission, Ministry of Communications, Customs Administration, and Ports Administration Office of the State Council to Vice Premier Li Lanqing, 2 August 1995.
13. Interview with the Deputy General Manager, July 2005.

REFERENCES

Yang, M.M. (1994), *Gifts, Favors and Banquets: The Art of Social Relationships in China*, Ithaca, NY: Cornell University Press.
Zheng, J. (2009), *My Memorable Days at Yantian Port* (in Chinese), Beijing: Social and Economic Publishers.

APPENDIX

'Five Directives from China State Council to Simplify Yantian Customs Procedures'. Official English Translation of Appendix to the 1993 Master Contract between HPH and Dong Peng Industry Company Limited (later named Yantian Port Group), October 1993.

Attachment:

Provisional Plan Regarding the Simplified Port Inspection Formalities of Yantian Port

1)   Import/export procedures of international liners will be handled in advance by the shipping company or its agents with the relevant inspection units. Generally inspection units will not conduct on-board inspection except under special circumstances.
2)   Hygiene and quarantine authorities will implement radio quarantine with respect to those international liners coming from non-epidemic areas. For those coming from epidemic areas, berth quarantine or anchorage quarantine may be implemented based on circumstances.

3) Transhipment containers imported or exported via the sea will not be opened for examination if the container body and the seal are intact and the situation is normal.

4) Transhipment containers transported via the land will not be opened for examination if sealing is carried out by the customs at the place of entry into China, and the container body and the seal are intact and the situation is normal.

5) Customs formalities and other inspection and examination procedures for import/export containers may be handled by inland customs if the owner lodge such an application and the conditions are deemed satisfied by the inspection units.

PART III

Co-evolution: theory and practice

8.   Forms of co-evolution

Chapter 2 identified two broad interpretations that can be given to the concept of corporate co-evolution. The first interpretation is that co-evolution signifies the development of a firm alongside that of its environment largely through a process of the former adapting to the latter. This may be regarded as an 'asymmetrical' type of co-evolution in that changes in the environment are its primary driver. It is consistent with the traditional evolutionary view that a firm has to fit environmental conditions or requirements in order to survive. This fit is seen to be achieved either through the natural selection of the 'fittest' firms or through firms learning to adapt to the external situation.

The second interpretation regards co-evolution as a process in which the firm and entities in its environment both actively influence the evolution of the other. This is a more 'symmetrical' kind of co-evolution in that it is driven by developments in the environment and by the actions that a firm takes reflecting the intentions of its leading managers. While symmetrical co-evolution allows for the possibility that over time external factors may influence the way a firm evolves, it envisages that initiatives taken by corporate leadership can impact on the evolution of the environment as well.

Each of these two forms of co-evolution is evident in the history of YICT. This chapter addresses the first research question posed in Chapter 3: 'to what extent did YICT and its environment co-evolve?' It begins with an overview of relevant factors at different system levels: macro, meso and micro. It then highlights distinctive features of the Chinese emerging economy environment in which YICT was located, before indicating the developments in that environment which were consequential for the evolution of the Chinese port industry and for YICT in particular. Faced with unfamiliar market and governmental contexts, YICT's strategic managers had to learn to adapt to them. Partly as a result of this learning process, they came to articulate a clear set of strategic intentions and, over time, found ways of approaching its environment proactively with a view to getting those intentions implemented. Many of these management initiatives have already been described in Chapters 6 and 7. In the last section of this chapter, we focus on the sequence of actions taken both by actors in the firm and in its external field over the key issue of in-port practices and standards. These actions and their consequences provide a clear example of symmetrical co-evolution. They have already been described in the last section of Chapter 7; our purpose in this chapter is to trace their sequence more precisely in order to illustrate the co-evolutionary process.

SYSTEM COMPONENTS IN THE CO-EVOLUTION OF YICT AND ITS ENVIRONMENT

Lewin et al. (1999) offer an analysis of organizational co-evolution that 'attempts to integrate the interplay between the adaptation of individual organizations, their competitive dynamics and the dynamics of the institutional systems within which firms and industries are embedded. The theory assumes that organizations, industries (populations) and environments (institutional and extra-institutional) co-evolve, that their rate, pace and patterns of change are distinct and interdependent, and that the direction of these changes is not unidirectional' (Lewin et al., 1999: 536).[1] The YICT study provides a longitudinal case study that illustrates the complex interrelationships at play. Figure 8.1, adapted from Lewin et al. (1999: 537), schematically identifies the relevant components of the macro (country level), meso (sector level) and micro (organization level) systems that were involved.

Within this broad co-evolutionary framework, the features of the macro and meso environments that were contextual to the company can be broadly classified into developing country factors, shipping and port industry dynamics, and international joint venture ownership factors. The developing country factors featured an imperfect market situation, immature legal framework, government control and intervention, and bureaucratic administration with underdeveloped rules and practices. To these common features of transition economies could be added the implications for business of China's specific historical and cultural legacy (Child and Tse, 2001). These characteristics constituted a complex macro picture against which business organizations in China had to function.

In the meso environment, the dynamics of the shipping and port industry were characterized by oligopolistic competition in Hong Kong and South China. Hong Kong was a mature development, while Yantian, as a new offspring from a Hong Kong parent, tried to establish itself as an entity in the oligopoly of a few players. In all infrastructure developments, barriers to entry are artificially high because of their nature as capital intensive investments and the need for government involvement in

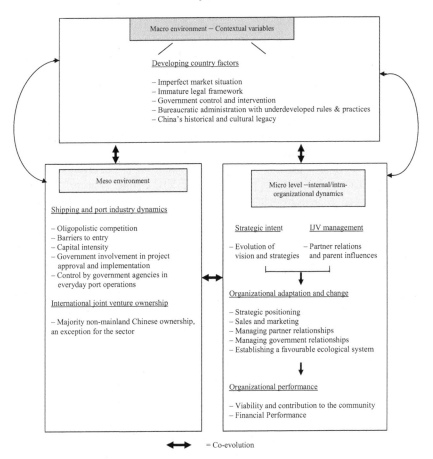

Figure 8.1   Macro, meso and micro system components in the co-evolution of YICT and its environment

approvals and implementation. In these particular circumstances, the initial barrier to entry was manifest in the difficulties of establishing a market position and operational viability. In the industry environment, government involvement also took the form of regulatory agencies forming an outer ring of the service package through the controls they could exercise over everyday port operations. The majority non-Mainland ownership of the joint venture was also significant because it constituted a major and unique departure from the sector norm. It was a feature that coloured the views of some government members towards YICT and which inspired external pressures for change in control of the company, particularly at the time of the Phase 3 negotiations.

The government organizations that had a close bearing on YICT's evolution were located at both macro and micro levels. At the macro level, relevant ministries were the Ministry of Communications [MOC] in charge of the port sector, the National Development and Reform Commission [NDRC] which had to approve all major investment projects, and the regulatory bureaux in charge of customs, frontier inspection, and quarantine. At the local mcso level, the important players were the local regulatory bodies together with the Shenzhen SEZ government which was also a minority-owning partner in the YICT joint venture. We have already noted instances where vertical relationships within this broad governmental sector were significant for the firm and its development. One example was that the government agencies within the port for several years resisted implementation of the five directives for reform in customs and clearance at Yantian issued by the top tier of government itself – the State Council.

The micro level also comprised several interacting organizations. 'The firm'– YICT – was an equity joint venture consisting of managers and a board nominated by its two main parent companies, HPH and YPG. This meant that relationships of a horizontal kind within the joint venture as well as those with its parent companies were critical for its successful evolution. The two key factors giving rise to the firm's evolution through organizational adaptation and change were the strategic intent of senior management and the relationships between the joint venture partners and with the higher levels to which they reported – respectively Hutchison Port Holdings and the Shenzhen government [YPG]. Chapters 6 and 7 described the management initiatives taken at the micro level to adapt and change the company and the ways they impacted on the company's environment. They included strategic positioning as a world-class port with commensurate investment and practices to achieve a leading level of productivity and service, innovations in port sales and marketing, managing partner and government relationships, and establishing a favourable ecological system. The fact that YICT was organized as an international joint venture introduced factors such as differences in partner objectives, differences in their capabilities and familiarity with advanced practices, as well as some contrasts in management culture and style. The tensions as well as the synergies that could arise because of these factors accounted for some of the dynamics in the company's evolution. Evolution at the micro level, first in terms of first establishing cooperative relationships within the firm and second in reaching consensus on a common strategy, had a major influence on the company's performance.

Table 8.1 summarizes developments and initiatives stemming from both the environment ('external parties') and the firm which contributed to the co-evolution between the two. Many of these events have already been described in the preceding chapters. The table groups them into two broad categories: (1) changes and initiatives in YICT's environment which had consequences for the evolution of the Chinese port industry or for the evolution of the firm; and (2) initiatives taken by the firm which had consequences for its own evolution or for that of the port industry or other external entities.

A DEVELOPING COUNTRY ENVIRONMENT

It goes without saying that environments are profoundly significant for organizations. For the management theorist as well as the practitioner, a deep understanding of the competitive and institutional environment is a critical ingredient of a successful strategy. Grant (2002: 65), for example, states that 'Developing strategies and appraising strategy are all about seeing the "big picture" – looking at the firm as a whole and within the context of its industry environment'.

Environments in transitional developing economies can present many complexities. In such economies, the environment has particular significance for organizational development because it tends to create difficulties for the conduct of business. These difficulties result largely from the under-development of institutions such as those that protect market transactions and property rights, as well as from political intervention (World Bank, 2012). The consequence is a greater degree of uncertainty and risk, as well as the need for managers to engage more intensively with politicians and officials than they may be used to doing in a developed economy. Austin's (1990) argument that the difference of managing in developing countries lies in the distinctive nature of the business environment is echoed by other analysts who have examined the peculiarities of the environment in transitional economies (Child and Tse, 2001; Peng, 2000; Warner et al., 2005). For this reason, Austin (1990: 3) takes the view that 'A distinguishing feature of more successful companies in developing countries is their superior ability to understand and interact with their business environment'.

In addition to these sources of uncertainty, emerging and transitional economies tend to experience a higher rate of change, and often growth, than is the case with more developed economies. However, although these factors can create additional uncertainty, they also provide excellent opportunities for firms to influence aspects of their environments. As

Table 8.1 *Examples of initiatives by external parties and the firm in the co-evolutionary process*

Source of initiative	Initiative	Effect
Initiatives by *external parties* with consequences for their own evolution or that of the port industry	Official recognition that unreformed ports would stifle China's economic growth; central government approval of free trade zones close to ports	Government commitment to economic reform (market liberalization) and pursuit of growth after 1992 stimulated expansion and modernization of China's port industry.
	Official adoption of YICT innovations as industry standard	Opened the possibility for developments at Yantian to disseminate to other ports
Initiatives by *external parties* with consequences for the evolution of the firm	Modernization became official policy	Encouraged search for international partner for port development both at Shanghai and Yantian
	Designation of YICT as pilot port for reform; public recognition through awards	Provided official endorsement of YICT as world-class port and the green light for its further evolution
	Market liberalization encouraged growth in South China; founding of Shenzhen SEZ	Provided economic justification for YICT to invest long term for world-class standards and practices; favourable to subsequent expansion and innovation by YICT
	Growing competition in South China ports	Encouraged YICT to undertake further competitive initiatives such as offering an integrated transport, warehouse and port service
	Political campaign against majority non-Mainland ownership of YICT	Extracted 'concessions' from HPH affecting YICT such as reduced ownership share and purchase of loss-making Pingyan Railway which was then used to enlarge YICT's hinterland

Initiatives by *the firm* with consequences for its own evolution	Lobbying of government to ease in-port regulatory restrictions	Once successful, this enabled new practices and supporting technologies to be implemented in Yantian port
	Decision to overcome an initially inertial market environment	Innovation of 'end-user marketing' to cargo owners
Initiatives by *the firm* with consequences for the evolution of the port industry or other external parties	Lobbying and financing of study groups that produced specific proposals for China's port reform	New arrangements for in-port government regulation, pioneered at YICT, were adopted throughout the industry
	YICT pioneered the application of new concepts, such as 'megaport', 'world-class port', 'hygienic port', 'virtual free port', 'green port', higher quayside construction standards, and new environmental protection standards	YICT's status as a pilot site for port reform, plus its winning of awards, enhanced the influence of its innovations on the evolution of the industry as a whole
	YICT pioneered and funded coordinated logistics and traffic systems in its immediate environment – the 'Easyport' concept	Assisted Shenzhen to become an advanced logistics centre

economies move towards more comprehensive market systems, and institutions go through reforms in support of economic development, the very fact that the rules of the game are not fully developed and implemented provides scope for companies to take the initiative in influencing and negotiating these external conditions. The Yantian port development has provided clear evidence of this.

In China, the influence of the 'mega force' (Austin, 1990) was potentially overwhelming. This term refers to the government of a developing country and its various agencies, and associated social, political and legal arrangements (Baron, 2000). It is well recognized that government influence and control in the business system is particularly strong and pervasive in China (Redding and Witt, 2007; Lin, 2011). As Table 8.1 indicates, the policies and decisions of the Chinese government and its agencies had profound consequences for the evolution of the country's port industry and for the specific evolution of YICT.

At the macro-meso levels, the government's clear commitment from 1992 onwards to economic reform and the opening of the economy and economic growth provided the fundamental stimulus to the expansion and modernization of China's port industry. The authorities realized that an export-led path of rapid development could not be achieved without considerable expansion and improvement of its ports. Other policy initiatives such as the establishment of free trade zones close to ports also stimulated port development. The establishment of special economic zones, which were concentrated in southern China, encouraged the rapid development of light industries such as toys, furniture and electronics which were highly suited to containerization.

At the micro level, governmental influences prevailed in very significant ways both over YICT's core operations, through the presence of the local partner and in-port regulatory agencies, as well as in the firm's interactions with external authorities, such as when it required government approval for expansion. The adoption of Yantian port as the official pilot for establishing new efficiency standards and associated reforms in in-port practices, including those of government regulatory agencies, sanctioned YICT's aspirations to evolve the port into a 'world-class' facility and gave a green light for the port's further evolution both in scale and in efficiency. Official recognition and endorsement also stimulated a process whereby practices at Yantian were taken up by other Chinese ports, especially newly developed ones such as Ningbo, Tainjin and Xiamen.

ADAPTING TO THE ENVIRONMENT

Any successful strategy development on YICT's part had to take those factors into consideration, in addition to dealing with market forces such as through positioning, pricing and promotions. Secondly, gaining entry and proving operational viability required strategies for dealing with and changing the environmental agencies. Environmental organizations like the regulatory agencies exercised a direct impact on the market supply and demand situation. For example, the demand for port services would be either enhanced or impaired according to the combined influence of the regulatory agencies and the company over the service package offered to the market. The regulatory authorities directly influenced the flow of cargo through the port and had the power to halt it if they deemed fit. Thirdly, to achieve long-term growth and development, the organization had to meet the expectations of its various stakeholders, prominent among which was again the joint venture's government partner. Within an institutionalized environment, social and political agendas could be as important as economic ones for infrastructure projects such as a major port.

YICT could never afford to underestimate the importance of its interactions with this environment. Unlike a purely commercial concern, a firm operating within a highly institutionalized environment would find strategies framed only in terms of competitive market dynamics to be insufficient (Rodrigues and Child, 2003; 2008). Without trying to impact on its institutional environment, the company could not progress, as the previous three chapters have shown. While many formal aspects of the institutional environment were deeply embedded, it was at the same time in a state of flux due to the reform programme and because China was determined to make adjustments necessary for it to secure accession to the WTO. This meant that many aspects of the environment, such as moves towards a decentralized market system, were evolving in directions favourable to the realization of YICT's goals. Moreover, most senior government officials were committed to improving the system and hence receptive to new proposals, especially ones which could add some specific substance to the watchwords of the reform programme.

Right from the start, the Chinese partner had clear ideas about the port's strategic role. It recognized the port's importance to the city of Shenzhen. Former Mayor and Party Secretary Li Hao described the city's intention 'to fly with both wings, namely seaport and airport' as part of a key strategy for the development of Shenzhen.[2] Li (1999) saw port development as critical to the city gaining entry to the 'world league'.

This is why he supported the bold move to allow an international consortium to have majority ownership and management of such a strategic asset. Allowing majority ownership by the international consortium had not happened before in China's port industry, Li Hao succeeded in getting it approved with the blessing of Premier Li Peng who attended the signing ceremony of the joint venture agreement on 5 October 1993.

The intentions of the international consortium headed by Hutchison-Whampoa were initially less clearly articulated. Their understanding of the strategic role of the new Yantian port development was largely framed in terms of its implications for Hong Kong rather than in terms of the special features of the Mainland China environment. For Hutchison, majority ownership was important partly to protect its 'home base' – the Hong Kong port – and partly to take out an option in the event that the new site prospered. The Hutchison Group, and particularly its politically seasoned and economically astute Chairman, read the overall political and economic signs of China positively. It was convinced of the future opportunities both for Hong Kong and the region to develop as hubs for South China trade. The other shareholders, Maersk Shipping Line and COSCO (China's shipping line), invested in the project as part of their corporate investment portfolio. Maersk Line sold their shares in Hong Kong's Modern Terminals to acquire a 10 per cent stake in YICT, and this expressed a strategic intent to move as a pioneer across the Hong Kong border. So management was given the task of making the new port work with an existing business model and a relatively simple strategy – namely, market the hardware and facilities at a slightly reduced price compared to Hong Kong. The early crisis of the first two years when the port was operating well below the planned levels showed, much to management's surprise, that simply providing new facilities was not enough. The existing model was not working. Apparently there was no plan to take into account the specifics of the 'China factor'. The General Manager's 1995 Report to the Board and other documents at that critical period indicate a growing realization that inertia towards changing the status quo was enough to stall the ambitions of the new entity.

With the benefit of hindsight, it was evident that the business model then being followed by the international consortium based in Hong Kong had not taken into consideration the unique features of the environment in which the new joint venture found itself. YICT management was following the tried and tested route of business development in a developed economy, namely Hong Kong. It underestimated the need to push and provide support for change in a developing country environment. It underrated the importance of addressing government relationships in China. YICT management might have understood that change had to be incremental, but, with success being dependent on achieving a critical mass, it was surprised by the difficulties of persuading customers to make the first move. Managers conducting business in China often discussed its bureaucracy and red tape, and it was clearly a concern for customers as well. However, YICT management in the early days had no plans to tackle this particular challenge. At this stage of the port's development, the Mainland environment seemed to be wearing down all the players in the industry. This was not only peculiar to Yantian; the same inertial forces were at work in the western Shenzhen ports, Shekou and Chiwan, which had begun operations a few years before Yantian.

As YICT managers grappled with the problem, they began to re-define it. First, they came to see their task as being to manage a change process, and in particular one of helping customers to change. Second, they recognized the significance of the government's influence over the port's competitive attractiveness. This re-definition encouraged management to take the initiatives that were described in Chapters 6 and 7 and which created the possibility for YICT to evolve. In retrospect, two initiatives were particularly significant. The first was aimed at overcoming the initially inertial market environment; this was the innovation of 'end-user marketing' to cargo owners. The other was the firm's lobbying of government to ease in-port regulatory restrictions. Once this began to bear fruit after 1995, it opened the way for new efficiency-enhancing practices and supporting technologies to be implemented within Yantian port.

These initiatives reveal that YICT's management had grasped the complexities of coping with environmental forces. It now paid special attention to the special challenges of operating an international joint venture in a developing country. Over time, the management learned to appreciate the macro and meso environmental dynamics they were facing and began to think in terms of addressing the political and institutional environment in addition to attending to the market. In fact, they came quite quickly to appreciate how the complications and restrictions imposed by Chinese government agencies were a handicap in attracting business to the new port. The insights they gained included the need to deal proactively with the involvement of government port agencies in their dual role of 'control and service provision' as well as the need to re-shape the industry as a whole through innovations in marketing and managing partner expectations. Learning from continuous feedback from the market and from political associates during the first few years, YICT management identified that the key requirement for the company to evolve was to have an impact on its environment. In other words, the company had to effect changes proactively in that environment for it to survive and succeed.

In Chapter 2 we suggested that the conjunction of initial conditions and subsequent learning implies that corporate evolution is likely to be characterized by both continuity and change. The initial conditions present when YICT was founded were potential sources of strength. They included a favourable economic environment; the availability of Hutchison-Whampoa's accumulated expertise in port operations and its willingness to invest heavily; and a Chinese partner eager to assist the port's development and expansion. These conditions persisted, despite occasional differences between the joint venture's partners, and they led to a degree of path-dependence. They engendered the continuities in the company's evolution seen in terms of an emphasis on growth and continuous improvement, and sustained them through the vision of becoming a 'world-class port'. On the other hand, the crisis of YICT's early years provoked the innovation of some important practices, and the company's management went through a major learning process in having to adapt to unforeseen circumstances. Its strategy became an emerging one which introduced dis-continuities with past thinking and practice in the port industry. This learning undoubtedly encouraged openness to the further stream of innovations in subsequent years that made the port into an industry leader. At the same time, the implementation of these innovations required measures to secure a relaxation of environmental restrictions. The process was not one of simply adapting to the environment; it also required actions to influence that environment.

INFLUENCING THE ENVIRONMENT

Intentional proactivity by management has emerged as a common theme among organizations breaking away from environmental constraints in China. For example, Warner et al. (2005) investigated how 12 SOEs (state-owned enterprises), FOEs (foreign-owned enterprises) and DOEs (domestic-owned enterprises) responded to the Chinese reform and WTO entry. They found that enterprises responding actively through innovative strategies and new management practices (described as proactive) achieved markedly better performance than those which were passive and less dynamic towards new challenges (described as reactive).

The extent to which YICT's managers appreciated the special nature of its environmental context conditioned their ability to conceptualize and design an appropriate response. Most significant of all was their recognition that if the organization was going to survive and succeed it had to influence the environment in a systematic manner. That was the beginning of the emergence of a coherent strategy.

For YICT, initiatives aimed at influencing its institutional environment were of much greater significance than initiatives aimed at its competitive environment. As noted in Chapters 4 and 5, Yantian did face competition from terminals in Hong Kong and from those in west Shenzhen. In its early days, the reluctance of many shipping companies to transfer business from Hong Kong to Yantian presented a major challenge to the viability of the new port. This was overcome largely through the innovation of direct 'end-user marketing' to cargo owners. The dominant position that Yantian enjoyed among Shenzhen terminals meant that local competition never posed an over-riding threat. The trigger-point mechanism ensured that there would be no serious competition brought about by overcapacity. However, the growth of competing ports did stimulate YICT to introduce certain initiatives aimed at enhancing its market attraction such as offering the integrated transport, warehouse and port service noted in Chapter 6. The company's initiative in developing an 'ecological system' around the port had an impact on its wider meso environment in that it assisted Shenzhen to become a logistics centre.

Most of YICT management's attention was devoted to confronting the institutional constraints which faced the company. The first requirement for pursuing a proactive stance in a highly institutionalized environment is to recognize the agencies and groups that are particularly relevant to the business and then establish a framework for dialogue with them. In the case of YICT, different government agencies were involved in the structure of the company, in the control of its business activities, and in the quality of service it could provide.

Government Participation in the Structure of the Company

In the early stages of its opening to the world, one of China's main methods of attracting foreign direct investment [FDI] was to involve foreign capital and management in international joint ventures. Most international investors in infrastructural and strategic sectors took a minority interest or a 50/50 joint venture with the Chinese partner. YICT was an exception by which the international party had been permitted to hold a majority shareholding.

The structure of the company, an equity joint venture, brought the Shenzhen SEZ government as a local partner into the business. The Shenzhen government necessarily had a different set of priorities, culture and organizational norms to those brought to the company by the main international partner, Hutchison. As well as requiring its cooperation for the smooth running of the port, the approval of the Shenzhen partner had to be gained for major developments such as expansion of the port and for provision of complementary infrastructure. The local partner also proved to be of invaluable assistance in opening doors to higher levels of the Chinese government and for supporting proposals that YICT was putting to them.

The Control of Business Activities

All enterprises in China had to apply for a business licence in which the scope of their business was defined. In addition the amount of investment was stipulated as agreed during the negotiations. Approvals of licences and investment had to be obtained from a level of government consistent with the importance of the project and amount of the investment. Generally, investments above RMB 30 million (US$3.7 million) or projects of a strategic nature had to be approved by the Ministry of Foreign Trade and Economic Cooperation [MOFTEC] in Beijing. In the case of the Yantian port development, the project size was relatively large (US$3 billion) and strategic, therefore requiring approval from Beijing ministries for all the steps in its development and growth. Specifically, the Ministry of Communications was the overseer of all transportation activities, while the Ministry of Foreign Trade and Economic Cooperation was in charge of FDI. From an overall planning perspective, the State Planning Commission (later known as the National Development and Reform Commission – NDRC) provided administration and guidance on developments of a strategic nature. There were parallel arrangements at the local government level. The conduct of business attracted numerous government bureaucracies engaged in monitoring and approving specific activities, be they of a business or developmental nature.

Regulatory Controls Over Business Activities

In China, all business enterprises are subject to a range of controls exercised by government ministries both in their day-to-day activities and in their development. Many of these applied to YICT even though in the negotiations to establish the joint venture Hutchison had managed to secure agreement that it would enjoy managerial autonomy in the setting of its prices and in its employment practices. Regulatory agencies enforce the laws of the country and execute policies set by central and local governments. In the port environment, the Customs Administration, Frontier Inspectorate and Quarantine Inspectorate are in place to enforce regulations related to their functions which govern the import and export of goods and cargoes through the port. They form a layer of government control around the port and an outer ring of 'control and service provision', a term used by these regulators to describe their dual roles in the port.

Quality of Service

The quality of service that the port could offer was therefore directly affected by regulatory agencies that enforce the laws of the country and execute policies set by the central and local governments. We noted in Chapter 7 how major advances achieved proactively by YICT, with backing from HPH, eased the negative impact that the administration of such regulations had on the efficiency and quality of service that the port could offer, and how the reforms accomplished at Yantian then became exemplars for the whole Chinese port sector.

The regulatory constraints imposed by external institutions were complemented by normative and cognitive features evident in the different business concepts held by the international operators, on the one hand, and by the partners and agencies in the port's institutional environment on the other hand (Scott, 2001). While the business-oriented port management focused on client satisfaction, business development and company growth, the local Chinese agencies and partners tended to focus on social and political considerations appropriate for the time, such as employment creation and use of the latest technologies for the sake of demonstrating development. Furthermore, the company had to operate in a Chinese environment with all the associated cultural norms and practices in human relations prevalent at the time. The regulatory, normative and cognitive characteristics of its environment were the reality facing the company. Its initial business model did not fully appreciate this reality and therefore did not work as well as the company had hoped.

Faced with such institutional constraints, firms could succumb to environmental forces and allow them to dictate, even jeopardize, their developmental paths. There are certainly cases where this has happened in China (Clissold, 2004). Alternatively, their managements could demonstrate a clear intent to be proactive towards external factors. As Chapter 7 described, YICT developed proactive strategies towards managing partner relations and those with other arms of government. The effectiveness of these strategies had one common factor which is that they took into account the special political, social and cultural factors embedded in the Chinese environment. In managing the partner relationship, for example, YICT management paid special attention to the human factors of the Chinese partner organization, particularly the psychology of its leaders wishing to satisfy both their organizational and personal needs. Driven by the prestige of being at the leading edge, China's political leaders tended to pursue hub port status, sometimes regardless of its feasibility. It was fortunate for Yantian that the necessary physical and economic conditions were present. The YICT planners were therefore able to design a strategy for Yantian to become a 'mega port' which satisfied both business and psychological needs.

Table 8.1 lists initiatives taken by YICT which had consequences for the evolution in its environment. As part of its lobbying of government, the company assisted by its parent HPH produced specific proposals for the reform of in-port practices which eventually led to new arrangements that were adopted throughout the sector. Another example concerns the innovation, or at least adoption, by YICT and HPH of new concepts and standards that were not only applied in a pioneering way within Yantian but which were also adopted in many instances by other Chinese ports. Prominent among the new concepts were the 'mega port', the 'world-class port', the 'hygienic port', the 'virtual free port' and the 'green port'. Examples of new standards applied by YICT which subsequently influenced the evolution of other Chinese ports were the higher quayside construction specifications and the introduction of rigorous environmental protection standards associated with the 'green port' concept. These were described in Chapter 6.

Likewise, YICT's dealings with the regulatory agencies demonstrated an approach towards change that was well accepted because the process was incremental, followed a path of least resistance with immediate gains and low risk for both the organizations and individuals involved. As described in Chapter 7, when handling developmental projects like Phase 3 and Phase 3E, YICT management orchestrated a detailed relationship management programme involving top leaders and stakeholders in lobbying for political support with government agencies, as well as an incremental process of persuasion and compromise in the lengthy negotiations with the joint venture partner.

As time went on, this managerial approach served to accumulate goodwill and influence for YICT among both its partner and external governmental authorities. This permitted a transition from asymmetrical co-evolution towards that of a more symmetrical nature. How managerial initiatives came to be directed towards actively influencing the evolution of its environment so as to facilitate the achievement of the company's strategic objectives was illustrated by the issue of port practices, described in the last section of Chapter 7. There was a sequence of initiatives and events which led to co-evolution between the firm and organizations in its environment. These enabled the evolution of practices at Yantian port and also shaped Chinese government port policy, transformed the practices of port-based regulatory bodies, and led to significant changes throughout the whole Chinese port industry. Taken together, they provide a clear instance of 'symmetrical' co-evolution.

The ways in which YICT and HPH managed relationships with government regulatory authorities were described in Chapter 7. Table 8.2 lists the sequence of key events connected with the co-evolution of port practices at Yantian and other ports. They are categorized according to the three system levels identified at the beginning of this chapter: macro, meso and micro. It is apparent, however, that some important actors, such as Hutchison Group Chairman Li Kashing and former Shenzhen Party Secretary Li Hao, played important roles that crossed system levels. Although Li Kashing represented the firm, he also had direct access to the top levels of the Chinese government. Similarly, Li Hao provided a circuit between meso and macro levels through his personal connections in Beijing.

Previous chapters have described the events that took place, and Table 8.2 sets out their sequence. To recap: in the early 1990s, once economic reform, growth and opening to the outside world returned to the official agenda, senior government figures let it be known that investment from Hong Kong would be welcome to develop China's inadequate port system. This was the trigger for the negotiations that led to the establishment of the YICT joint venture and for agreement in principle to a reform in customs and port clearance at Yantian. Building on this, HPH put forward the case for YICT to be treated as an official pilot site for modern port practice in China, but this was only formally agreed in November 1995 after considerable lobbying by HPH and YICT, backed up by a study group and its report. The report put the case for Yantian to become an official pilot for trying out new customs procedures. At the same time, the company had embarked on an active policy of 'relationship management' and formulated the vision of Yantian becoming a 'world-class port' in support of attaining international standards of performance. The report received the endorsement of a vice premier and the head of the Customs Administration. Nevertheless, the implementation of reforms in regulatory agency practices were actually only implemented at Yantian following additional study group work and a further report produced under the vice premier's sponsorship.

From 1997 onward, a co-evolutionary process unfolded in which, in collaboration with its in-port regulatory agencies, YICT's management initiated a series of best practices which are listed in the 'micro' column of Table 8.2. As the port achieved very visible success, attracted visits by

Table 8.2   The sequence of events in corporate co-evolution focusing on in-port practices

Date	Macro (Central Government)	Meso (Port sector and Shenzhen SEZ)	Micro (YICT and its JV partners)
1991–92	Renewal of government's programme of reform and opening following Deng Xiaoping's 'Journey to the South' in early 1992.	1991: Zhu Rongji (then Mayor of Shanghai) invited Li Kashing (Hutchison Group Chairman) to reform the Shanghai ports, unusually offering a 50% ownership stake.	1992: Li Kashing decided to commit investment to China rather than just donations. Opening of negotiations to establish YICT July 1992. Li led the negotiation using his and Hutchison's reference power to obtain favourable terms.
1993	The established relationship networks with top government circles enabled Chinese governmental endorsement of YICT by the personal presence of both President and Premier at the signing ceremony establishing YICT, October 1993. The State Council in principle regarded establishment of Yantian port as a pilot project for port reform in China.	The Maersk shipping line, the major customer and minority shareholder, strongly supported plans for YICT to become an advanced 'mega' port. Multinationals began to establish a stronger presence in China, after a period of testing the water with a beachhead strategy in the late 1980s.	Hutchison's aim is for YICT to be treated as a 'pilot site' for modern port management. Customs reform was on Li Kashing's change agenda as his port investment portfolio in China became more important. Hutchison pressed for a specification of port administration reforms as a condition for signing the contract for the YICT joint venture. The contract was signed October 1993 accompanied by five directives for reform in customs and port clearance at Yantian. HPH in a detailed report put forward the case for YICT to be treated as a 'pilot site' for modern port management in China. It also started on plans to develop YICT into an advanced 'mega port'.
1994		Backed by support from the Hutchison Group, a senior government delegation led by Shenzhen's Vice Mayor visited six European countries to learn international port practices.	

1995	As a result of personal lobbying in the Ministry of Communications and Transportation [MOC] by HPH and YICT, an official study group was established which visited Yantian and Shenzhen. In August 1995 it reported on the impact of government agencies on the performance of the port. The report requested permission to try out new customs procedures in YICT as a pilot. The report passed up through the Chinese government system (various ministries and levels) finally gaining the official endorsement of Vice Premier Li Lanqing. Li Lanqing then passed the report with positive comments to another Vice Premier Zhou Jiahua and the head of Customs Administration Chien Kunlin. Hutchison and YICT also approached Chien for help through ex-Shenzhen Party Secretary Li Hou. This resulted in the MOU of November 1995 (see under 'micro').	November 1995, Yantian port formally designated as the 'pilot site' for national reforms in port customs administration.	1994–95: Formal announcement of YICT's intention to become a 'world-class port'. Implementation of port reform directives was initially resisted by government agencies within the Yantian port. YICT incurred losses and frustration. YICT established an advisory group on government relations, consisting of retired senior officials, with help from HPH. YICT funded a study group on port reform consisting of middle-level officials from government agencies (see under 'macro'). It also formed a China Affairs Department to conduct 'relationship management'. November 1995: Customs Administration and YICT sign MOU to simplify transit and clearance procedures at Yantian port. First round of reforms initiated with 'green lanes' and cargo release at the gates, and 'bonded transit'' of imports and exports.
1996	Central government initiative under Vice Premier Li Lanqing which produced a report on reform in China's ports. It recommended: consolidating government agencies operating within ports; raising efficiency by applying 'scientific' techniques; adopting international practices.	Following the Li Lanqing report, six government agencies operating within Chinese ports were consolidated into three. They came under different ministries but the central government endorsed initiatives to implement reforms in their port practices.	During the preparation of the Li Lanqing report, HPH facilitated visits by the government study group to foreign ports to review 'best practices'. Completion of this report created opportunities for YICT to agree with government agencies on implementing reforms within the Yantian port.

Date	Macro (Central Government)	Meso (Port sector and Shenzhen SEZ)	Micro (YICT and its JV partners)
1997+	Trade-related reforms increasingly motivated by China's wish to gain entry to the WTO. Visits by central government ministers and commissioners endorsed developments at Yantian port. Deputy Minister of Communications and his colleagues increasingly consulted YICT senior managers for advice. 1999: Premier Zhu Rongi initiated a freeze on headcount in regulatory authorities; this encouraged them to accept YICT's investment in labour and time-saving technology in the context of rapid growth in the port's throughput.	Dissemination of YICT initiatives to some other ports in China, especially newly developed ones such as Ningbo, Tianjin and Xiamen. For example, internal documents from the Customs Administration asked other customs districts to adopt similar reform procedures in the light of the YICT pilot experience. Dissemination was facilitated by national awards to YICT indicating endorsement of its standards and performance by the sector in China. 1999–2003: Non-Mainland majority ownership of YICT became a live political issue triggered by negotiations to approve Yantian port Phase 3.	After 1997: YICT's successful marketing to end users created higher port service demands. That in turn increased the pressure on the Customs Administration for further practice reforms. 1998: electronic customs application introduced. 1999–2003: negotiations over approval of Yantian port expansion [Phase 3]: threat from some government officials to establish competing terminal facility.

2001+	China's accession to the WTO led to an increased volume of trade, enhancing both the strategic importance and profitability of the Yantian port. Further development of intra-Asia trade as well as recognition of the growing importance of China's domestic trade in the economic growth of the country.	2000–2003: closer cooperation among Shenzhen port operators to demand greater port clearance efficiency. At the same time YICT faced increasing competition from other Shenzhen ports.	2001: YICT joint project with the Frontier Inspectorate resulted in speeding of port clearance.
			2001+ YICT gained series of national awards. From 2002 Yantian port introduced several best practices in collaboration with regulatory authorities to improve the quality of its services: e.g., introduction of paperless fully automated international trans-shipment system; pre-clearance of empty import containers; same day clearance of inspections and application of the 'hygienic port' concept. It also invested in supporting technologies for inspection and surveillance.
			2004: MOU signed with Customs on increasing efficiency and with Frontier Inspectorate on vessel clearance. Electronic gate control system introduced.
		2005: YICT chosen by the Global Institute of Logistics to be the 'Global Terminal of the Year'. In the same year, YICT was recognised by the Ministry of Communications as a top port for productivity, efficiency and service to customers.	2005: Development of China hub strategy to cater for mega vessels. The port further developed as a showcase for Shenzhen.
			2007–08: Application of the 'hygienic port' process; implementation of paperless declaration system for selected enterprises; installation of the FS 3000 system for security inspection.
		Investments by competitors (the Wharf Group amongst others) into Chanwan, a 10 terminal facility in the western part of Shenzhen, gathered momentum.	2008: Fast clearance of empty boxes system in place.
			2008: Further efficiency of tractor clearance system with pre-advice, shortening time taken to enter and exit the terminal.
			2008: Pilot study of "Easyport" implementation to provide additional on time information to port users.
			2009: A new FS 3000 system installed to scan full boxes for security sensitive cargo.
			2009: Further easing of procedures for inland transit clearance, thus facilitating domestic cargo transhipment.
			2010: Further relaxation and automation of inspection requirements for "Reliable Enterprises"

central government ministers and commissioners, and secured a series of major awards, its standards and practices received clear public endorsement.[3] This encouraged government authorities to press for YICT's initiatives to be disseminated among other Chinese ports and for the local regulatory authorities in other ports to follow the lead taken by their branches at Yantian. The development of competing terminals in west Shenzhen, especially after 2000, provided an external stimulus for YICT management to press on further with the development of service improvements.

In retrospect, these events appear to have a rational momentum focused around the mutual acceptance of a 'win-win' strategy of port development accepted by all the parties concerned. However, the reality was by no means as straightforward or the process of co-evolution as inevitable as this. In particular, considerable political activity was required to give them momentum. This is the theme of Chapter 9 which puts forward a political perspective on corporate co-evolution in light of events in the YICT case.

NOTES

1. As noted in Chapters 1 and 2, the most influential constituents of the institutional environment of firms are normally government ministries and regulatory agencies, and public bodies such as those forming the legal system. The most significant 'extra-institutional' aspects of a firm's environment are normally its market(s), relevant technologies and know-how.
2. Interview with Li Hao, August 2005.
3. See the Appendix at the end of this chapter for a list of the main national and international awards gained by YICT.

REFERENCES

Austin, J.E. (1990), *Managing in Developing Countries: Strategic Analysis and Operating Techniques*, New York: Free Press.

Baron, D.P. (2000), *Business and its Environment* (3rd edition), Englewood Cliffs, NJ: Prentice Hall.

Child, J. and D. Tse (2001), 'China's transition and its implications for international business', *Journal of International Business Studies*, **32**, 5–21.

Clissold, T. (2004), *Mr. China*, London: Robinson.

Donaldson, L. (2001), *The Contingency Theory of Organizations*, Thousand Oaks, CA: Sage.

Grant, R.M. (2002), *Contemporary Strategy Analysis: Concepts, Techniques, Applications* (4th edition), Oxford: Blackwell.

Lewin, A.Y., C.P. Long and T.N. Carroll (1999), 'The coevolution of new organizational forms', *Organization Science*, **10**, 535–50.

Lewin, A.Y. and H.W. Volberda (1999), 'Prolegomena on coevolution: a framework for research on strategy and new organizational forms', *Organization Science*, **10**, 519–34.

Li, H. (1999), *The Work of Li Hao in Shenzhen* (in Chinese), Beijing: Central Publishing Company.

Lin, N. (2011), 'Capitalism in China: a centrally managed capitalism (CMC) and its future', *Management and Organization Review*, **7**, 63–96.

Peng, M.W. (2000), *Business Strategies in Transition Economies*, Thousand Oaks, CA: Sage.

Redding, G. and M.A. Witt (2007), *The Future of Chinese Capitalism*, Oxford: Oxford University Press.

Rodrigues, S.B. and J. Child (2003), 'Co-evolution in an institutionalized environment', *Journal of Management Studies*, **40** (8), 2137–62.

Rodrigues, S.B. and J. Child (2008), *Corporate Co-evolution: A Political Perspective*, Chichester: Wiley.

Scott, W.R. (2001), *Institutions and Organizations* (2nd edition), Thousand Oaks, CA: Sage.

Warner, M., V. Edwards, G. Polonsky, D. Pucko and Y. Zhu (2005), *Management in Transitional Economies*, London: Routledge Curzon.

World Bank (2012), *Doing Business 2012: Doing Business in a More Transparent World*, accessed at http://www.doingbusiness.org/reports/global-reports/doing-business-2012.

APPENDIX

Major National and International Awards Granted to YICT

2001: Yantian port Phase 2 awarded 'Luban Prize' in quality construction – by the Ministry of Construction PRC and the Architectural Association of China (Luban was the name of the most admired architect in ancient China. The Prize was the most coveted prize in recognition of the building quality of civil construction projects in China).

2003: YICT elected to fifth place in the '100 Star Overseas Chinese Invested Enterprises 2000–2002' – by the Office of Overseas Chinese Affairs, the State Council PRC.

2003: The third China Freight Industry Awards – Excellent Container Port in the categories of Comprehensive Service and Transport Networks – by *China Shipping Gazette*, a national shipping journal.

2005: Best container terminal China – by *Cargonews China*, an English language magazine published in Asia.

2005: Best port – Gold Prize – in the fourth China Freight Industry Awards – by *China Shipping Gazette*.

2005: Global Container Port of the Year 2005–2006 – by the Global Institute of Logistics, a global association of logistics providers headquartered in New York.

2006: 100 Star Overseas Chinese Invested Enterprises in China – by the Office of Overseas Affairs, the State Council PRC.

2007: Luban Prize for YICT Phase 3 project – by Ministry of Construction PRC and the Architecture Association of China.

2007: Environmental protection certificate from the Shenzhen Pengcheng Waste Reduction Steering Committee for efforts to reduce waste and protect the environment.

2008: International hygienic port – by the World Health Organization (WHO) and the General Administration of Quality Supervision, Inspection and Quarantine of the PRC.

2004–2009: For five consecutive years, YICT was awarded the following by the Container Branch, China Ports Association, the national association of ports and terminals:

- First prize – Top 10 ports in China
- Best container terminal in China in terminal productivity
- First prize – Excellent terminal in China in quay crane rate.

9. The political dynamics of corporate co-evolution[1]

Corporate co-evolution implies that there is interdependence in the respective development of firms and their environments. This was clearly evident in the case of YICT within its China context. The successful evolution of YICT within its China environment, and the ways in which this also contributed to the evolution of the country's port sector as a whole, demonstrate how co-evolution based on collaboration can provide significant benefits to all parties. It has become clear, however, that this progressive outcome did not arise spontaneously. Rather it resulted from lengthy and sometimes arduous political processes in which both the company and various organs of government strove to influence the other through the relationships between them. Moreover, this relational framework had to be constructed and maintained. The structure of the framework was partly shaped by the system of approvals and regulations that applied to Chinese ports. It was also importantly developed through 'relationship management' initiatives by the firm and encouraged by key actors at both local and central levels of government. This chapter examines these processes and, in doing so, addresses the second research question raised in Chapter 3: 'what were the processes through which co-evolution took place?'

Studies have provided evidence of corporate co-evolution, mainly with reference to the strategies and practices of firms and industries (for example, Jones, 2001; Flier et al., 2003). So we know that co-evolution can take place, but we know much less about how this happens. The way in which this interdependence plays out necessarily lies at the heart of any theorizing on the subject (Volberda and Lewin, 2003). An important question concerns how co-evolution is driven forward. We noted in Chapter 2 that there has been a longstanding debate in the study of organizational evolution over the role of environmental determinism versus firm-level initiatives (White et al., 1997). The co-evolutionary perspective has been motivated by a realization that the managerial intentions, strategies and initiatives, both of a firm and of external bodies, can act as evolutionary drivers in addition to given situational factors. What requires further exploration is how intentionality gives rise to change. For example, in discussing the co-evolution of multinational enterprises [MNEs] and institutions, Cantwell et al. (2010: 572) refer to both MNE experimentation and institutional entrepreneurship as potential drivers, but they do not go further into the processes by which co-evolution might come about. While they identify the role of 'change agents' in co-evolution, they pass over the political process whereby such agents mobilize support and accumulate sufficient influence to have an impact.

Only recently have co-evolutionary studies come to refer to the political processes that may be involved (for example, Dieleman and Sachs, 2008; Rodrigues and Child, 2008; Dieleman and Boddewyn, 2012). There is scope to progress further towards a systematic political analysis of corporate co-evolution. Power and its use lies at the heart of a political perspective, which therefore would focus on how the power and influence held by firms and relevant external parties impact on the evolution of their respective activities and organizations. It is the aim of the present chapter to develop a political perspective further. It uses the YICT story to show the additional insights that a political approach to corporate co-evolution can offer. We shall develop a political analysis that recognizes how the power bases available to firms and external organizations provide platforms for exercising influence, and that translating that influence into actual change requires initiatives to mobilize support and build legitimacy. Our intention is that this analysis will provide a useful foundation on which further investigations of corporate co-evolution can build, as well as a basis for drawing out the practical implications offered in Chapter 10.

We shall begin by arguing the case for taking into account the political relations that firms have with their environments, rather than just concentrating on their market relations as much of the existing scholarship has done. This case is particularly strong for emerging economies which, as Chapter 8 noted, tend to be characterized by an active exercise of governmental and institutional power over markets and business activities. Having raised the need to take power into account, we discuss how this somewhat nebulous concept can be defined and applied to real-life cases like that of YICT. We then illustrate how power and influence entered into the events described in previous chapters, concluding with the insights that arise from the analysis.

THE CASE FOR A POLITICAL PERSPECTIVE

Economic logics have dominated co-evolutionary studies, and strategy analyses in general – the logic of markets, transaction costs and resource capabilities (Dopfer, 2005). This is understandable given that the construction of most co-evolutionary (and evolutionary) theorizing about firms has been informed by the paradigm of the free market economy in which other firms are the key external players (for example, Aldrich and Ruef, 2006). Studies of corporate co-evolution have therefore generally considered the growth strategies companies have taken in their marketplaces rather than how they relate with governments and institutions (for example, Burgelman, 2002; Santos and Eisenhardt, 2009). The focus on markets readily assumes that the role of institutions external to the firm, especially the various arms of government, is normally one of being relatively passive guardians of the rules of the market game rather than active players in that game. This assumption has never been wholly tenable, even in paragons of free-market neo-liberalism like the United States. Lewin et al. (1999) recognize that the institutional environment of firms impacts on the non-institutional environment through laws, regulations, and policies affecting markets. Recent years have seen more direct government interventions in the world of business in response to crises in developed countries, as well as the growing importance of emerging economies with highly interventionist governments and bureaucracies. The importance of the institutional environment even in the USA is also indicated by the way that corporations endeavour to use a variety of channels to influence government policy and political opinion (Barley, 2010).

For these reasons, valid theorizing and useful policy guidance both require a complementary perspective that takes into account the essentially political relationships between firms and the actors in their institutional environments. This would incorporate power and its exercise through political action into the analysis of co-evolutionary dynamics, and would be consistent with the realist tradition of political science which regards politics as being fundamentally concerned with the gaining and use of power to further particular interests (Morgenthau, 1948; Vasquez, 1998). This perspective would be particularly apposite to contexts like China and others where government agencies have a significant involvement in systems of business (Lin, 2011).

Power in Relationships Between Firms and Government Institutions

Chapter 2 introduced the concept of a 'relational framework' comprising the social and political relations between firms and relevant external agencies (Scott and Meyer, 1983). A relational framework provides the means through which the parties can exercise influence in ways that potentially affect both their evolutionary paths. It identifies a playing field where actors, who may be situated at different organizational levels, compete to advance their interests and goals. This corresponds to what Fligstein (1996) called a 'strategic action field'. Thus, a relational framework provides the means through which the parties can exercise influence in ways that potentially affect their evolutionary paths. More specifically, a relational framework is also relevant to co-evolution as a conduit through which firms can voice their claims and advance their interests to institutional bodies, while it also allows institutional bodies to express approval or otherwise of particular corporate policies and practices. It encompasses arrangements such as joint government-business committees, consultative arrangements and lobbying channels (Hadjikhani and Ghauri, 2001).

The relational framework YICT had with relevant external parties in China was described in Chapter 7. The government initiated that framework through its initiatives to encourage investment by the Hutchison Group and it was also shaped by the regulatory system applied to port investment and operations. For the company's part, YICT and HPH made considerable efforts to develop and use the framework, especially to lobby branches of government to permit or assist evolutionary changes.

Firms and external agencies vary in how strong a basis they possess for exercising power over each other, as do their abilities to mobilize and apply such strengths effectively (Child and Rodrigues, 2011). In other words, while power resources act as initial or baseline conditions, how effectively these are utilized within a relational framework may depend on other factors such as the ability of the actors to mobilize support, present their case and negotiate skilfully. Chapter 2 described how the concept of 'bargaining power' draws attention to the ways in which the parties of a negotiation or a relationship can build on their baseline sources of power to enhance their influence. For this reason it is helpful to distinguish between 'power' referring to having the potential to ensure the compliance of others, and 'influence' referring to the exercise of power. The question then arises as to what view of power and how it is exercised can most usefully be applied to the task of better understanding the co-evolution of firms and institutional environments.

Power is not a one-dimensional entity (Haugaard and Clegg, 2009). Three types of power are commonly identified: 'power over', 'power to' and 'power with' (Göhler, 2009). An early and widely accepted view is that power is manifested when one agent enforces its views or desires onto another, even against the latter's will (Dahl, 1957). This is the notion of having 'power over' which is often associated with the material basis of power – stemming from the possession of resources which others do not have. Nye (2004) has called this kind of power 'hard power'. The asymmetrical possession of resources gives a person or organization the ability to control rewards offered to, and costs incurred by, other people, as well as the instruments to articulate and control information (Emerson, 1962; Pfeffer and Salancik, 1978). Another perspective, associated with Parsons (1964), refers to power based on authority, in which 'power is the legitimate mechanism regulating commitments' (Clegg et al., 2006: 193). This is consistent with the notion of having normatively approved 'power to' accomplish socially accepted purposes. It draws attention to the ways in which legitimacy is socially constructed as a foundation of power (Gordon, 2009). A third concept is that of 'power with' whereby action possibilities are created through people's willingness to pool their resources, be co-opted, or to mobilize their efforts collectively (Follett, 1924). This willingness could be founded on a mutual identification and perceived mutual benefit between the parties concerned. 'Power to' and 'power with' are consistent with Nye's concept of 'soft power'. Different types of power can be combined, such as in what Courpasson (2000) has called 'soft bureaucracies'.

The distinctions between 'power over', 'power to', and 'power with' are germane to the analysis of corporate co-evolution. They serve to identify different power resources or 'bases' of power. Sources of power may be of a material nature involving the ability to offer rewards or exert coercion. They may also be of a more ideational or normative nature whereby power derives from having legitimacy, the ability to attract identification, and acknowledged expertise.[2] 'Power over' tends to be based on material and coercive resources; 'power to' on legitimacy and expertise; and 'power with' on identification. Moreover, distinguishing the different types of power draws attention to the possibility of a progression from hard power to soft power, and perhaps from conflict to cooperation, as the relationship between a firm and external bodies develops (Kostova and Zaheer, 1999; Moon and Lado, 2000). Thus the relations between co-evolving parties may themselves evolve from being initially based on legal and contractual provisions to becoming increasingly based on mutual confidence and trust.

In attempting to analyse corporate co-evolution from a political perspective, a framework which takes into account the range of power sources identified by the different types of power promises to be useful. In this respect, French and Raven's (1960) classification of 'the bases of social power', although dated, provides a comprehensive and useful classification which covers a range of power sources. French and Raven appreciated that different bases of power could apply in different circumstances and that only rarely would a given empirical instance of power be limited to one source. As the title of their article indicates, French and Raven also recognized that power is a social phenomenon that is activated through relationships. Their five bases of power are: (1) possession of *material* resources which provide 'the ability to reward';[3] (2) *coercion* which can include force and also the withholding of reward; (3) *legitimacy*, whereby the exercise of power is regarded as rightful by other parties (Bierstedt, 1964); (4) *reference*, in which the basis of a person's or unit's power lies in the identification of others with the power-holder; and (5) *expertise*, whereby the expertise held by, or attributed to, a person creates a willingness to accept his or her authority. These bases of power can be considered to be 'power resources'. Relevant actors may possess several of these power bases, and indeed they can be mutually reinforcing. In particular, material resources can enhance other bases of power.

A firm may be able to increase its bargaining power within the co-evolutionary process through: (1) *mobilization*, such as establishing coalitions with other parties and lobbying; and (2) developing the *legitimacy* of its position through inter alia articulating socially acceptable goals (Welch and Wilkinson, 2004; Hadjikhani et al., 2008). Whereas mobilization relies on an appeal to common interests, legitimacy also relies on establishing cognitive bridges to other parties especially to institutions (Suchman, 1995). Political capital can be a key asset for developing and maintaining the relational framework required to achieve a mobilization of support for actions that firms prefer (McCarthy and Wolfson, 1996; Frynas et al., 2006). Research on corporate behaviour indicates that firms possessing greater resources are more likely to be politically active (Hillman and Hitt, 1999). Galang (2012) similarly suggests from a review of available studies that the appropriateness of different firm responses to government corruption will depend on the political resources they possess. In order to create strategic opportunities and reduce competitive threats, firms are increasingly creating professional structures to deal with governments and institutions that regulate their activities, for example, lobbying government agencies (McLaughlin et al., 1993; Getz, 1997; Hadjikhani, 2000; Hadjikhani and Ghauri, 2001; Hadjikhani et al., 2008).

Governments, for their part, cannot be regarded as passive players. Relationships between governments and firms construct an arena of mutual influence where the limits of government of enforcement depends on the firms' economic power and where firms' power is restricted by the powers of governments to mediate those firms' opportunities and sources of competitive advantage. Outcomes are partly dependent on each party's negotiation skills and their ability to mobilize support for their respective objectives (Boddewyn and Brewer, 1994). However, the maintenance of firms' bargaining power and performance requires that they preserve strategic independence in their relations with government. For example, the possession by firms of indirect ties to government, such as through state enterprises having ownership stakes and board places in them (as is the case with YICT), was found in Russian banks to result in higher performance than having direct ties, probably because the latter introduces pressures on firms to evolve according to political agendas (Okhmatovskiy, 2010).

The foregoing discussion gives rise to four fundamental assumptions that underpin a political perspective on corporate co-evolution. The first is that we should take into account a range of power resources, the relative significance of which may change over time. The second assumption is that power operates through relationships and 'is inseparable from interaction' (Clegg et al., 2006: 6). The third assumption is that power is a capacity rather than the exercise of that capacity (Lukes, 2005). In other words, holding a power resource provides the potential for achieving influence but the outcome will depend on the dynamics of relations with the other parties involved. In order to affect both their own evolution and that of other parties, firms and external units have to translate sources of power into effective power (influence). The fourth assumption is that this translation is effected through activities within the relational framework between a firm and its relevant external parties.

POWER AND CO-EVOLUTION IN THE CASE OF YICT

The perspective just developed implies that an examination of how power impinges on co-evolutionary dynamics should proceed through three stages. The first stage would consider the power resources that apply and which create *initial conditions* for the organizations involved to exercise influence on one another's evolution. The second stage would examine how corporate leaders and external actors *construct and use a relational framework* to exercise influence. The third stage would consider how such influence advances the course of *co-evolution*. We now proceed through these three stages referring to the case of YICT.

ANALYSIS STAGE 1: BASES OF POWER

Table 5.1 in Chapter 5 listed the key players in YICT's co-evolution and their relevance. To infer the power resources of these key players, we used data from both interviews and documents. Inference was relatively straightforward for resources of a material and coercive nature, because these were clearly evidenced by features such as investment funds and formal legal rights respectively. Expertise could also be assessed relatively easily. For example, there was a consensus in the port industry press and circles about HPH's advanced practices, which Mainland Chinese ports clearly lacked when YICT was founded. Inference of legitimacy and reference-based power relied more on deductive reasoning supported by interviewee comments. For instance, the alignment of YICT's stated objectives with China's national development objectives was deduced to be conducive to the firm gaining legitimacy in governmental circles, and this was borne out subsequently by events such as public awards and approving visits to the port by Mainland VIPs.[4] On the government side, legitimacy to influence the company's evolution was formally based on legal and ownership rights. The presence of referent power was inferred from evidence that others identified with the focal party. Thus the referent power accorded to the firm through its parent company Chairman, Li Kashing, was presumed from evidence such as the public praise he was given by senior Mainland actors (for example, Li, 2010) and from their behaviour, such as accepting his personal hospitality. The Mainland government's identification with local Chinese players, and the support this gave to their mobilization were apparent in statements made at a time of tension in their relationship with the 'foreign' parent such as over the re-negotiation of YICT's ownership structure in 1999–2002.

Table 9.1 summarizes the power bases available to both YICT and key external government organizations in their co-evolutionary development. We arrived at the categories in the table by: (1) identifying the attributes that indicated the possession of power; and (2) applying the French and Raven scheme to classify those attributes. The second column of the table refers to sources of power available to the firm and which furnished the potential to influence the environment and its evolution. The third column refers to sources of power available to external parties and which provided the potential to influence the firm's evolution.

Sources of Power Available to the Company

Offering material inducements

The most significant material inducement that the company could offer to ensure compliance with its desired policies was its outlay of investment dollars. The initial tranche of HK$2.5 billion to develop Phase 1 of the port was quickly followed by an additional HK$4.7 billion in developing Phase 2. This took place ahead of the planned schedule, which also served to enhance the company's legitimacy with government. At a time when China had no experience in port development, and Shenzhen was only a small city, this material commitment was seen as a strong endorsement of both and a clear commitment to develop a modern international port. Since 2000, additional investment has amounted to HK$22 billion. To date the whole project has involved an investment of around HK$30 billion (US$3.8 billion). With the success brought by YICT's development, Shenzhen became a significant port city. From a greenfield site, Shenzhen grew into one of the largest hubs in South China, and the fourth largest port operator in the world, just after Singapore, Hong Kong and Shanghai. Such investment effectively put Yantian on the world map of container transportation in a matter of only 15 years.

One major use of the investment dollars was in the purchase of existing land and into reclamation and construction projects, including road and rail development. Other uses included provision of supporting facilities for agencies such as the customs and other inspectorates. As the investment projects progressed, and their success becoming evident, they generated other business activities and income associated with the port, such as taxes from ships calling, import and export taxes collected at the port, container repair, depot business, tug boat activities, export and import cargo consolidation business. An economic impact study identified a multiplier of seven in the income generated in the community for every dollar of income for the port operator.

Through other direct material contributions, YICT was partly responsible for bringing about the modernization of the inspection processes aided by a high level of computerization and automation. For example, materially assisted by the company, the Yantian Customs was the first in China to introduce the highly computerized electronic gates for customs control. With the company's financial aid, the port's branch of the Quarantine Inspectorate was one of the first to introduce new technology

Table 9.1 Bases for power and influence in YICT's co-evolution

Bases for power and influence: 'power resources'	Examples of YICT power resources	Examples of external (primarily government) organizations' power resources
Material resources: 'Possession of material resources which provide "the ability to reward" and confer benefits'	Significant outlay of investment dollars, both in basic facilities and in systems to support reforms in the practices of government agencies in the port Provision of tax and other public revenues Financing of local infrastructural developments Willingness to transfer advanced technology and practices	Concessions on tax and operational benefits, including majority ownership, freedom over pricing and employment policies Provision of in-port services such as customs
Coercion: 'Based on the ability to enforce conditions, and to withhold benefits and rewards'	Capacity to enforce contractual terms, specifically insisting on 'agreed conditions being met precedent to payment'	The right to withdraw concessions Sanction over granting of licences or permissions for YICT's future development The right of in-port regulatory agencies to halt throughput of cargo Constraints on YICT strategy imposed by competing ports in the region
Legitimacy: 'The exercise of power is regarded as rightful by all parties'	Alignment between the firm's vision of 'world-class' standards and national development objectives Providing funds and other support for agreed developments ahead of schedule and over and above formal expectations	Government intervention legitimated by laws (e.g. customs regulations) and by the official status of its agencies Shenzhen government's participation in YICT's strategic decision making was legitimated by its stake in ownership

Reference: 'The basis of a person's or unit's power lies in the identification of others with the power-holder'	High reputation in China of Li Kashing, Chairman of parent company [HPH] Parent company [HPH] is world's largest port operator: a 'famous name' in its industry	Government as guardian of national interests, especially in the abnormal situation of a majority 'foreign-owned' major infrastructural facility
Expertise: 'The expertise held by, or attributed to, a person or organization creates a willingness to accept his or her authority'	HPH (and increasingly YICT) was publicly recognized by the international industry as an expert organization in cargo handling, IT and management systems	Logistical operations in development of the hinterland. However, government at both local and central levels lacked modern port expertise. Competing ports also lagged behind YICT's practices and technology

Note: Definitions of bases for power are adapted from French and Raven (1960).

into hygiene control as part of certification for China's first 'hygienic port'. YICT was also one of the first to install X-ray machines for customs inspection, and, in the post 9/11 security conscious environment, the first to put in an automated system for security checking. In all these initiatives, YICT worked closely with the agencies in using technology and applying it to the port systems. Sometimes, additional investments from the port company were necessary and were offered in anticipation of future needs. More important, however, was what the General Manager termed 'thought leadership' in understanding the trends, the needs and the soft and hard technology involved in bringing about successes in the projects. This is an example of where material and ideational sources of influence worked together to secure compliance with the organization's wish to evolve into a world-class port. While the Yantian port made material progress in becoming one of the most modern and well recognized ports in the world, its management gained legitimacy and expert credibility through leading port development in Shenzhen. This combination of material and ideational bases of power became self-reinforcing over time, a process enhanced by the company's own initiatives to construct a relational framework with government bodies.

It is worth noting that YICT management's strategy of obtaining support for its service improvement and project development efforts were guided by an economic business model. This was based on the premise that the port's expansion and continuous investment was only possible if it was successful in providing a service to customers, and that service improvement is only achieved when all units and government agencies lend their support to the port operator. This positions the operator at the centre of integrating all the service elements in pursuit of the desired 'world-class' status. In numerous government-led operations meetings, the theme was always: 'how we can improve our service to obtain more throughput so that we can continue to grow?' The most senior government official in attendance, usually the Deputy Major acting in the interest of the Shenzhen city government and the Chinese joint venture partner, was able to leverage his influence over the government side with this economic message of growth and development.

Coercion

In a business relationship, it is unlikely that either the firm or its external parties can use direct coercion to force anything to happen. However, as the reverse of material inducements, coercion can be an option. It is especially powerful in enforcing agreed terms and conditions within a contract when such terms are well written and when the context is conducive to respecting the legal conditions of the contracts. In the case of YICT, the contracts were written tightly with specifications and mutual obligations clearly stated. For example, in contracts governing the payment of investment dollars to the Chinese partner, the 'conditions precedent to payment' were specified in very strict terms, so ensuring that certain conditions were met before cash changed hands. These conditions specified that given reforms in the port agencies should have taken place, or that construction work like provision of electricity or railway connections had to be completed, before effecting payment of money or proceeding to the next stage of development. However, the negotiation of such conditions needed to be very carefully handled lest they created too much tension between the joint venture partners and between the joint venture and the government.

Gaining legitimacy

Alignment of the company's policies and developments with the values of the community in which it functioned gained it legitimacy. The vision of a 'world-class port', which HPH and YICT publically espoused on the back of their investment, was a particularly strong source of influence because it positioned the firm as a leader in port development, not only in China but internationally. This ideational vision was strongly supported by Maersk, YICT's major customer and a minority shareholder.[5] It both constituted a claim to superior knowledge and created a social rationale for the port of considerable appeal to China's developmental aspirations. As quoted in Chapter 7, YICT's General Manager clearly expressed the view in 1997 that the company should lead with objectives that were consistent with China's national development agenda in order 'for the officials to be able to lend their support'.

Right from the start Hutchison had a high profile in the international port industry and was a 'famous brand'. As YICT advanced in terms of operational performance and profitability, it also took on this mantle – a facility that China could be proud of, with which leaders at different levels would like to be associated. There was a succession of VIP visits to YICT along with publicly approving statements, made by high officials including President Hu Jintou, Premier Wen Jiabo, Premier Li Peng and Premier Zhu Rongji. All this strengthened the company's public legitimacy. This made it easier to justify official support for YICT, whose majority non-Mainland equity share deviated from government policy on the ownership of infrastructure assets. The consistent securing of awards after 2001 from the Ministry of Communication's Chinese Port Association, and becoming the first China port to secure a global award in 2005, added further public recognition. Another boost to YICT's legitimacy stemmed from the way it provided funds and other support for agreed developments ahead of schedule and in excess of formal requirements. Legitimacy of this sort opened up opportunities for YICT to secure official recognition as the 'pilot' for modern port practice in China. This facilitated the evolution that the company desired and helped it to push for service improvements with government agencies.

The company's vision informed its policies on port construction and operations, as well as investment decisions. It dictated the specifications for port construction (for example, a 17 metre draft alongside quay decks), equipment level (the number of quay cranes and yard cranes and their specifications), the level of automation (degree of sophistication in the computer system) and operational excellence (productivity require-ments in terms of number of moves per operating hour), marketing, public relations, as well as human resources training and development. In these ways, the means by which the company gained legitimacy as a basis of power also enhanced other foundations such as the emergence of the company as an admired point of reference for its sector as a whole.

Referent power

In 2012, Hutchison Port Holdings (HPH) was operating 315 berths in 52 ports across 26 countries. It is a proven entity in port operations. The Chairman of the Hutchison-Whampoa holdings group, Li Kashing, enjoys extraordinary respect in China.[6] From the start, Hutchison there-fore served as a powerful referent for YICT. As events turned out, the port's ability to attract the world's largest shipping lines became well recognized. Even at an early stage when YICT was struggling to survive, questions were not asked by potential customers about its ability to handle vessels, but rather about its capacity to manage Chinese red tape. After an initial period of establishing itself, YICT proved to be a terminal that could handle high volumes with rapid turnaround in a manner that key shipping lines like Maersk and APL endorsed. YICT has been handling mega vessels consistently at 35 moves per crane hour, meeting and exceeding operational requirements of the carriers. Satisfied with the service it had been receiving at YICT, the Maersk line launched the world's largest container vessels using Yantian as a hub. YICT has for many years been known as the largest exporting port to the USA.

With the credibility to operate efficiently and service world-class clients, and with the conscious publicizing of this achievement, YICT gained the reputation as the most modern port in China. Its status as an industry referent was evidenced by the large number of visitors from all walks of life who visited the port. VIPs visiting the Shenzhen SEZ made a point of visiting the terminal and were favourably impressed. Moreover, because of the various pilot schemes that YICT organized with its relevant government agencies, they gained the prestige of having state-of-the-art units at the forefront of experimentation in the movement towards modernization. VIPs from these government departments were invited to see the port, as well as showcases like X-ray machines, CCTV control centres, security systems, and computer links. Heads of the local units gained recognition in front of their superiors. In contrast to the opposition they had shown in the mid-1990s, government agencies in the port subsequently demonstrated a growing commitment to supporting YICT in its forward evolution. The common thread running through these developments is that YICT secured leverage for its own evolution and also influenced that of external agencies through developing referent power.

Expert power
The power that YICT derived from being seen as an expert operator within its international sector was closely associated with its emerging status as an admired point of reference. Being perceived and recognized by the industry as an expert helped YICT to seek government support in maintaining the terminal's 'world-class' status. Its acknowledged expertise was sustained both by investment in the most advanced technology and by taking the initiative in introducing advanced management techniques and cultivating an association with centres of learning.

As Chapter 6 described, YICT invested in the latest technology in computer and mechanical handling systems, planning and operations. Its size – by 2007 it became the largest single terminal in the world – meant that it could afford to invest in new technology, such as in dual hoist handling and tandem lift quay cranes. These cranes helped raise the port's operating efficiency. YICT also employed the latest IT systems in yard management so that it could handle the large number of containers stored in the yard – at times over 100 000 boxes – and still maintain high efficiency during the peak season. The company invested in Six Sigma processes, approaching General Electric and Motorola directly to obtain the relevant know-how. The introduction of new practices such as this assumed wider significance because they ensured that a continuous improvement culture prevailed in the company's operations. It also maintained active links with various business schools and other educational institutions, offering itself as a site for research projects which its managers regarded as valuable learning opportunities. YICT became recognized externally as a hub of expertise and in some areas, its level of expertise exceeding that of its Hong Kong parent. In negotiations to promote an evolution of both attitude and practice within the company and among external parties, this expertise was a source of respect and influence.

Sources of Power Available to External Parties

By far the most significant category of player in its environment in terms of influence over YICT's evolution is the Chinese government in the form of various official bodies at central and local levels. These bodies exercised influence primarily through their potentially coercive powers. These were formally legitimized by law and also received some referent support in terms of reflecting national interests. Expert power was not relevant, since government at both central and local levels lacked expertise of a technical and managerial kind in the running of modern ports. In addition, as YICT came to face growing competition from other new South China ports, its strategic choices were to a degree also constrained by that source, particularly with regard to pricing.

Offering material inducements
Its location in an SEZ meant that YICT was offered various favourable material inducements, such as a 100 per cent exemption from profit tax for the first five years followed by a 50 per cent exemption for the next five years. This was standard for companies located in SEZs. More discretionary, and therefore more at risk of being rescinded, were the provisions of a special support programme for the joint venture. These included the acceptance of non-Mainland majority ownership, granting the right to YICT to set prices for its services, and to hire and fire according to commercial principles. Although basically regulatory in purpose, the provision of in-port government services could also be seen as a material power resource.

Coercion
Chinese government authorities had coercive powers which could potentially impact on YICT's evolution. These were wide-ranging and concerned both its mode of operation and future expansion. Government agencies exercised considerable influence over the port's everyday operations in terms of what could be done or not done concerning ship and cargo clearance, tax and payment of duties, customs and quarantine checks. This last not only involved possible taxes and fines, but also impacted on the throughput times that the port could achieve. As we have seen, YICT's management went to considerable efforts to negotiate changes in customs procedures which were handicapping its ability to compete and to evolve toward achieving the goal of a world-class port.

Regarding its longer-term evolution, each stage of the port's expansion had to have prior approval from both local and national governments. Many ministries were involved. The state planning commission examined economic feasibility, the trade ministry looked at international trade aspects, the finance ministry investigated foreign exchange implications, the investment ministry looked at investment needs, and the ministry of transportation and communications went into the technical aspects of logistics and the like. Every other agency concerned with the port also had to approve a new development since this required them to invest in additional resources and support. A great amount of lobbying and negotiation had to take place for any new phase of the port's expansion to be approved. Literally hundreds of 'chops' were required from both the SEZ and the central government.

Another 'coercive' influence on YICT's evolution derived from the increasing competition that it faced. As YICT became more successful after 2000, new entrants were drawn into the South China port sector and competition became keener. This competition had several effects on YICT's evolution. It reduced YICT's initial monopolistic market power. In the early period (1995–2000), YICT was virtually the only international port of call in Shenzhen. Hutchison's operations in Hong Kong were the main competitor. YICT charged a tariff slightly below Hong Kong's, but at a significant premium (25–30 per cent) over what other port operators in the region commanded. Growing competition raised the cost of development for subsequent phases of YICT because it had to retain the edge in service level – such as increasing the size of container vessel that could be accommodated. However, as the number of players increased, the companies concerned became more isomorphic in their actions and applied the Hong Kong tradition of 'oligopolistic interdependence' (Cheng and Wong, 1997). They learned that any extreme action taken by one player would affect all the players in the industry in areas such as labour negotiations, competitive pricing and offering incentives to port agencies. The ports in the area also joined forces under YICT's leadership to lobby on issues of common concern such as getting the local government to initiate a programme for port security and to improve the road infrastructure.

Legitimacy and referent power
There is a long history in China, predating the Communist regime, of government intervention and ownership in business and industry (Faure, 2006). As Redding and Witt observe (2007: 43), 'the assumption that only a central government power was appropriate was implanted from the beginning and has survived to the present day'. We have noted the powers that government agencies had to intervene in both YICT's operations and expansion plans. These were legitimated by law and by the undisputed authority that such agencies enjoy in the Chinese business

system. In addition to the rights attaching to the jurisdictions of government agencies, in the case of YICT the Shenzhen local government has the right to participate in decisions on the company's evolution by virtue of its ownership share and its representation on the joint venture's Board of Directors. The Shenzhen partner used YICT's dependence on it, and on the approvals of central government agencies, as leverage to negotiate a higher ownership stake as a condition for agreeing to investment in the port's further expansion.

Some of the power enjoyed by the government agencies with which YICT had to deal was also of a referent nature, though this source overlapped with the legitimacy they enjoyed. YICT was in the highly abnormal position of being an infrastructural facility of strategic national importance under the majority ownership and managerial control of a non-Mainland multinational corporation. In this situation, government agencies were not only exercising their normal rights to confer approval on throughput in the port; they were additionally playing the role of national guardian in so doing. They could, and did, question whether YICT was evolving in the best interests of China by maintaining HPH's majority shareholding in the later stages of the port's development. This issue became increasingly acute as YICT gained an influential position in the Chinese port industry. Chapter 5 noted how, during the negotiations over Phase 3 development, some Chinese officials actually urged the local partner to establish a competing facility.

ANALYSIS STAGE 2: THE EXERCISE OF INFLUENCE IN A RELATIONAL FRAMEWORK

Having identified initial conditions giving the players in the YICT case the potential to exercise influence, we now turn to evidence of how a relational framework between them was created and used to advance their preferred evolutionary paths. This is illustrated primarily with the events described in Chapter 8 concerning the evolution of government agency practices both within the Yantian port and in the Chinese port sector as a whole. We shall also refer to another salient issue which, although it bears particularly on co-evolution, illustrates how influence was exercised within the relational framework between the firm and external agencies. This was the question of ownership which arose during the negotiations over the Phase 3 expansion.

The process of co-evolution in this area advanced through events at three system levels: 'macro' (central government), 'meso' (local government and the port sector in China) and 'micro' (YICT and its parent company HPH). The first two levels are external to the firm, although in practice distinctions between the levels are not always clear-cut. For example, central government agencies operated within the port, and the special access to central government that Li Kashing enjoyed blurs the distinction between micro and macro levels. Table 8.2 in Chapter 8 summarized the main events occurring during the period from 1991 to 2010. It is evident that the relationship between the firm and government was particularly active at certain periods (such as 1993, 1995–96 and 1999–2003) when key issues were at stake. However, the rapid rate of change never allowed it to become dormant.

Table 9.2 re-categorizes key events within the relational framework between the firm and government bodies ('environment') according to the power resources in play. The table shows how the principal actors used their sources of power to take initiatives which promoted the evolution both of the firm and also of its environment. There is clear evidence of intentionality among actors at all levels. Some senior government actors as well as those in Shenzhen were committed to a reform agenda. Senior management in YICT and HPH also had a clear agenda to secure reforms that permitted advance toward their vision of a world-class port. However, intentionality toward co-evolution was qualified. There was not always clarity or agreement among government officials over port reform and they needed persuading to permit the reforms at Yantian. Although YICT, as the official pilot project, did influence the evolution of the wider port system, the prime intentionality of its management was to improve the firm's own operating circumstances – as the General Manager put it, 'YICT was after commercial success, not national influence'.[7]

An initial exercise of influence came when Zhu Rongi in 1991 invited Li Kashing as HPH Chairman to modernize the Shanghai ports. This opened new opportunities for HPH to evolve into Mainland China on favourable terms, which resulted in the 1993 joint venture agreement establishing YICT. The agreement's granting of majority non-Mainland ownership of a major infrastructural facility and its five directives for reform of in-port government agency practices were both significant departures from precedent – a clear break from path-dependence. The firm's intention was then to work with the government agencies to initiate in-port reforms, legitimated by the central government's signing of the JV agreement as well as by support from Maersk, a major customer. The fact that these met with initial resistance led to preparations for the negotiations of 1995 and 1996 to secure implementation as well as simplification of the government agency structure. Official recognition in November 1995 of Yantian as the 'pilot site' for national

Table 9.2   Power resources relevant to initiatives in the co-evolution of the firm and its environment[1]

Initiatives by the firm	Initiatives from the environment
Material	
1991–92: Li Kashing decides to commit investment to China rather than just donations.	The Maersk shipping line, a major customer, takes a 10% stake in YICT and strongly supports plans for Yantian to become a major port.
1992: Opening of negotiations to establish YICT. Li is the lead negotiator using his and HPH's high investment offer and reference power to negotiate favourable terms.	1996: Central government initiative under Vice Premier Li Lanqing reorganizes government agencies operating within Chinese ports.
1993+ HPH invests heavily in the expansion of Yantian port.	
1995/6: In preparation of the Li Lanqing report, HPH facilitates visits by a senior government study group to foreign ports to witness international port 'best practice'.	
2002+ YICT invested in new technologies to support government port authorities activities.	
Coercive	
1997+ YICT's successful marketing to end users created higher port service demands. That in turn increased pressure on the Customs Administration for further reforms of practice.	1994+ Implementation of port reform directives is initially resisted by government agencies within the Yantian port. Regulatory controls threatened YICT's ability to grow through attracting customers.
	1999: Premier Zhu Rongi initiates a freeze on headcount in regulatory authorities; this encourages them to accept YICT's investment in labour and time-saving technology in the context of rapid growth in the port's throughput.
	1999–2003: negotiations over approval of Yantian port expansion [Phase 3]: threat from some government officials to establish competing terminal facility.
	2000+ Increasing competition from other Shenzhen ports.

Legitimatory

1995: Formal announcement of YICT's intention to become a 'world class port'.

1995: YICT signs an MOU with government to become the 'pilot site' for national reforms in port customs administration.

2001+ YICT wins series of national awards. In 2005 YICT was recognized by the Global Institute of Logistics as the 'Global Terminal of the Year'.

2005: Development of China hub strategy to cater for mega vessels. The port further developed as a showcase for Shenzhen.

1991: Zhu Rongji (then Mayor of Shanghai) invites Li Kashing (HPH Chairman) to modernize the Shanghai ports, unusually offering a 50% ownership stake.

1993: Public governmental endorsement of YICT by the personal presence of both President and Premier at the signing ceremony establishing YICT, October 1993.

1993: The State Council considers establishing Yantian port as a pilot project for port reform in China.

1995: Customs Administration and YICT sign MOU to simplify transit and clearance procedures at Yantian port, November.

1996+ Visits by central government ministers and commissioners endorsed developments at Yantian port. Deputy Minister of Communications and his colleagues increasingly consult YICT senior managers for advice.

1999: Maersk endorses YICT's plans to build mega port capability.

Reference

1992–93: Li Kashing leads for Hutchison in negotiation to establish YICT – his reference power helps secure unprecedented terms on ownership and management rights.

1996+ YICT becomes official point of reference for China's port reform.

Initiatives by the firm	Initiatives from the environment
	Expert
1993: HPH through a detailed report puts forward the case for YICT to be treated as a 'pilot site' for modern port management. HPH starts on plans to develop YICT into an advanced 'mega' port.	1999+ Dissemination of practices pioneered by YICT to other container ports in China, especially newly developed ones such as Ningbo, Tianjin and Xiamen. Other Shenzhen ports and Shanghai adopted systems similar to Yantian's.
1994–95: HPH and YICT lobby the Ministry of Communications, resulting in an official study group which visited Yantian and Shenzhen.	
1995: YICT signs an MOU with government to become the 'pilot site' for national reforms in port customs administration.	
1995–96: In preparation of the Li Lanqing report, HPH facilitates visits by a senior government study group to foreign ports to witness international port 'best practice'.	
2001: YICT joint project with the Frontier Inspectorate resulted in speeding of port clearance.	
2002+ YICT introduced several best practices to improve the quality of its services: e.g. introduction of paperless fully automated international trans-shipment system; pre-clearance of empty import containers; same day clearance of inspections and application of the 'hygienic port' concept. It also invested in supporting technologies for inspection and surveillance.	

Note: ¹The 'firm' refers to YICT and its majority parent company, HPH. The 'environment' refers primarily to Chinese government units at a central level (for example, Ministry) and local level (for example, Shenzhen SEZ government). To a lesser extent it refers to competitors and customers.

234

port administration reforms was a major breakthrough legitimizing YICT's aim to develop a 'world-class port' and its leading status in the Chinese port system. It opened up a wider programme of port reform in China as a whole.

Another feature of the power resources underlying the relational process between the company and government clearly emerges from Table 9.2. The company (YICT and HPH) was able primarily to marshal material and expert power resources to support its objectives, though both categories of resource were also sources of its growing legitimacy in the eyes of the Chinese authorities. These authorities for their part relied primarily on a combination of their coercive powers and their ability to confer legitimacy to the firm. They were lacking in expert power and, in light of the country's official policy to reform and open the Chinese economy, this created a dependency on the firm as a leader of port improvement both through the investment it was willing to commit and in the concepts and practices it applied.

ANALYSIS STAGE 3: INFLUENCE WORKING THROUGH A RELATIONAL FRAMEWORK AS A DRIVER OF CO-EVOLUTION

As indicated by Table 8.1 in Chapter 8, both external parties (primarily governmental) and the firm were drivers of some evolutionary developments within each other's domain as well as within their own domains. External parties initiated actions that led to or enabled their own evolution or the evolution of the firm. Similarly, the firm initiated actions that led to or enabled its own evolution. It also initiated some actions that led to or enabled the evolution of aspects of its environment, namely China's port sector or relevant Chinese government policies. It is significant that, with the notable exception of China's reform and opening programme, virtually all of the developments noted in Table 8.1 resulted from or were substantially shaped by interaction between the firm and external bodies. This illustrates how mutual influence within the relational framework between the parties played a central role in their co-evolution.

Official commitment to the policy of economic reform and opening to the outside world created a climate that was conducive to the introduction of reforms in China's port practice. Lack of reforms in the country's antiquated ports would seriously inhibit the growth of trade necessary to support economic growth. Part of that reform concerned the standard of physical facilities and part concerned the organization and practices of in-port regulatory authorities.

In these respects, a change in the external macro environment established drivers for evolution in the port sector as a whole as well as in that domain of government concerned with the sector. These contextual changes had consequences also for evolution at the more specific level of YICT and its Yantian port. The rapid rate of economic growth that China achieved after 1992, led by South China, provided an economic justification for YICT to invest long term for world-class standards and practices. Moreover, an important instrument of China's economic reform was the establishment of the SEZs, including Shenzhen. The desire of the Shenzhen government to make its city a beacon of modernization favoured YICT's proclaimed aim of becoming a world-class port. It encouraged the company's Shenzhen joint venture partner to back many of the company's proposals for developing the port. This support often took the form of active engagement alongside the company in lobbying higher governmental authorities. Subsequent recognition of Yantian as the country's official pilot site for port reform, complemented by high level visits, public praise and awards, lent further backing to the evolution of the port as the leader in its field.

The macro environment was therefore positive for an evolution in port practices and standards. It led the government to be favourably disposed to co-opting Hutchison and other leading non-Mainland multinationals to provide support for the reform programme. This is a highly significant point because it recalls that the impact of the reform on firm-level practice came about largely through the medium of cooperation with the government – through the relational framework that developed. Government took the crucial initiating steps, such as the Shenzhen government's initiative in securing investment for Yantian's Phase 1 and Zhu Rongi's 1991 invitation to Li Kashing to help with the modernization of Shanghai port. Subsequently, YICT with the backing of its parent company played a proactive role in developing a relational framework with government. To make the appropriate connections, YICT's management secured the help of key influential figures within government circles to reach ministry chiefs to conduct lobbying.

Li Kashing was a key agent in YICT's evolution. On major issues Li maintained personal contact with national leaders who regularly visited him. He could therefore represent the firm's case on such matters. According to informants, his role at the time of YICT's founding, and throughout its evolution, was threefold. It combined articulating a vision, authorizing investment decisions, and opening top-level government doors to create or sustain a relational framework. As the YICT General Manager explained:

> In broad terms, the Chairman would tell the implementers the big ideas – overall strategies like we must secure development rights to Phase 3, have controlling shares in the joint venture, reasonable land prices – leaving details to implementers. The broad guidelines then became the umbrella for investment decisions in support of 'world-class' standards and the mega hub strategy advocated by YICT management ... The Chairman was very conscious of his influence and worked hard at cultivating his capability to do so. He kept an active list of contacts with government, at both local and national levels, and was included in most of the relevant economic and political committees reserved for influential Hong Kong leaders. In fact, he was regarded as the leading Hong Kong businessman with an international reputation and influence. Normally quite low profile, he appeared high profile on the right issues to ensure he and the Group appeared in a favourable light in front of the national leaders. They also made regular visits to see him. He hosted President Jiang Zemin's visit to Hong Kong in his hotel during the 1997 Hong Kong handover ceremony. He became the best known business person in China and among all leading Chinese officials. For some less senior officials, having an audience with K.S. Li was an honour in itself. As a subsidiary of the Hutchison Group, YICT learned to leverage the Chairman's influence.[8]

Other network links were also important. To gain access and cultivate the necessary relationships, the YICT management also secured the help of key influential figures within government circles to reach ministry chiefs to conduct lobbying. For example, through the introduction of the former Shenzhen Party Secretary and Mayor, a personal friend of the head of the China Customs Administration, the YICT team met the top customs officers in Beijing and secured the opportunity to explain the importance of customs reforms for port development. That eventually led to the November 1995 signing of the Port Reform MOU in Shenzhen, attended personally by the National Commissioner of Customs Administration. YICT's Advisory Group, which was largely composed of former senior government officials, and its China Affairs Department, worked on the company's behalf in enlarging and deepening the relational framework with government officials – what the company called 'relationship management'. Using insider knowledge, the former helped to open doors at the higher level while the latter concentrated on middle levels.[9]

Securing all the necessary approvals for major port developments typically took three to five years of lobbying and follow-up by company staff (sometimes whole departments) dedicated to the task. One interviewee described how the process passed through different government levels:

First of all, the agenda for change is set at the local level in discussions with the local government chief. To get his agreement, we have to work on the details of implementation to ensure that the local team is comfortable with the potential success of the change. Then we have to sell it upstairs. We must use powerful people to help us connect to the top.[10]

In addition to actual project costs, the YICT Board allocated an annual budget to the General Manager's office for lobbying and supporting activities such as commissioning reports. According to the General Manager:

Lobbying and negotiation with partners and government occupied senior management's attention more than the operational aspects of running the company's day-to-day business. Without a doubt they were the job number one for top management. Executives were assigned specific responsibilities to contact and build relationships with different government bureaucracies and officials within them.[11]

The firm's intention to work with the government agencies to initiate in-port reforms was legitimated by the central government's endorsement of the JV agreement as well as by support from Maersk, a major customer. The fact that these reforms met with initial resistance led to preparations for the negotiations of 1995 and 1996 to secure implementation as well as simplification of the government agency structure. Official recognition in November 1995 of Yantian as the 'pilot site' for national port administration reforms was a major breakthrough in legitimizing YICT's aim to develop a world-class port and its leading status in the Chinese port system. It opened up a wider programme of port reform in China as a whole.

In the course of a few years, the YICT team developed a full agenda for reform in government agency port practice ranging from simplification of procedures to innovations in controls employing the latest computer technology. The company formulated specific programme objectives, examined existing procedures, and then proposed and drafted new procedures and detailed implementation plans. The intention behind these was firstly that the firm's agenda supported the country's broad reform objectives of growth and development; secondly, that the proposed changes were low risk and implementable; and thirdly, that the frontline government officials charged with implementation had a sense of owning the reforms. Its willingness to provide supporting investment and technology not only made these initiatives possible but also helped to secure legitimacy for them. These changes, previously set out in Chapter 8 (Table 8.2), enabled the young port to handle the volume of trade attracted to use its facilities which grew at over 30 per cent per annum in some years. As also noted in Chapter 8, the changes introduced at Yantian, in turn, had an impact on the evolution of the sector environment through their subsequent dissemination to other Chinese ports. The status of official pilot site was undoubtedly a supportive factor, but so also was the success of the port itself which was increasingly recognized through a stream of public awards. In this way, a mutually-supportive co-evolution got underway.[12] As a precondition for this development, it had been necessary to establish a relational framework between YICT and government agencies, both at the local level and centrally. Although the initial moves in establishing this framework had been made by government ministers and Li Kashing, YICT's management had to invest considerable effort in deepening and expanding it, often with significant help from its advisors and Shenzhen party and government officials.

In the YICT case, corporate co-evolution occurred insofar as the nature of the focal firm as well as characteristics of its environment were altered over time as the result of interaction between the two. The process exhibited several of the features identified by Lewin and Volberda (1999). Change was promoted by mutual direct interactions between the firm and external agencies and hence manifested multidirectional causality. It also proceeded across several levels (Baum and Singh, 1994), both across the divide between macro (central and local government, the port sector) and micro (YICT and its majority-owning parent) as well as within each category. Moreover, it is possible to identify key initiating events, such as Zhu Rongi's 1991 invitation to Li Kashing and the 1993 joint venture agreement. However, while these were breakthroughs, it could be argued that the combination of China's official reform programme with HPH's overall port developmental strategy delineated the path along which subsequent incremental evolution proceeded along increasingly collaborative lines. Positive feedback loops reinforced this trend. For, despite the conflict over the Phase 3 development, as the fruits of modernization and reformed practices became evident, the relationship between firm and units of government exhibited more 'power with' and less 'power over'.

THE POLITICAL DYNAMICS OF CORPORATE CO-EVOLUTION

The YICT case validates and augments the political perspective on corporate co-evolution advanced in the first part of this chapter. It suggests that while a power 'base' provides the potential for exercising influence, and is an essential initial condition, translating that influence into actual evolution requires a more elaborate process. Power resources per se are not sufficient to bring about co-evolution. Both YICT (supported by its main parent company) and relevant Chinese officials had to be far-sighted and accommodating in their use of the power resources at their disposal. In addition a relational framework had to be established for them to negotiate, receive proposals, and discuss together. Over time, this framework, set within benign economic circumstances, enabled their relationship to take on a 'power with' nature.

Various power resources were utilized by both the firm and external organizations to create propitious grounds for each to realize its objectives through engendering change by the other party. As set out in Table 9.1 and illustrated in Table 9.2, these power resources consisted of *a combination of material and ideational factors, which tended to be mutually reinforcing*. However, power resources by themselves do not necessarily generate co-evolution between a firm and external organizations. For this to happen, the case suggests that two conditions have to be present. First, there has to be a *relational framework* between the actors, which will take time and effort to develop. In the YICT case, a relational framework was established through several initiatives taken both by senior government officials and by the HPH chairman. The leaders of the firm then initiated a series of actions to enlarge and deepen that relational framework over time. These actions gave them access to decision-makers higher up in the system and facilitated acceptance of their objectives. The ability to open up a relational framework, and to translate power resources into effective influence, also depends upon the successful mobilization of support from key players in the system. Mobilization requires a series of initiatives. YICT's management made efforts to develop the relational frameworks initiated by the HPH Chairman in order to undertake informal lobbying for support from key external actors. It often secured the support of the company's local partner, effectively the Shenzhen SEZ government, when lobbying central government ministries. The relationship between the firm and government was particularly active at certain periods (such as 1993, 1995–96 and 1999–2003) when key issues were at stake, such as resistance by government agencies to port reform and negotiations over the approval of port expansion respectively.

The second condition for co-evolution to occur is that there needs to be specific proposals for change in both the firm and its environment. Cognitive framing around ideas such as 'a world-class port' was translated into proposals that largely emanated from YICT. These were couched within the general ambit of China's reform and were presented as conforming to the principles of that reform. Together with its parent group, YICT's management sponsored studies that led to specific plans, which it backed with offers of investment. Thus, while the resources available to a focal organization may encourage, even oblige, other organizations to enter a relational framework with it, the exercise of influence on the evolution of these other parties is strengthened by *initiatives expressed in tangible proposals* that appeal to the interests and/or beliefs of the other parties and so help to mobilize their support and establish legitimacy in their eyes.

The process of mobilizing support for evolutionary change also depended on managing the power dynamics between different levels. YICT is embedded at the nexus of an external environment, which has dual central and local regulatory levels, and an internal context created by the duality of HPH and YPG. In this respect, it is a hybrid organization. This created a kind of 'institutional duality' (Kostova and Roth, 2002) or more precisely an 'institutional plurality' which denied YICT full autonomy of action. YICT and its parent companies each had its own identity in dealing with the external environment. These identities merged into one when it came to lobbying for expansion and support of the port, lobbying for government support especially to secure customs reforms, and in promoting the brand name. At other times, however, conflicts between various actors at different levels posed a critical threat to YICT's evolution at several points, such as resistance to the port's rapid expansion within HPH, and conflicts between the parent companies during the Phase 3 negotiations. Another example of a multi-level process was the need for the firm to lobby for central government directives in order to obtain the cooperation of local regulatory bodies to implement in-port reforms. Despite the risk of conflicts, a high degree of interpenetration across system levels of this kind may prove to be particularly propitious for co-evolution to take place since it allows for strong relational frameworks.

The notion of co-evolution simply being between a 'firm' and its 'environment' can mask these more complex power dynamics between organizational pluralities. There were on-going subsidiary interactions within the broader co-evolution of YICT and the governmental environment: between the firm and its parent companies, and between different levels and agencies of government. It is therefore not necessarily possible to provide straightforward answers concerning 'what co-evolves with what?' or concerning the nature of the relational framework within which co-evolutionary links are forged.

The YICT case also illustrates feedback loops within the co-evolutionary process. As the co-evolutionary dynamic between YICT and external organizations – both governmental as well as competitors – progressed, the company's high levels of performance based on advanced practices enhanced both its legitimacy and its ability to mobilize support for the evolutionary path it sought to travel. Not only did the company achieve outstanding levels of performance in its own operations, but also the reforms it initiated and helped to disseminate as a pilot demonstration project within its sector directly influenced the evolution of that sector and in so doing contributed to China's wider economic and social development. The success of these reforms helped to legitimate the company's actions further in the eyes of government and to mobilize support within higher governmental circles, as demonstrated publicly by top level visits to the port. Its tangible and substantial material investments lent credibility to, and trust in, its ideational claim to be a world-class port. Investment in advanced facilities and state-of-the-art technologies also gave esteem to senior officials which encouraged their co-optation. Thus the customs office at Yantian became the most advanced in China and the techniques introduced by YICT management provided government officials with inputs they could use to formulate proposals for reform across their different agencies.

The YICT case suggests that material power resources always play an essential role in corporate co-evolution because of the fundamentally economic nature of the focal organization. The role of material resources is likely to be most crucial in the early stages of co-evolution before other resources have been developed. The mutual attractiveness of material benefits is often the basis on which a relational framework is initiated. Even in YICT's case where the establishment of that framework owed much to Li Kashing's reference power – based on his prestige and status in Mainland China – it was HPH's capacity to contribute materially to the development of China's port system that was the initial attractor for both firm and government. While non-material power resources can operate from the start of the relational process, such as HPH's acknowledged expertise, they are likely to grow in significance over the course of co-evolution as and when the relational framework deepens. Although material and coercive resources did not cease to be relevant to the co-evolutionary process, particularly when major expansions were proposed, the significance of ideational resources grew in a way that is somewhat parallel to models of trust development (for example, Lewicki and Bunker, 1996). This is part and parcel of being far-sighted in the use of initial power resources so as to build up approval and identification between the co-evolving parties.

Despite points of conflict such as the regulatory agencies' initial resistance to reform, over time the relationship between the company and government bodies became primarily a process of 'power with'. This meant that both the company and government agencies were able to rely increasingly on 'soft power' (Nye, 2004). The process of co-evolution progressed through an augmentation of the social capital between firm and external agencies in which their relationship came to embody greater consensus and mutual confidence. Even when the politically sensitive issue of ownership arose again with the port's Phase 3 expansion, there was sufficient mutual goodwill to result in an agreed compromise solution. Several reasons can be proffered for this trend. The continued commitment of material resources by HPH to YICT, even in the early loss-making period, demonstrated the good faith of its intentions. Equally, the growing flexibility of the government authorities to countenance reforms provided a platform for goodwill in the firm's eyes. The firm itself learned the importance of publicly articulating a mission, which accorded well with national aspirations, and it also learned to devote resources to managing its relations with external bodies. This enriching of the relations between firm and government is consistent with the tendency in East Asia to favour 'governed interdependence' in which collaboration between state and industry enhance the capabilities of both (Weiss, 1995).

Figure 9.1 models the process whereby the dynamics of influence enter into corporate co-evolution as indicated by the insights just noted. For simplicity, we present the model to focus on actions taken by the firm. It articulates the view that, contrary to the inexorable environmental determinism of the Darwinian tradition, corporate co-evolution can at least under some circumstances be driven by corporate initiatives. Also, in contrast to Darwinism, our analysis implies that there is a range of possible outcomes to the co-evolutionary process. There is no denying that some firms survive while others fail, but this is at least partly a consequence of how successful their leaders are in exercising strategic choice through political initiatives (Child, 1997). A political perspective injects a degree of uncertainty into the process of co-evolution. It draws to attention the fact that relationships between firms and organizations in their environments rest upon different symmetries of power and are characterized by open-ended processes of mobilization and negotiation. Although we have emphasized the role of relational frameworks in facilitating co-evolution, not all interactions within them lead to co-evolution. Our argument is that actions building on sources of power to create influence are the ones most likely to drive co-evolution. We noted, for example, how HPH combined material, referential and expert power with skilful negotiation to secure the establishment of YICT on terms that were politically extraordinary at the time and that triggered a

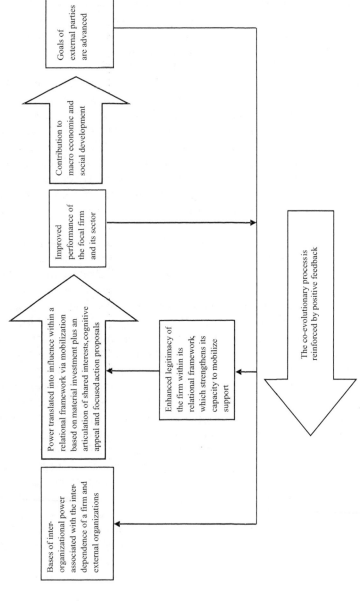

Figure 9.1 The processes of organizational influence in corporate co-evolution

process of reform in the wider Chinese port sector. Later on, public recognition of the world-leading performance achieved by the port enhanced its legitimacy as a pilot for sector-wide reforms.

CONCLUSION

This chapter has offered a political perspective that contributes to unpacking the dynamics of corporate co-evolution. It does so by highlighting the importance of relational frameworks through which an organization and significant external parties can exercise influence on each other by mobilizing and legitimating identifiable sources of power. It also indicates that the concept of 'corporate' co-evolution can helpfully indicate the role that firm-level initiatives can play in the evolution of a whole sector (population). In the case studied, co-evolution arose from a combination of social actions and was reinforced by positive performance effects. While the presence of a favourable economic environment was a fundamental condition for this co-evolution, insight into more specific conditions emerged from examining the relational framework that developed between key corporate and external power-holders. One such condition is the necessity not just to have relevant power resources but also to know how to use them.

Another contribution of this study lies in its demonstration of Lewin and Volberda's (1999) argument that the co-evolutionary process spans different levels of analysis that have become conventional distinctions within organizational and strategic studies. The relational framework or network of relationships that was central to YICT's co-evolution crossed a number of levels including the company itself, its international owning group, the Chinese port sector, local government and central government. Moreover, it was not just relationships that spanned these levels. It was also essential for successful co-evolution that there was a cognitive bridging as well; that the actors concerned understood how developments at the company level carried implications for those at the sector and national levels and vice versa.

Prevailing co-evolutionary theories tend to treat institutions and firms as distinct entities. The YICT case demonstrates that this boundary is not necessarily clear-cut. The firm in question is a joint venture between HPH, an MNC ultimately controlled by Li Kashing, and the Yantian Port Group which is an arm of the Shenzhen city government. While the joint venture is legally a firm and operates like one, at the same time it could be considered as one of the several interpenetrations of firm and state that occur in this case study. Moreover, the Yantian Port Group is simultaneously a firm and a local state actor in competition with other state (municipally) owned ports such as Shanghai. Similarly, Li Kashing, a key player, is a firm owner but also highly integrated into China's institutional fabric having direct access to the corridors of power in Beijing. So conventional theoretical identities based on levels of analysis are conflated. However, this is not so much a problem of methodology but, rather, it points to the limitations of theory derived from 'western' situations in which these boundaries are more discrete than is the case in China where, as noted, government interpenetrates business to a high degree. A high degree of interpenetration across system levels of this kind may prove to be particularly propitious for co-evolution to take place since it allows for strong and active relational frameworks. This is an issue which further studies in comparable environments may serve to clarify.

Our thesis in the writing of this book is that a political perspective is valuable for an understanding of corporate co-evolution. However, this still leaves the question of how this perspective matches up against alternative explanations. It is possible to argue that the main paths of evolution at macro and micro levels would have come about in any case because of fundamental economic forces. China's coastal economy boomed after 1992. This inevitably placed a premium on building additional port capacity and improving the productivity of existing capacity. So it can be maintained that the demand for container port services would have attracted new entrants, who would have introduced world-class standards which would have eventually diffused throughout the sector in China entailing, among other changes, reforms in government port procedures. In other words, economic forces would have led to co-evolution anyway.

While the economics cannot be denied, a purely economic explanation cannot take into account the actions that had to be taken, even the struggles that had to be endured, to make these changes happen at different levels of the system. Economic forces might eventually catch up with inertia, but they do not readily explain how proactive change comes about. They do not provide any insight into how change was accomplished through interaction with conservative bureaucratic agencies. Without reference to political factors, a large part of the story would be missing. This missing element is precisely the part that is of particular value to would-be change agents who need to know what can be done to take co-evolution forward and how to do it. It is instructive here to compare the situation in Brazil where the country's potential for rapid growth in international trade is being severely handicapped by largely unreformed port practices (Noble, 2010; IBAdev, 2011). This suggests that economic rationality does not necessarily bring about co-evolutionary change and that political obstacles can stand in the way.

Considering their rarity and their potential for offering fresh insights, there can be little question about the desirability of further studies on the processes of change involved in corporate co-evolution. It would be particularly valuable to compare such processes in situations which contrast both in environments and in the proactive moves made by firms. However, such studies face two significant challenges. One is the practical problem of obtaining sufficient and valid information about what goes on in the relations between key organizational actors and key external actors. Such information is normally confidential and carefully guarded from the prying eyes of investigators. This is not an easy obstacle to address and doing so may depend largely on finding participants in the process who appreciate the value of collaborating with scholars. The second obstacle is more of our own making. This is the inadequate conceptualization and theorization of the subject and in particular the theoretical myopia of single-discipline explanations. Recognizing this, the present chapter has advanced a fresh perspective that can usefully add to current theorizing on organizational change and co-evolution.

NOTES

1. This chapter draws in part from Child, Rodrigues and Tse (2012).
2. The differentiation between material and ideational sources of power derives from Weber's analysis of socio-economic development (Mommsen, 1989).
3. French and Raven call this 'reward power'.
4. See the Appendix in Chapter 8 for a list of the most significant national and international awards conferred on YICT.
5. Interview with Maersk's Henrik Zeuthen, *South China Morning Post: Freight and Shipping Post*, p. 3, 28 November 1994.
6. An indication of this respect and how it contributed to creating a relational framework between Hutchison (and therefore YICT) and the Chinese government is provided by former Vice Premier Li Lanqing (2010) in his book *Breaking Through: The Birth of China's Opening-up Policy*. Li Lanqing mentions a list of powerful HK businessmen who donated money and invested in China's economic zones, saying that 'some have become my personal friends' (Lanqing, 2010: 252). Li Kashing was one of them.
7. Correspondence with John Child, 2009.
8. Written statement provided by YICT's General Manager to John Child, 2009.
9. Interview with Deputy General Manager, July 2005.
10. Interview with Deputy General Manager, July 2005.
11. YICT General Manager's correspondence with John Child, 2010. The annual budget for lobbying and related activities was substantial, but its size is confidential.

12. This view was expressed by interviewees from both of the joint venture partners, including the General Manager and the Shenzhen Director of the Ministry of Communications.

REFERENCES

Aldrich, H.E. and M. Ruef (2006), *Organizations Evolving* (2nd edition), Thousand Oaks, CA: Sage.
Barley, S.R. (2010), 'Building an institutional field to corral a government: a case to set an agenda for organization studies', *Organization Studies*, **31**, 777–805.
Barney, J.B. and S. Zhang (2009), 'The future of Chinese management research: a theory of Chinese management versus a Chinese theory of management', *Management and Organization Review*, **5**, 15–28.
Baum, J.A.C. and J.V. Singh (eds) (1994), *Evolutionary Dynamics of Organizations*, New York: Oxford University Press.
Bierstedt, R. (1964), 'Legitimacy', in J. Gould and W.L. Kolb (eds), *A Dictionary of the Social Sciences*, Glencoe, IL: Free Press, pp. 386–7.
Boddewyn, J. and T. Brewer (1994), 'International-business political behavior: new theoretical directions', *Academy of Management Review*, **19**, 119–43.
Burgelman, R.A. (2002), *Strategy Is Destiny: How Strategy-Making Shapes a Company's Future*, New York: Free Press.
Cantwell, J., J.H. Dunning and S.M. Lundan (2010), 'An evolutionary approach to understanding international business activity: the co-evolution of MNEs and the institutional environment', *Journal of International Business Studies*, **41**, 567–86.
Cheng, K.H. and Y.J. Wong (1997), *Port Infrastructure and Container Terminal Business* (in Chinese), Hong Kong: Commercial Press.
Child, J. (1972), 'Organizational structure, environment and performance: the role of strategic choice', *Sociology*, **6**, 1–22.
Child, J. (1997), 'Strategic choice in the analysis of action, structure, organizations and environment: retrospect and prospect', *Organization Studies*, **18**, 43–76.
Child, J. and S.B. Rodrigues (2011), 'How organizations engage with external complexity: a political action perspective', *Organization Studies*, **32**, 803–24.
Child, J., S.B. Rodrigues and K.T. Tse (2012), 'The dynamics of influence in corporate co-evolution', *Journal of Management Studies*, **49**, 1246–1273.
Clegg, S.R., D. Courpasson and N. Phillips (2006), *Power and Organizations*, Thousand Oaks, CA: Sage.
Courpasson, D. (2000), 'Managerial strategies of domination: power in soft bureaucracies', *Organization Studies*, **21**, 141–61.
Dahl, R. (1957), 'The concept of power', *Behavioral Science*, **2**, 201–15.
Dieleman, M. and J. Boddewyn (2012), 'Using organization structure to buffer political ties in emerging markets: a case study', *Organization Studies*, **33**, 71–95.

Dieleman, M. and W.M. Sachs (2008), 'Coevolution of institutions and corporations in emerging economies: how the Salim Group morphed into an institution of Suharto's crony regime', *Journal of Management Studies*, **45**, 1274–1300.

Dopfer, K. (ed.) (2005), *The Evolutionary Foundation of Economics*, Cambridge: Cambridge University Press.

Eisenhardt, K.M. (1989), 'Building theories from case study research', *Academy of Management Review*, **14**, 532–50.

Emerson, R.M. (1962), 'Power-dependence relations', *American Sociological Review*, **27**, 31–41.

Faure, D. (2006), *China and Capitalism: A History of Business Enterprise in Modern China*, Hong Kong: Hong Kong University Press.

Flier, B., F.A.J. Van Den Bosch and H.W. Volberda (2003), 'Co-evolution in strategic renewal behaviour of British, Dutch and French financial incumbents', *Journal of Management Studies*, **40**, 2163–87.

Fligstein, N. (1996), 'Markets as politics: a political-cultural approach to market institutions', *American Sociological Review*, **61**, 656–73.

Follett, M.P. (1924), *Creative Experience*, New York: Longman, Green.

French (Jr), J.R.P. and B. Raven (1960), 'The bases of social power', in D. Cartwright and A. Zander (eds), *Group Dynamics: Research and Theory*, New York: Harper and Row, pp. 607–23.

Frynas, J.G., K. Mellahi and G.A. Pigman (2006), 'First mover advantages in international business and firm-specific political resources', *Strategic Management Journal*, **27**, 321–45.

Galang, R.M.N. (2012), 'Victim or victimizer: firm responses to government corruption', *Journal of Management Studies*, **49**, 429–62.

Getz, K. (1997), 'Research in corporate political action: integration and assessment', *Business and Society*, **36**, 32–72.

Göhler, G. (2009), '"Power to" and "power over"', in S.R. Clegg and M. Haugaard (eds), *The Sage Handbook of Power*, London: Sage, pp. 27–39.

Gordon, R. (2009), 'Power and legitimacy: from Weber to contemporary theory', in S.R. Clegg and M. Haugaard (eds), *The Sage Handbook of Power*, London: Sage, pp. 256–73.

Hadjikhani, A. (2000), 'The political behavior of business actors: the case of Swedish MNCs and the EU', *International Studies of Management and Organization*, **30**, 93–117.

Hadjikhani, A. and P.N. Ghauri (2001), 'The behavior of international firms in socio-political environments in the European Union', *Journal of Business Research*, **52**, 263–75.

Hadjikhani, A., J.-W. Joong-Woo Lee and P.N. Ghauri (2008), 'Network view of MNCs' socio-political behaviour', *Journal of Business Research*, **61**, 912–24.

Haugaard, M. and S.R. Clegg (2009), 'Introduction: why power is the central concept of the social sciences', in S.R. Clegg and M. Haugaard (eds), *The Sage Handbook of Power*, London: Sage, pp. 1–24.

Hillman, A. and M. Hitt (1999), 'Corporate political strategy formulation: a model of approach, participation, and strategy decisions', *Academy of Management Review*, **24**, 825–42.

IBAdev (International Business Academy for Development) (2011), *Building the Consensus Needed to Meet the Challenges of Brazil's Ports*, London and Rio de Janeiro: IBAdev.

Jones, C. (2001), 'Co-evolution of entrepreneurial careers, institutional rules and competitive dynamics in American film, 1985–1920', *Organization Studies*, **22**, 911–44.

Kostova, T. and K. Roth (2002), 'Adoption of an organizational practice by subsidiaries of multinational corporations: institutional and relational effects', *Academy of Management Journal*, **45**, 215–33.

Kostova, T. and S. Zaheer (1999), 'Organizational legitimacy under conditions of complexity: the case of the multinational enterprise', *Academy of Management Review*, **24**, 64–81.

Lewicki, R.J. and B.B. Bunker (1996), 'Developing and maintaining trust in work relationships', in R.M. Kramer and T.R. Tyler (eds), *Trust in Organizations: Frontiers of Theory and Research*, Thousand Oaks, CA: Sage, pp. 114–39.

Lewin, A.Y. and H.W. Volberda (1999), 'Prolegomena on coevolution: a framework for research on strategy and new organizational forms', *Organization Science*, **10**, 519–34.

Lewin, A.Y., C.P. Long and T.N. Carroll (1999), 'The coevolution of new organizational forms', *Organization Science*, **10**, 535–50.

Li, L. (2010), *Breaking Through: The Birth of China's Opening-up Policy*, New York: Oxford University Press.

Lin, N. (2011), 'Capitalism in China: a centrally managed capitalism (CMC) and its future', *Management and Organization Review*, **7**, 63–96.

Lord, M.D. (2000), 'Corporate political strategy and legislative decision making', *Business and Society*, **39**, 76–93.

Lukes, S. (2005), *Power: A Radical* View (2nd edition), Basingstoke: Palgrave Macmillan.

McCarthy, J.D. and M. Wolfson (1996), 'Resource mobilization by local social movement organizations: agency, strategy and organization', *American Sociological Review*, **61**, 1070–88.

McLaughlin, A., G. Jordan and W. Maloney (1993), 'Corporate lobbying in the European Community', *Journal of Common Market Studies*, **31**, 192–212.

Mommsen, W.J. (1989), 'The two dimensions of social change in Max Weber's sociological theory', in W.J. Mommsen, *The Political and Social Theory of Max Weber: Collected Essays*, Oxford: Polity Press, pp. 145–65.

Moon, C.W. and A.A. Lado (2000), 'MNC-host government bargaining power relationship: a critique and extension within the resource-based view', *Journal of Management*, **26**, 85–117.

Morgenthau, H.J. (1948), *Politics Among Nations*, New York: McGraw-Hill.

Murmann, J.P., H.E. Aldrich, D. Levinthal and S.G. Winter (2003), 'Evolutionary thought in management and organization theory at the beginning of the new millennium', *Journal of Management Inquiry*, **12**, 22–40.

Noble, J. (2010), 'Brazil's ports in a storm', *Financial Times*, accessed 9 July 2011 at http://blogs.ft.com/beyond-brics/#axzz270nPDExn.

Nye, J.S. (2004), *Soft Power: The Means to Success in World Politics*, Cambridge, MA: Public Affairs.

Ocasio, W. (1997), 'Towards an attention-based view of the firm', *Strategic Management Journal*, **18**, 187–206.

Okhmatovskiy, I. (2010), 'Performance implications of ties to the government and SOEs: a political embeddedness perspective', *Journal of Management Studies*, **47**, 1020–47.

Parsons, T. (1964), *Essays in Sociological Theory*, New York: Free Press.

Pettigrew, A.M. (1973), *The Politics of Organizational Decision-Making*, London: Tavistock.

Pettigrew, A.M. (1977), 'Strategy formulation as a political process', *International Studies of Management and Organization*, **7**, 78–87.

Pfeffer, J. and G.R. Salancik (1978), *The External Control of Organizations*, New York: Harper and Row.

Puffer, S. and D. McCarthy (2007), 'Can Russia's state managed network capitalism be competitive? Institutional pull versus institutional push', *Journal of World Business*, **42**, 1–13.

Redding, G. and M.A. Witt (2007), *The Future of Chinese Capitalism*, Oxford: Oxford University Press.

Rodrigues, S.B. and J. Child (2008), *Corporate Co-evolution: A Political Perspective*, Chichester: Wiley.

Santos, F.M. and K.M. Eisenhardt (2009), 'Constructing markets and shaping boundaries: entrepreneurial power in nascent fields', *Academy of Management Journal*, **52**, 643–71.

Scott, W.R. and J. Meyer (1983), 'The organization of societal sectors', in W.R. Scott and J. Meyer (eds), *Organizational Environments: Ritual and Rationality*, Beverley Hills, CA: Sage, pp. 129–153.

Suchman, M.C. (1995), 'Managing legitimacy: strategic and institutional approaches', *Academy of Management Review*, **20**, 571–611.

Vasquez, J.A. (1998), *The Power of Power Politics*, Cambridge: Cambridge University Press.

Volberda, H.W. and A.Y. Lewin (2003), 'Co-evolutionary dynamics within and between firms: from evolution to co-evolution', *Journal of Management Studies*, **40**, 2111–36.

Weiss, L. (1995), 'Governed interdependence: rethinking the government-business relationship in East Asia', *The Pacific Review*, **8**, 589–616.

Welch, C. and I. Wilkinson (2004), 'The political embeddedness of international business networks', *International Marketing Review*, **21**, 216–31.

White, M.C., D.B. Marin, D.V. Brazeal and W.H. Friedman (1997), 'The evolution of organizations: suggestions from complexity theory about the interplay between natural selection and adaption', *Human Relations*, **50**, 1383–1402.

Yin, R.K. (2009), *Case Study Research: Design and Methods* (4th edition), Thousand Oaks, CA: Sage.

10. Lessons for managers operating in a complex environment

We have seen how the newly-established YICT struggled to survive, how it was turned around and how it then progressed towards the fulfilment of its mission within a complex environment. The question naturally arises whether there are lessons to be learned from the 'thick description' (Geertz, 1973) we have presented of this particular case that have more general relevance for managerial practice. This closing chapter maintains that some 'naturalistic generalization' (Stake, 2000: 22) is possible from the YICT case and that there are implications which are transferable especially for practitioners who find themselves operating in a similar environment. We attempt to articulate the key themes that have emerged inductively from the case study as practical lessons.

'THICK DESCRIPTION' AND 'NATURALISTIC GENERALIZATION'

Chapter 3 argued for the importance of case studies in understanding management in action. Fortuitously, the cooperation between two scholars and a practitioner has enabled this longitudinal study to emerge in its present form, with a co-evolutionary framework guiding a study which enjoyed a high level of insider insight. Social scientists have long argued whether case studies have any contribution to make towards generalization, except for disconfirming conventional wisdom or prevailing hypotheses. A major advantage of the case study approach lies in its ability to study the particular in detail against its specific context so as to produce a rich understanding, or 'thick description' (Geertz, 1973). The solution to the tension between understanding the particular in detail and the ability to abstract the lessons learned lies in an appreciation of similarities in the context of the case and other contexts. If a context against which the particular lesson is drawn is comparable in its significant features to certain other contexts, this offers the possibility of generalization regarding those contexts in order to promote the transfer of knowledge and practice.

Stake (2000) calls this procedure 'naturalistic generalization', which is 'arrived at by recognizing the similarities of objects and issues in and out of context and by sensing the natural co-variations of happenings. To generalize this way is to be both intuitive and empirical ... Then the demands for typicality and representativeness yield to needs for assurance that the target case is properly described. As readers recognize essential similarities among cases of interest to them, they establish the basis for naturalistic generalization' (Stake, 2000: 22–3). The potential for generalizability and transferability can best be illustrated by the power of the engaging narrative to help people develop vicarious experiences in a foreign context – in effect to create a virtual reality (Donmoyer, 2000). The extent to which the experience is turned into learning, however, depends on the recipients of the information and their ability to effect the transfer to their context. Often, such learning is tacit and situational, implied rather than explicit.

What are the particular contexts within which this case study is situated? What parallels can be drawn with what can be considered as 'similar environments'?

The YICT case happened in a transitional economy during a period of great change. China in the early 1990s was characterized by a mixed command and free market economy, with the old and the new often co-existing. In this transitional period, the old institutional rules of the command economy still constrained development, while new forces emerging from the reform and opening programmes struggled to become established. Government, the 'mega force', was present in many areas of the economy and exercised a major influence on the day-to-day conduct of business affairs. Although this influence formed the bedrock of a business culture that worked against new developments, constant and rapid changes generated by the reform and opening movement quickly gathered momentum. As the new market forces took shape, they produced a surge of economic gains to emergent benefactors. Old institutional rules began to lose their grip on the system as successive pilot projects moved the change forward. In the South China context, industrial migration was also taking place, rapidly and extensively. Within 20 years, in the 1980s and 1990s, Hong Kong's light industrial production had moved to the neighbouring Guangdong province and the growth of the supporting transportation industry in South China immediately followed such migration. The environment undergoing these changes simultaneously produced great challenges and opportunities.

The context in which YICT evolved therefore had two key defining characteristics, both of which rendered its environment quite complex

(Child and Rodrigues, 2011). One was the high involvement of government and its associated institutions in the business system. The other was the high rate of change accompanying a rapid transition toward a market economy. The possibilities of naturalistic generalization from the YICT case depend on whether this context contains some similarities to other developing countries. In Chapter 3 we concluded that many other emerging economies, including Brazil, Indonesia and Russia, share the first characteristic, namely an extensive involvement of government and its agencies in business through heavy regulation and political intervention. Regarding the second defining characteristic, although relatively few other emerging economies have undergone a transition from a planned economy, most share with China the experience of rapid change associated with institutional reform and high growth. With these similarities in mind, we can now proceed to draw some lessons for managers from the YICT experience.

IMPLICATIONS FOR THE MANAGEMENT PRACTITIONER

The YICT story offers guidelines for managers operating in complex environments like those of China and some other major emerging countries. Its experience illustrates how to survive and prosper in a complex environment through employing approaches such as taking a holistic view of the environment by reading it politically as well as economically, proactively managing its relational framework with external agencies, being innovative, mobilizing organizational and other resources, developing collaboration based on 'power with', building a sustainable business eco-system, and learning consistently in the crafting of strategies. These seven approaches, together with the gains they produce, offer the prospect of generating a positive cycle of co-evolution over time. They will now be summarized in turn.

Read the Environment Holistically for First Mover Advantages

To read the business dynamics of an emerging economy accurately, management must be sensitive to the political as well as the economic forces at play, noting that, because of institutional immaturity and ambiguity, the constantly changing environment of a transitional economy offers unique opportunities for first mover advantages.

We have observed that the leaders of YICT and the Hutchison Group were able initially to capture a new opportunity ahead of competition and then to manage the port so that it provided a cost efficient service and built capacities of the right kind in a timely manner. As a result, the company enjoyed significant first mover advantages. At the outset it established a unique position with special terms and conditions for doing business in its new environment. It subsequently captured a sizeable market share and created high value for its stakeholders. This can only be achieved by correctly interpreting political as well as economic signals coming from an economy undergoing turbulent changes. Against all odds, in the initial start-up stage, the Hutchison Group invested the right resources for Yantian to grow. Its Chairman had the foresight to ensure that its investment in ports was at the right place at the right time during China's reform and opening. Given the political turbulence of the immediately preceding years and the problems for efficient port operation posed by Chinese government bureaucracy, this required political insight as well as economic judgement.

In managing YICT's survival and growth phases, the company's management placed a lot of emphasis on non-market forces in a developing economy, such as managing strategic relationships with government and its agencies, as well as with the local joint venture partner. Indeed, the turnaround of the vicious cycle to a virtuous one was the result of a systemic process of simultaneous interventions in innovative marketing (end-user marketing as well as marketing to its immediate customers), strategic pricing (initial partnership arrangement with anchored customers), relationship management (with government agencies and the joint venture partner), service and productivity development (emphasis on pilot projects and risk reduction) and unconventional development initiatives (building programmes ahead of requirements and employment of international standards). These were all based on an accurate and open-minded holistic reading of the environment with appropriate emphasis on its 'developing country' character.

It is also worth noting that the ambiguities and relative immaturity of institutions in the transitional state provided some unique opportunities for pre-emptive strategies. In dealing with government regulatory bureaucracies, for example, YICT took initiatives to influence them in the direction of more transparency and standardization or, in the terminology of the day, 'meeting international practices halfway'. Framing a vision for the port and conceptualizing specific initiatives that were informed by it gave rise to successive change agendas and MOUs signed between YICT and the regulators. These in turn signalled to the business community that change was on the horizon and that the new port was receiving support from the reformers in government. Its public relations initiatives were immediately followed by detailed implementation, supported by investment in hardware and processes.

These systematic interventions finally led to steady progress in the reform of regulatory practices, thus confirming the confidence of the experimenters and attracting the interest of followers. The turnaround of the vicious cycle was in a way the result of a discovery of an opening in the institutional 'iron cage' that emerged after a series of trials and errors. YICT's many experiments in marketing, in relationship management and in service development challenged the traditional business model of port development. Breaking away from accepted wisdom early on, and replacing it with an open agenda, paid dividends. Reading the environment holistically, considering non-market as well as market factors, opened the door to new possibilities.

Manage Key External Relationships Proactively

Environmental complexity requires well articulated and coordinated relationship management to help the firm satisfy the demands of its stakeholders and to open up a developmental path. In an emerging economy, with several channels of governmental influence at play, relationship management is multi-faceted. It requires careful attention to several sectors of government as well as to customers who may have concerns about the quality of service that can be offered in an emerging economy.

Given the complex environmental conditions facing an infrastructure business operated by an international joint venture in a transitional economy, its senior managers are obliged to focus on multi-faceted relationship management. In the case of YICT, the complex relationship structure consisted of the joint venture partner, regulatory, local and national government relationships, on the one hand, and immediate and second-order customers (shippers and the owners of freight respectively) on the other. We have noted how in managing these multi-faceted relationships, YICT management adopted a coherent, win-win, yet pragmatic philosophy. Applying this philosophy to specific areas meant employing a 'pull' rather than a 'push' strategy in the sense of trying to capitalize on movements created by changes in the environment.

In practice, this approach had a number of salient features. YICT senior management involved the joint venture partners as equals in decision making, through consistent practices such as consulting minority shareholders before Board meetings. It also expended energy and effort on building personal trust within the mixed executive team, communicating regularly informally as well as formally, sharing the benefits of a profitable business, and growing together in subsequent phases of the port's development. As a result, it was possible to achieve effective collaboration despite the political sensitivity of non-Mainland majority ownership and management, and despite cultural and organizational differences.

In the case of the regulators, YICT fashioned an awareness of new possibilities by initiating reforms and improvements and then supporting their implementation with hardware and software investment. Almost without exception, every successful change in improving the regulatory environment involved a painstaking step-by-step process of investigating change opportunities, educating the stakeholders at various levels in the hierarchy, planning and managing perceived risks during the change process, and supporting the change programmes with human and technical resources. YICT recognized that the regulatory environment defined a large part of the service package to customers. It was faced by the fact that its potential customers were initially very sceptical that the regulators would permit a hassle-free service if they used a Mainland port rather than Hong Kong. YICT therefore developed its approach to securing institutional change out of necessity, although when analyzing the experience it becomes clear that the process adopted closely resembles that of many successful change programmes. Influencing government is a matter of bringing about change and many of the organizational change management insights can be applied in that context.

YICT's managers practised the art of persuasion and creating legitimacy within a relational framework with both local and central government. As one of the first investors in China's port industry, Hutchison secured some special concessions, such as majority ownership by an international business group and the freedom to price. YICT was able to capitalize on these to become a pilot showcase for the Chinese port industry. For over a decade, YICT held the position of an industry leader in Shenzhen as well as in China nationally, partly because of its size but more importantly because of its business and management practices in service, productivity and port development. The local Shenzhen government regarded YICT as one of the FDI success stories and a cornerstone of the city's development as a world city. The central authorities in Beijing viewed the port favourably as one of the most advanced in handling mega vessels, a sign that China had become truly connected to the world.

Such positioning required careful nurturing and implementation. This was manifest in the detailed planning of timely investments (like Phases

2 and 3), foresight in employing new technologies in developing the infrastructure (like the mega vessel strategy in port development), and developing and sustaining the perception of its leadership position in the industry. YICT had a well developed relationship map – details of departments and personnel to contact and lobby for support. It had a process of proposing developments, supporting them with careful analysis, and mobilizing appropriate support resources such as advisory services for liaison and consultation and, when necessary, utilizing the doors that were open to the Hutchison Group Chairman. That it achieved significant influence with both the local and national government testified to the success of its investment in the building of relationships and the company's credibility.

Regarding customers, given the strength of Hutchison's business relationship with major carriers, YICT was able to build an anchored base of business partners, like the Maersk, COSCO and Evergreen shipping groups. When the export market boomed in the early 2000s, these carriers brought double digit growth to the port and created the much envied critical mass for port development. YICT's brand of direct marketing to end users, developed initially out of necessity, also contributed to strengthening and extending its customer relationships.

Innovate to Survive and Break the Vicious Cycle

Because of the changing nature of the turbulent environment, firms have to innovate continuously in marketing and service development and in managing their internal and organizational functions. In the case of YICT, challenging traditional wisdom in a start-up situation with an open mind towards development helped break the vicious cycle in which it was initially caught.

Developing markets call for innovations. Developing markets in a transitional economy require an even higher level of innovation. At the same time, that type of environment permits such innovations to take place. It provides ample space and opportunities for such to flourish partly because of the immaturity of the market and partly because of the particular form of transitions the economy is going through. YICT experienced an initial period of inertia and the onset of a vicious cycle, described in Chapter 5, in which shippers wanted to use a port not beset by problems of cargo clearance, while at the same time complaining about the lack of shipping frequency that resulted from their hesitancy to use the new port. In order to break out of this vicious cycle, YICT's management developed a marketing strategy that was innovative for the industry – breaking new ground by directly approaching indirect customers – cargo owners – so creating more 'stickiness in the value chain'. YICT adopted this approach at a time when the trend was in its favour with the rapid growth of manufacturing in Southern China encouraging interest in exporting via a Chinese port. The immediate customers – the shipping lines – initially sensed some intrusion into their own 'backyard' business relationships, but soon appreciated that they could benefit from collaboration to develop the new market. YICT adopted a systemic approach and conducted parallel experiments in marketing, pricing, product/service delivery and relationship management. Together, these activities challenged the accepted wisdom enshrined in the traditional model of port development and managed gradually to turn around the vicious cycle.

In service delivery, YICT was able to benefit from the mature experience of its international parent company. However, it adapted many practices to its local environment in ways that yielded impressive results, such as collaborating closely with Customers in trial shipments, and micromanaging the relationship with Customs. These experiments paid handsome dividends to YICT, in capturing and maintaining market share in a developing market, and commanding a premium rate from customers. To summarize, these events indicate that, while recognizing the uniqueness of each market, efforts to innovate beyond traditional approaches can benefit managements working in a developing country context.

Mobilize Organizational Resources to Meet Growth Challenges

While focusing on maintaining external flexibility, management must also pay timely attention to developing its internal system efficiently and implement operational and human resources programmes in support of its overall strategy.

To keep the system in synch, timely attention must be placed on developing internal support while firms push for external opportunities. In YICT, the company's ability to develop a cost effective production system, with the right kind of human resources system in support, ensured that it kept pace with the demands of growth. For a very short period of time, in 2002 and 2003, its ability to cope was in doubt at a time when the market grew at an annual rate of 40 per cent and 30 per cent respectively. However, management quickly mobilized both internal and external resources to expand the port's capacities following an extraordinary growth trajectory that market observers watched with awe.

It achieved operational excellence through process and people management, which enabled the company to expand and operate efficiently and
keep a large portion of the value created.

Growing organizations in quantitative terms is itself a challenge in a
developing world as the resource constraints such as lack of the right
human resources can set in easily; growing them in quality terms in a
short period of time poses tremendous problems. In YICT, management
paid determined and consistent attention to the 'growth problems'. Its
emphasis on training and development for operators, supervisors and
managers started early in the history of the firm, partly from a tradition
of excellence in this area on the part of the parent company, and partly
from a top management commitment to developing local talent. YICT's
mission statement identifies people development as a key element in
becoming world-class. After the early survival period, the company soon
searched for process excellence tools and it began to implement 'process
innovation initiatives' using the Six Sigma methodology. Management
was insistent on building an organization with a culture of continuous
improvement. Its internal institutionalization of stated core values
required a considerable commitment of energy and resources. The result
was that YICT grew as an organization in terms not just of size but also
of productivity and quality. This enabled it to capture the opportunities
presented by the rapid growth and internationalization of the Chinese
economy.

Develop Collaboration Based on 'Power With'

*The ability to dovetail the interests of joint venture partners and adapt to
new and evolving structures of governance is key to managing collaboration with significant partners. It calls for willingness to compromise and
an understanding of how a synergistic partnership benefits the firm in
significant ways.*

The structures of international joint ventures are governed by the legal
and regulatory framework of the environments in which they are located.
However, the process of turning what appears to be an institutional
constraint into a competitive strength is key to realizing the synergistic
potential of the partnership. Because the firm is operating in a developing
country, a partner from the indigenous environment brings in a skill set
of managing local and government affairs at a level not readily accessed
and understood by international managers. At YICT, the person seconded
from the local partner, a port development specialist as well as a senior
government servant, proved to be invaluable in setting out the framework

and principles of relationship management. The group of advisors and the staff at the China Affairs Department, who were charged with the responsibility of ensuring smooth relationships, were a major asset in terms of local expertise. Their commitment to the tasks at hand was in no small way a result of the quality of collaboration between the two key members (representing the international and local partners) in the management structure. The ability to apply the skills of international managers to customers and those of Mainland managers to the local relationships worked very well for the young enterprise.

Later, as the terminal grew in size and profitability and the local partner wanted a bigger share of the now-profitable pie, there was the potential for conflict as we witnessed in the negotiations around the development of Phase 3 and beyond. The willingness to find a solution and 'think outside the box' towards a new shareholding allocation (from 70/30 to 65/35) and to agree joint operations in the various development phases manifested the goodwill and flexibility of both partners. They realized that it was in their mutual interest to collaborate rather than to compete and cause problems for each other. The strengthening of the collaboration brought further benefits to both partners. YICT was hailed as a good example of how inward FDI could be managed in collaboration with local partners. The Yantian Port Group was highly rated as a successful example of infrastructure development. Good quality collaboration also ensured that further expansion could proceed ahead of the competition.

Build a Sustainable Business Ecosystem

Exploiting the environment, leading firms can blend in their own success by contributing to developing a beneficial ecological system for the industry, making their own evolution part and parcel of an evolving 'eco system'.

The idea of out-competing other players in an industry by developing an ecological system is not a new management concept. However, the creative adoption and implementation of the idea remains in its infancy. We see such approaches more and more in the hi-tech and logistics industries. In the case of YICT, its success can partly be explained by its contributions to the development of related industries like warehousing, trucking and container repairs that have grown more or less in step. During the course of its history, YICT made some conscious decisions aimed at fostering the growth of supportive industries by promoting logistics-related activities. Out of necessity, it approached end users and tried to understand the value chain in the logistics of changing from using Hong Kong to Yantian. YICT's investment in smoothing the customs declaration procedures was important to filling gaps in the institutional voids of underdeveloped intermediary agencies. Hutchison's investment in the inland container depot, one of the first of its kind in the area, together with the deployment of technologies like the Global Positioning System for tracking cargo, helped create confidence among customs administrators concerning the port's management of transport-ation. With Phase 3, YICT also invested in the port railway, aiming to penetrate into China's interior with an environmentally friendlier trans-port mode than road trucking. Even though green marketing was at an infant stage, it signified the coming of new concepts and developments. By virtue of the fact that YICT represented the largest investment in the area, its continuous investment in logistics and related industries over the last 15 years provided symbolic leadership for the other investors in building warehouses, consolidation centres and other logistical infrastruc-ture businesses. In doing so, the industrial leader was not just building competitive advantages around its own firm strategies but also engaging various players in the value chain to increase the competitiveness along the whole chain. In an environment where an industry is in its infancy, nurturing and growing strong linkages can strengthen the chain such that the players all occupy special niches that benefit from the synergy between them. In a transitional economy, where industry structures are relatively fluid, such opportunities are available.

Learn Consistently in the Crafting of Strategies

The process of strategy formulation and implementation involves continu-ous learning from experimentation. A compelling vision at the outset based on correct reading of the environment can guide its management along the path of 'trial and error'. It is a learning mindset that drives the strategy-crafting process towards achieving coherence and effectiveness.

Is strategy embodied in a plan based on a detailed analysis of the environment and competitors? Or does it evolve through a fluid process of experimentation and learning and further experimentation and learn-ing? To the practitioner, the answer often appears to be a combination of both processes. In YICT's case, the 'plan' took the form of a vision and the specifications attached to this. At the same time, Mintzberg's (1987) perspective of 'crafting strategy' was evident in the process of continuous learning that the company pursued. Early in its history, YICT espoused a vision of becoming 'China's first world-class port' (Mission Statement,

1995) in economic contribution, level of service, and people development. That served as a guiding principle in equipping the port and
developing its software and management practices. The company went
through a period of struggling to survive, followed by a period of fast
growth, diversity and consolidation. Each stage had its particular challenges and lessons to be learnt.

Looking back and judging from the effectiveness of the various
programmes and results, YICT seemed to have a coherent strategy
guiding their implementation. However, as our interviews with the
management team revealed, its thinking at the time was actually characterized by the perception of needs as they arose. This set out an evolving
agenda for learning. The company displayed continuing learning and
experimentation guided by its overall 'world-class' vision. Its learning
experience suggests that it is possible when interacting with a changing
environment to formulate and apply a proactive approach to overcoming
constraints and developing opportunities. This amounts to crafting strategies along the way.

THE PRACTICALITY OF POLITICAL INITIATIVE

The types of initiative taken by YICT's management to promote its
evolution have clear relevance for the ways in which a firm can, through
political initiatives and their 'routinization', generate sufficient influence
within its environment to permit implementation of its desired corporate
strategies. In fact, as we have seen, this influence even contributed to the
evolution of that environment. The generation of influence requires a
sequence of relationship management actions that builds upon the
material and ideational power resources available to the firm. This
sequence of actions can be summarized as the following steps. First,
analyze the bases of power the firm has vis-à-vis the environment and
formulate strategies and tactics to leverage the firm's relative advantages
that potentially stem from these power bases. Second, develop relational
frameworks in appropriate domains so that influencing efforts can target
appropriate personnel and policy agencies. Third, articulate a goal or
vision that is compatible with the agenda of key external players. Fourth,
bearing in mind the need to mobilize support and secure legitimacy,
develop lobbying and influence programmes aimed at expounding the
potential contribution of the firm's desired evolution to that of the wider
economy and society. Fifth, establish specialist organizational roles or
units to focus on the planning and execution of these influencing efforts.
Sixth, secure agreement with influential external parties to initiate and

manage low risk experimentation, preferably in partnership with them. Seventh, critically assess the outcomes of such initiatives and consolidate the gains from them. It is important here to ensure that there are appropriate loops across levels (micro to meso and macro) to feed back information on the gains, bearing in mind that influence is a continuing process, not a just a one-off project. Finally, incorporate these 'relationship management' programmes into the core strategy of the firm.

REFERENCES

Child, J. and S.B. Rodrigues (2011), 'How organizations engage with external complexity: a political action perspective', *Organization Studies*, **32**, 803–24.
Donmoyer, R. (2000), *Case Study Method*, London: Sage.
Geertz, C. (1973), 'Thick description: toward an interpretative theory of culture', in C. Geertz (ed.), *The Interpretation of Culture: Selected Essays*, New York: Basic Books, pp. 3–32.
Mintzberg, H. (1987), 'Crafting strategy', *Harvard Business Review*, July–August, 66–75.
Stake, R.E. (2000), 'The case study method in social enquiry', in R. Gomm, M. Hammersley and P. Foster (eds), *Case Study Method*, London: Sage, pp. 19–26.

Appendix. Reflexivity of the participant researcher Kenneth Tse, Managing Director, Yantian International Container Terminals, 1993–2009

Seale, commenting on reflexivity and writing in *The Quality of Qualitative Research*, concludes that:

> There is no substitute for presenting the evidence that has led to particular conclusions, giving the fullest possible details about the contexts in which research accounts arise. In the last analysis, writers must then trust in their readers' capacity to make their own judgements (Seale, 1999: 177).

Throughout this book, the study of YICT is presented as an independent report, with my role as ethnographer or participant observer largely placed in the background. This has been done to avoid cluttering the flow of the book with detours into methodological discussions about the possible bias of the participant researcher and how validation and triangulation procedures have mediated the possible impact. However, we need to stress that one of the unusual features and key strengths of this book lies in the fact that it has benefitted from my active involvement as the first chief executive of the company who lived through the first 16 years of its history. My personal involvement at a strategic level helped piece together missing parts of the story, and it has added to the significant interpretative understanding of how the company co-evolved and why. The coincidence of being a researcher and a key participant means that, for me, this has amounted to a piece of ethnographic research. I think it is therefore appropriate and informative to reflect on my beliefs and interpretations and how these might have influenced the study from my perspective as the ethnographic researcher within the team of authors.

Hammersley and Atkinson define ethnography as follows:

> In its most characteristic form it involves the ethnographer participating, overtly or covertly, in people's daily lives for an extended period of time, watching what happens, listening to what is said, asking questions – in fact,

collecting whatever data are available to throw light on the issues that are the focus of the research (Hammersley and Atkinson, 1995: 1).

In this case, I had indeed spent considerable time in the field with those being researched. I participated overtly in the activities studied and exercised more than a marginal influence on the people and issues involved. So in this Appendix I discuss the relevance of my role in relation to three issues. These are:

1. The researcher-key actor dilemma in conducting and presenting ethnographic research.
2. Validation and triangulation.
3. My reflection on my values, beliefs and assumptions during the intellectual journey of undertaking research into my own company's co-evolution.

As this is a personal account of reflexivity, an attempt in bending back upon oneself to provide 'thoughtful, self-aware analysis of the inter-subjective dynamics between researcher and the researched' (Finlay and Gough, 2003: ix), I shall in this section adopt a personal writing style rather than the third-party mode that characterizes the book as a whole.

THE RESEARCHER-KEY ACTOR DILEMMA

As a piece of ethnographic research, this study is characterized by one special feature that defines both its major strength as well as a potential weakness: the researcher and key actor dilemma. The backbone of this study, the YICT case reported in detail in Chapters 4, 5, 6 and 7, draws from over 16 years of my direct involvement as a key participant in the case study. As the first chief executive (Director and General Manager of the joint venture), I have followed the history and development of the port closely and have acquired intimate knowledge of the processes from the vantage point of an insider, indeed one of the key actors in the case. Very often, I was the main architect of the development plans and strategies, especially on the day-to-day basis on which strategies were executed while being formulated – the crafting processes. In a significant way, I developed the 'world-class port' vision and gave it specific meaning in execution (YICT Business Plans for the years 1995–2000). The joint venture's shareholders only articulated broad expectations, leaving policies and execution largely to the executive team headed by the General Manager. My freedom to act, especially in the early years, was almost total, as the Hutchison Port Holdings Group [HPH] had not yet been formed and the Hutchison-Whampoa Group [HWL] had only limited experience in managing international joint ventures. Even after HPH was formed, the ports under its control were managed as a portfolio of units, each with its own characteristics and specific application of its shareholders' intentions to its particular environment. Each entity was empowered to exercise a wide range of options in marketing, business development and human resources, as well as in partner and government relationships.

As the YICT joint venture became more successful through the years, my freedom to act was enhanced by being able to generate significant financial returns and capitalize on development opportunities. Through the years, therefore, I have found myself in a unique position able to articulate the concepts and processes behind YICT's strategy development, evolution of its policies and tactics as well as its interactions with the environment. Experienced first-hand or observed at close quarters, I saw the events that took place from their inception to their execution and evaluation. This means that not only was I able to capture the essence of the case study from a conceptual standpoint, but I was also able to provide personal details of the linkages and rationales behind the headlines and the reports. In management research, such experience is valuable as it allows me, as a researcher, to access the thinking processes of the key actors and the executive team. This is especially valuable in a study of the strategic aspects of corporate evolution. As researchers, we all admire Burgelman's unique experience of his ten-year association with Intel's CEO Andy Grove while conducting his research on the company's strategy development, which resulted in his book *Strategy Is Destiny* (Burgelman, 2002). Such in-depth understanding is often denied to management researchers who get limited access and can only rely on published information or sketchy details obtained from one or two executive interviews. I did not have the same problem. Because of my involvement, my opportunity to undertake research on YICT represented an insider advantage not dissimilar to that which Burgelman enjoyed in his study.

However, this advantageous position as an executive in the case posed a number of challenges to my other role as a researcher. The first challenge was the danger of personal bias. My views on appropriate research questions and methodology, and on relevant data for analysis, might have introduced a bias toward my conception of what the results should be. As a key actor in the case, I had my own personal explanations for the findings. In the event, working with the two other authors of this book, one of whom was also my main doctoral supervisor, helped me to approach the question with an open mind.

The second challenge as the key participant in the case study holding a position of authority was that I ran the risk of compromising my role as researcher. There was the very real risk that I could have unwittingly exercised an undue influence on the views expressed by interview respondents who might be concerned about in some way offending me. I like to think that a combination of their professionalism and my own personal style reduced this risk, but this could be wishful thinking. A third issue arose because, in analyzing the evolution of the company against the evolution of the environment, my role as advocate of the ideas and plans as well as involvement in their execution rendered objectivity in interpreting the data and arriving at independent conclusions quite difficult, if not impossible. My action orientation as an executive might also have limited my perspective in approaching the research question. Indeed, one might pertinently raise the query of whether an independent researcher would have applied the co-evolutionary framework differently and come to some other conclusions. These challenges are very significant and, if unguarded, I might end up presenting only a subjective account of the case with a reduced contribution to learning.

In numerous discussions with the other authors, I was made keenly aware of these challenges. I can recall numerous discussions with them on the desirability and feasibility of appreciating where information was subjective, which involved interpreting the meaning of actions and events, and where it was more objective in nature. There are some features where objective data speaks for itself – for example the growth of the company's throughput and size, its financial strength as exhibited by profitability and other measures, as well as external recognitions and awards granted for the company's efforts in productivity improvements. These amount to tangible, factual information and the availability of archival information could indicate them objectively. In that respect, the challenge was to cover as full a picture as possible, without being selective of materials supportive of my own pre-meditated conclusions. However, in intangible areas such as assessing the influence of the company's strategies on the environment and vice versa, we could only rely on the interpretations of the people involved, particularly those of the key actors. As one of those actors I had to play the dual role of actor and reporter. As this is a study of strategy formulation and co-evolutionary processes, some subjectivity in interpretations of soft data by the key actors seems inevitable. In effect, I had to strike a balance between the privilege of insider knowledge and unwarranted editorial freedom. A keen awareness of the dual roles, sensitivity to the possibility of bias, presentation of alternative interpretations, and methodical triangulation procedures were the means I used to handle these challenges.

VALIDATION AND TRIANGULATION

My intention to study the development of Yantian port as a case study started around the year 2000, while I became aware of the effectiveness of some of the managerial practices in the unique environment I found YICT to be in. I believed that, if well documented, they could become useful to other practitioners in a similar environment. Nevertheless, while trying to conceptualize and synthesize my own practices and the practices of the YICT team, I was always unsure of the extent of their usefulness to others. I began debating with myself and colleagues, taking notes, collecting information and writing memos to myself, especially on key events such as the relationship management processes in securing the port's Phase 3 development (see Chapters 5 and 7). In reporting events, I consulted those records extensively to ensure the right linkages were in place and that I was expressing interpretations of views and events not just from my perspective but also from that of others involved. For example, I asked for detailed records to be made by my Special Project Manager who was closely involved in the Phase 3 Expansion process. At the conclusion of Phase 3 negotiations, I asked for his account of the process which I used to balance my own views. In fact, all the while during this period I was acting as a researcher while performing as an executive. I struggled between making things happen and observing as well as documenting what was happening. In retrospect, I believe that forcing myself to reflect in this way considerably improved my judgement as an executive.

Recognizing that I wanted to study the case for its managerial practices and draw lessons from it for other fellow practitioners as well as to make a contribution to learning, rather than to write an autobiographical story, I have become keenly aware of the need to keep full records and a professional distance in reporting. My co-authors have repeatedly reminded me, indeed demanded from me, that all claims I make must at least be partially supported by some forms of evidence, written in the records from company archives or from interview data. As noted in Chapter 3, triangulation has become an important feature in the study. Even though I was frequently reminded of the need to support conclusions with evidence and even though I employed a degree of triangulation, I still faced several dilemmas.

One dilemma was in selecting from the abundance of material available to me, what to include and what to leave out? The longitudinal study reported in this book covered some 15 years of the history of the port. Over these years, I have read literally thousands of documents, including some that I wrote myself. The question is: how do I select so as to report the story in a balanced manner? Indeed, is there a 'story-line', in the sense of an underlying logic to it?

There are obviously no definite answers to these questions. I started by collecting key tangible data such as production charts and financial figures from company reports and Board meeting minutes, as well as a compilation of key events in a Key Event Chronology cross-referenced by a similar chronology produced by the Chinese partner (produced in their 25th company anniversary publication). Then I used insights from interviews to interpret and connect the events. For example, the interviews with former Shenzhen Mayor Li Hao and the Deputy General Manager and chief representative of the Chinese partner, Liu Neng Fang, enabled me to explore the rationales they attached to observable developments. I tried to present the early history from the perspectives of both the international partner as well as the Chinese partner, and for these I relied heavily on interview data. For the port's later developments, as I personally became more and more involved, I made a special effort to cross-reference company documents and the opinions of the other executives interviewed. My purpose was to ensure that I did not rely purely on my memories simply to present my version of the story. In fact, consultation with my co-authors resulted in the review of much more documentary evidence than was originally envisaged so as to ensure that the chapters were more grounded and balanced.

It is easy to claim that I aimed to present different sides of the arguments effectively. The dilemma is how to do this. Listening to the interviews, I became aware that there are different ways of seeing history. For example, different interviewees classified the stages of development of the port differently. Regarding how YICT managed to cope with its early difficulties, there were also some differences in the importance attributed to different causes of the turnaround, for example, between the importance of commercial account development versus end-user marketing. As one might expect, different emphases were associated with the position that respondents held in the company. The solution adopted was to recognize as many different perspectives as possible. Efforts have been made to include a range of verbatim quotes from both my interviews and those conducted by Dr Chung. So there is mention of a range of factors considered by the interviewees to be important to the turnaround (Chapter 5), rather than just presenting my own judgement. Although this book argues for the importance of managerial intentionality, a rival explanation is also considered. When commenting on the effectiveness of managerial initiatives like the process innovation initiatives (Six Sigma), additional insights are used: such as those from studies conducted by other independent researchers, for example, the University of Birmingham Master's students (see Chapter 6).

There is also the question of how to avoid making unwarranted leaps from parallel sequences of events to attributing cause and effect to them. Here, the tension between being a key actor and a participant observer is more pronounced. In my executive role, almost of necessity, I held strong views about the causes and consequences of events. Otherwise I could not have mobilized the organization to implement its policies. For example, in my own mind there was no doubting the importance of the world-class vision, the strategic intent, end-user marketing and relationship management (partner and government) for the overall success of the project. However, in studying these factors, I had to take a big step away from the firing line and put forward evidence to justify my claims, often relying on both conceptual and reasoned arguments when empirical evidence seemed to be inconclusive. The inability of the social sciences to assert causal linkages conclusively is well recognized, but that should not stop good arguments being advanced as plausible hypotheses. Behind the justifications, there is always a voice that says maybe the alternative is also true. In this book, I join my co-authors in arguing for the relevance of the co-evolution of corporate strategy and environmental policies, and for the pertinence of managerial intentionality in highly institutionalized environments if advantage is taken of the relational frameworks they offer. To some degree, however, I also accept a different perspective – that maybe a highly institutionalized environment can be extremely constraining, and, in certain circumstances, these constraining forces could prove to be too strong to be overcome by individual organizational efforts. The use of the devil's advocate procedure is of interest here. In two of the meetings I had with the experienced practitioner, acting as devil's advocate, he questioned me on the critical success factors of the case and the extent to which the matching of the company's strategies with the collective psyche of nation building contributed to YICT's development. I presented my arguments, which he countered by arguing that, with China's opening to the world as the predominant force, success of the enterprise well positioned in the value chain would follow almost automatically. Consequently, both sides of this argument are presented in this book.

THE INTELLECTUAL JOURNEY

Reflecting on the intellectual journey I went through as actor/participant observer might also provide some additional insights into the conclusions

I have reached. As a practising manager, I have always espoused management ideas such as the importance of vision and mission in a value driven organization. I also believe in the potential of individuals in a participative management environment, as I have seen the power of such a belief in actual management situations throughout my 35-year business career. With a background in human resources management, consulting and marketing in a multinational company environment before being appointed as General Manager of YICT, I have always enjoyed strategizing on company positioning. This has been informed by Porter's ideas of the value chain and Pettigrew's ideas of change management and contextualization, as well as Mintzberg's concept of crafting strategy. Almost by instinct, most managers understand the power of contextualization and continuous learning, even though they might not know how to articulate such concepts. Consciously or unconsciously, managers are guided by their theories of business. I was no exception. In the practice of managing YICT, my focus was first of all to survive and to continue to succeed as a business, so I adopted whatever worked in those special circumstances, experimenting, summarizing and learning as we went along. Studying managerial practices and theorizing about them came later.

As I began this learning journey, I was first of all interested in strategy development, trying to find theoretical justifications for my practices and to expand the scope of conceptual understanding. I read the literature on strategy development, especially the writings of Ansoff, Porter, Pettigrew, Drucker and Mintzberg, until I came across Mintzberg's configuration of the ten schools of strategy formation. Awed by the breadth of the subject matter, I was impressed by Mintzberg's concept of 'emergent strategy' and his description of the 'crafting process' (Mintzberg, 1987a; 1987b). That is a powerful idea, I thought, because it explained the strategy formulation process better than other theories and it certainly seemed to apply in my own case. So emergent strategies, learning and crafting became my standard lenses through which I watched and described the world, armed with many other schools to guide me through the strategy safari.

However, the strategy formation process constituted only one part of the phenomenon I was trying to understand. The other major aspect was the organizational form – the international joint venture and how it works in the special environment. Cooperation became of interest as the case I was studying was situated in a joint venture environment in China. In this area, it was Child's work on cooperative strategy (for example, Child et al., 2005) and his earlier book on the Chinese environment (Child, 1994) that introduced me to a full range of ideas about the difficulties of managing international joint ventures in an emerging economy. Differences in partner objectives, developmental stages, cultures and managerial practices all contribute to the complexity. An economy in transition further complicates the environment as changes and unpredictability reign supreme. There, institutional influences play a more important role in the way business is done. The question is asked whether simple strategies without regard to those contextual forces would be effective. Indeed, I began to explore the question – what will constitute a good strategy given such an environment, for instance, institutionalized and in a joint venture situation? In this respect, Austin (1990) and Peng (2000) provided useful insights. Austin's idea of the governmental involvement as the mega force in a developing country helped me understand the situation that I found myself in. Peng's study of transitional economies shed light on the complexities of the coexistence of the old and new. Together, these ideas seemed to contextualize for me my own managerial practices. However, to put everything in the right perspective, I still had to search for an over-arching framework.

Ideas of evolution and later co-evolution between organizations and environments were introduced to me by John Child, as he continued his theoretical work on 'strategic choice' (Child, 1972; 1997) and on corporate co-evolution jointly with Suzana Rodrigues (Rodrigues and Child, 2003; Rodrigues and Child, 2008). The Rodrigues/Child study builds on the co-evolutionary framework developed by Lewin and his associates (Lewin et al., 1999; Lewin and Volberda, 1999; Lewin and Koza, 2001). I found the framework to be comprehensive and compelling as it allows for organizational understanding and strategic initiative under a complex set of realities in the macro and meso environments. It also depicts co-evolutionary, interdependent and mutually interacting forces at play. In their more recent treatment of co-evolution, Rodrigues and Child (2008) placed added emphasis on the political dimension, which enriched the framework considerably. Their political interest theory of corporate co-evolution represented a new dimension for understanding organizational realities. Delving into the theory of corporate co-evolution, and the Telemig case on which the Rodrigues and Child study was based, I was satisfied that the concepts of co-evolution helped me understand the YICT case I was studying, as it places all the components that I have considered important into the proper contexts, in addition to its holistic perspective. In terms of theory development, since the framework was still in the early days of definition and application, the potential of making a contribution to its advancement appeared more realizable. I thought that, because of the political initiatives my colleagues and I took in the process of corporate co-evolution (especially in creating and managing relationships within a relational framework), the YICT case could shed light on the detailed processes involved.

REFERENCES

Austin, J.E. (1990), *Managing in Developing Countries: Strategic Operating Techniques*, New York: The Free Press.

Burgelman, R.A. (2002), *Strategy is Destiny: How Strategy-Making Shapes a Company's Future*, New York: Free Press.

Child, J. (1972), 'Organizational structure, environment and performance: the role of strategic choice', *Sociology*, **6**, 1–22.

Child, J. (1994), *Management in China during the Age of Reform*, Cambridge: Cambridge University Press.

Child, J. (1997), 'Strategic choice in the analysis of action, structure, organizations and environment: retrospect and prospect', *Organization Studies*, **18**, 43–76.

Child, J., D. Faulkner and S.B. Tallman (2005), *Cooperative Strategy: Managing Alliances, Networks and Joint Ventures*, Oxford: Oxford University Press.

Finlay, L. and B. Gough (eds) (2003), *Reflexivity: A Practical Guide for Researchers in Health and Social Sciences*, Oxford: Blackwell.

Hammersley, M. and P. Atkinson (1995), *Ethnography: Principles in Practice* (2nd edition), London: Routledge.

Lewin, A.Y. and M.P. Koza (2001), 'Editorial – Empirical research in co-evolutionary processes of strategic adaptation and change: the promise and the challenge', *Organization Studies*, **22**, v–x.

Lewin, A.Y. and H.W. Volberda (1999), 'Prolegomena on coevolution: a framework for research on strategy and new organizational forms', *Organization Science*, **10**, 519–34.

Lewin, A.Y., C.P. Long and T.N. Carroll (1999), 'The co-evolution of new organizational forms', *Organization Science*, **10**, 535–50.

Mintzberg, H. (1987a), 'The strategy concept 1: five Ps for strategy', *California Management Review*, **30**, 11–24.

Mintzberg, H. (1987b), 'Crafting strategy', *Harvard Business Review*, July–August, 66–77.

Peng, M.W. (2000), *Business Strategies in Transition Economies*, Thousand Oaks, CA: Sage.

Rodrigues, S.B. and J. Child (2003), 'Co-evolution in an institutionalized environment', *Journal of Management Studies*, **40**, 2137–62.

Rodrigues, S.B. and J. Child (2008), *Corporate Co-evolution: A Political Perspective*, Chichester: Wiley.

Seale, C. (1999), *The Quality of Qualitative Research*, London: Sage.

Index